LYRICAL AND
ETHICAL SUBJECTS

SUNY SERIES IN CONTEMPORARY CONTINENTAL PHILOSOPHY

Dennis J. Schmidt, editor

LYRICAL AND ETHICAL SUBJECTS

*Essays on the Periphery
of the Word, Freedom, and History*

DENNIS J. SCHMIDT

STATE UNIVERSITY OF NEW YORK PRESS

Published by
STATE UNIVERSITY OF NEW YORK PRESS, ALBANY

© 2005 State University of New York

All rights reserved

Printed in the United States of America

No part of this book may be used or reproduced in any manner whatsoever without written permission. No part of this book may be stored in a retrieval system or transmitted in any form or by any means including electronic, electrostatic, magnetic tape, mechanical, photocopying, recording, or otherwise without the prior permission in writing of the publisher.

For information, address State University of New York Press,
194 Washington Avenue, Suite 305, Albany, NY 12210-2384

Production, Laurie Searl
Marketing, Anne M. Valentine

Library of Congress Cataloging-in-Publication Data

Schmidt, Dennis J.
  Lyrical and ethical subjects : essays on the periphery of the word, freedom, and history / Dennis J. Schmidt.
     p. cm. — (SUNY series in contemporary continental philosophy)
  Includes bibliographical references and index.
  ISBN 0-7914-6513-6 (hardcover : alk. paper) — ISBN 0-7914-6514-4 (pbk. : alk. paper)
  1. Language and ethics. I. Title. II. Series.

BJ44.S36 2005
149'.94—dc22

2004022565

10 9 8 7 6 5 4 3 2 1

Language, most dangerous of possessions, is given to human beings so that creating, destroying, perishing, and returning to the eternal mistress and mother, we might bear witness to who we are, having inherited and learned from her the most divine of her attributes, all-embracing love.

—Hölderlin, "Im Walde"

In Memory of

Hans-Georg Gadamer

CONTENTS

Acknowledgments	xi
Introduction	1
1 Lyrical and Ethical Subjects: Straining Communicability	7
2 Wozu Hermeneutik?: On Poetry and the Political	19
3 Between the Lines: On Language, Translation, and Tradition	33
4 On Blank Pages, Storms, and Other Images of History: Speaking and Imagining History	47
5 Time Made Loud: On Language and Music	61
6 What We Cannot Say: On Language and Freedom	77
7 "Two mouthfuls of silence": On Language and Pain	91
8 On the Dark Side of the Moon: On Language and Deafness	103
9 Speaking of Nature: On Language and the Unbidden World	117

10	Words on Paper: On Language and Script	131
11	"Like a fire that consumes all before it": On Language and Image	141
12	Language in the Age of Modern Technicity: Speaking of Freedom and Community Once Again	163

Appendix: "Monologue" by Novalis   191

Notes   193

Index   211

ACKNOWLEDGMENTS

The chapters in this volume have been presented and developed in a number of contexts. I would like to acknowledge the people who have participated in these forums and guided me in my own reflections. First, my students at Villanova University need to be recognized since many of these issues were explored in the context of seminars with them. Their interventions, comments, questions, and frequent objections have shaped me perhaps more than I have shaped them. I hope they have enjoyed working with me as much as I have enjoyed working with them. My arrival at the Pennsylvania State University occurred after this book was finished; nonetheless, the hospitality of my beginning here needs some acknowledgment. Many of the essays in these chapters were originally developed for two annual meetings: the Collegium Phaenomenologicum, which is held in Città di Castello, Italy, and the Hermeneutische Gespräche Forum held in Heidelberg, Germany. The conversations I was able to have at both events have been invaluable to me over the years.

A number of people have read and commented on these chapters. Some I will simply have to thank always since they continue to be my teachers by being my friends. I hope that everyone listed here sees that I have learned something from them. My thanks to Robert Bernasconi, Walter Brogan, Karin de Boer, Donatella di Ceseare, Hans-Georg Gadamer, Günter Figal, Rodolphe Gasché, Julie Klein, Jennifer Mensch, James Risser, Heidi Rose, John Sallis, Lawrence Schmidt, Susan Schoenbaum, Charles Scott, Daniela Vallega-Neu, and Alexjandro Vallega. Jennifer Mensch has been a special support as this book has worked its way through the publishing process. She belongs very much to its sources and keeps me close to them. Jane Bunker began as an editor with whom I worked and whose work I admired. That says much already, but I should add that she has become a friend as well. This book is dedicated to the memory of Hans-Georg Gadamer who was my teacher and my friend, and who will remain an inspiration.

Some of these chapters are based on articles previously published. In every case, the essays have been substantially rewritten. Nonetheless, they have retained the basic argument of their earlier form and so grateful acknowledgment is made to the following: "Wozu Hermeneutics?" (State University of New York Press, 1988), "On Blank Pages, Storms, and Other Images of History" and "Speaking of Nature" (*Research in Phenomenology*), "On the Dark Side of the Moon" (*Continental Philosophy Review*), and "Two Mouthfuls of Silence" (John Hopkins University Press).

Cy Twombly's *Fifty Days at Ilium* is reproduced here with the permission of the Philadelphia Museum of Art.

INTRODUCTION

> ... though the feeling of freedom is ingrained in every individual, the fact itself is by no means so near to the surface that merely to express it in words would not require more than common clarity and depth of perception.
>
> —Schelling, *Philosophical Investigations into the Essence of Human Freedom*

The following chapters are devoted to probing some of the ways in which we experience the fringes of language, and to highlighting the relation of both freedom and history to such experience. They are guided by the conviction that such reflections on the limits of language can open up something decisive for the effort to address the enigmas of ethical and political life and the challenges of judgment in those realms. To justify this conviction is one of the primary goals of this book. My contention is that when we arrive at experiences that press up against the unsayable, we find ourselves *claimed* by what, for lack of a better word, we might call an intuition. It is an intuition that *resists* any sublation or conceptualization; nonetheless, in the fact of this resistance we should recognize it as an intuition of what we most need to know about ourselves. It is the intuition of *freedom*. More precisely, it is an intuition of the abyssal freedom out of which we come to be who we are, and are not. It is because we can have such an experience of freedom that we know ourselves to be political beings who face ethical tasks and on whom the severe task of judgment is laid. Only beings defined by freedom can be challenged by ethical and political life, by the task of sharing life in time with other free beings. Consequently, only the radical experience of freedom opens up the depths of the realms of ethical and political life as beyond the reach of any economy of good and evil. When we begin to open the arenas of the ethical and the political from out of a radical sense of freedom, not a sense of freedom defined by the agency of a subject but a sense of freedom that lets something like a subject emerge at all, we escape the claims of an ethics or politics founded on the cherished assumptions of metaphysics. When this happens ethics is opened up independently of the claims of the autonomous subject and of the ideal of the good of a community.

The argument that I want to make in the following chapters is that reflection on the specific forms defining the *finitude* of human being illuminates in an original and unique manner how it is that such beings might find clues as to how to reply to the great riddles of ethical life. I also want to suggest that we will do this only once we have come to understand the question of the ethical in a more original manner than that which is framed by the presumptions of metaphysics and humanism. This can only happen if we come to appreciate the full reach and originality of freedom in such matters. The reason I believe that reflection on the forms of finitude can provide one of the avenues for doing that is precisely because such finitude is not—as it has so long been regarded—the other of freedom, but is rather the highest testimony to the reality of freedom. As we cease the effort to measure human being against some ideal of an infinite and omnipresent god who suffers no death—in other words, as we escape the ontotheological tradition and its presumptions—we will come to grasp the manner in which radical finitude opens the prospects for a new understanding of the issues of ethical life as they emerge from out of human freedom.

The phenomenological evidence for such finitude comes in many ways and is found in a variety of experiences. However, the form of finite life addressed here is chiefly language. It should also be added that language is addressed here not in the fullness of the question it puts to us as its speakers, but simply insofar as it bears witness to finitude. That other forms of such finitude are to be found should go without saying.

One of the assumptions animating the form that this argument takes in this book is that the relation of human being to language is so essential, so original, that it cannot even be thought as a *relation* at all. While it is true that language is the preeminent element of all relationality, such that we must say that there is relation only insofar as there is language, it is equally true that the notion of relationality cannot do justice to how it is that we belong to language. That which language opens up as a possibility cannot give an account of the being and force of language itself. Only language experienced *as* language can have this hope. The place of language in human being runs deeper than the notion of "relation," which implies distinct relata independent of one another, could ever hope to expose. Our being is saturated by language and needs to be thought from out of a consciousness of this saturation. But to do that and to make a serious effort to come to terms with the nature of language *as* language and with the horizon such a nature opens up for us, we must rigorously attend to the *performance* of language at work. Reflections that stay close to this performance of language do not remove themselves from language, but, so far as it is possible, stay close to the *way* language gives itself to be thought. A fidelity to the word itself, to the *way* words work as much as to *what* they say, is needed if such reflections are to pay due tribute to the experience of language as language. Such a fidelity would be very much like the fidelity to language of the poet or the translator, two important figures in the following chapters. In the context of the concerns that I want to trace, this fidelity means paying attention to the forms in which the performative capacity of language begins to approach its limits and break down. The sites that serve as the focal points of these chapters—translation, poetry, pain, music, images, history, community, deafness—each mark in their own way a point at which language arrives at the edge of its own possibilities and begins to yield to some other set of possibilities. Nowhere does the way of language make itself felt more than in approaching its own limits. This is also the point at which we recognize that even the limits of language are only opened up from out of an experience of language itself. We cannot move beyond, or outside, of the word in order to address its truth. At best we can dwell at the threshold that is the site of the advent of language.

Following the performance of language is not the same as theorizing *about* language. Being attentive to the performance of the word does not mean interpreting the meaning that is signified by any particular words. Such interpretations only function as a sort of noise that distracts us from the silent event of language speaking itself. Nor does it mean circumscribing the possibilities of meaning outlined by any particular language, or even language as such. There is an *intimacy* found in attending to the performance of language. It is too small, too delicate, to be a matter of language as such. We follow this intimacy of the word once we become attentive to *how* language *offers* something to be thought. Clearly, this requires that we cease regarding language as a human activity, as something that we control, and instead treat it as opening up the realm of that which we call the "human." Language speaks us. It does this in many ways, even to the point of shaping the faces we have since we exercise the muscles of our faces in the languages we speak and, as we all know, some muscles required by some languages have simply atrophied for those who do not speak those languages. The echo of this can be heard in the accents we have when we speak foreign languages for which our muscles have not been trained. We are in every way shaped by our language, and in much more far-reaching ways than simply shaping the face. Out of the strange contingency of the language we speak we come to be who we are. This is unsettling. But to let ourselves be unsettled by the depth, the reach, of the word is what is required for any serious reflection on the full experience of language as the site where we find something like the birthplace of the "human." In language we find the realization, the enactment of who we are.

Nietzsche was aware of this issue of performance, of the enactment of thinking in the word. When he wrote the self-critical preface to his *The Birth of Tragedy* some fourteen years after its initial publication, his most poignant criticism of his own accomplishments came in the form of the lament "It should have sung, this new voice—and not spoken! How sad that I did not risk saying as a poet what I had to say then: perhaps I could have done it." His lament is born of the sense that *style* cannot be separated from substance, and that his style in that book was simply too philosophical, too conceptual, to ever expose the intimacy of the thought it sought to present. Nietzsche's indictment of the conceptual language of philosophy is compelling for those who takee the performative dimension of language to heart.

But is there then still a place for conceptual reflection? Is it the case that the *only* way of finding rigorous fidelity to language is in performance? I believe that it is important not to forget that every performance of the word is a request for a reply, for a countering word, and that such a word of reflection can exhibit, in its own way, something of this intimacy of the word. The echo of the word of reflection can highlight and crystallize what might otherwise be lost in the noise of significations. There are those exceedingly rare figures—Hölderlin being among the greatest, and Nietzsche having struggled to arrive at this point—who have wedded performance and reflection. But those of us who do not have such gifts are left to celebrate them as they come to us and to see into them as much as we can.

The chapters that follow are dedicated to this task. They address a wide range of themes and figures; nonetheless, only a few assumptions govern all of the chapters. Perhaps the most basic assumption is that Kant is right when, in the third critique, he argues that there is a form of experience that moves us outside of the orbit of the language of the concept, the language of philosophizing. Aesthetic experience cannot be captured by the language of the concept and yet it is an experience for which language is constitutive. In aesthetic experience then we are put in a place that calls for a different relation to the word. He also argues that this experience, which opens up a sense of our subjectivity that is different from that which opens us up to the categorical imperative, is of fundamental importance for how we might answer the demands of ethical and political judgment. While the intention of these chapters is not to address Kant, or to provide a reading of the third critique, it is to pursue with the utmost fidelity the promise of that great insight driving the third critique. What I refer to as the "lyrical subject" is inspired by the idea of aesthetic subjectivity articulated by Kant. The "ethical subject" that I take to come into view by virtue of the appearance of this lyrical subjectivity is also akin to the sense of the ethical subjectivity forged in the third critique.

But three other figures do a great deal to shape the argument mounted in this book. It is important to see Nietzsche's insistence that thinking move beyond good and evil to be at work in everything said here. Nothing could be further removed from the sense of the ethical that I want to expose here than that which is able to see and understand itself in the framework of good and evil. The claim I want to make is precisely that, to the extent that it is properly understood and rigorously held in place, the realm of ethicality opened up by the experience of lyrical subjectivity *cannot* be translated into the framework of a metaphysics of moral life or the calculus of good and evil. Heidegger and Gadamer also shape the chapters here. In particular, their shared insistence on the primacy of language and the ineluctability of finitude conceived without reference to an infinite above it is important in what follows. Both also share Kant's conviction that truth belongs to the realm of the work of art, and both understand that such a conception of truth needs to be thought of as a matter of disclosure and performance.

There are, of course, other influences and assumptions at work in these chapters, but so far as is possible they are acknowledged as such. Although their range is rather wide, their overarching intention is specific and twofold: first, to open up a sense of language outside of the view that takes it as a matter of representation, and as an object of representation for itself in philosophizing; second, to follow out some of the consequences, some of the logic, of the finitude of language that emerges in this sense of language. More precisely, it is to try to demonstrate how the specific forms of this finitude bear on how we might come to understand ourselves as ethical subjects.

CHAPTER ONE

LYRICAL AND ETHICAL SUBJECTS: STRAINING COMMUNICABILITY

Die schöne Dinge zeigen an, daß der Mensch in die Welt passe.

—Kant, *Reflexionen*

The great discovery of the third critique is both stunning and yet intuitively compelling: that the form of reflection proper to the domain of aesthetic experience circumscribes a region that opens up onto an a priori. This is the region defined by the logic of aesthetic—or, as I want to call it, "lyrical"—subjectivity. Against every expectation, an experience marked by its relation to a peculiar form of pleasure—that otherwise most idiosyncratic of feelings—is shown to be the first clue to what is universal and necessary, but nonetheless found in no other form of experience. While it reaches far beyond the pleasure that is the first signal of taste, the initial entry into the aesthetic comes with the capacity to discriminate among pleasures: judgment begins with the judgment that a pleasure exceeds the privacy of pleasures that do not merit the claim of taste. Much is at stake in this claim and its consequences are dramatic, but among these consequences, perhaps the most surprising is that this a priori of the lyrical subject bears directly, and in an original manner, on the task of the ethical subject, namely, the task of making free, moral judgments.

Taking up the promise of Kant's insight in the third critique, there are two questions that I would like to address. The first is what, if anything, the capacity to recognize beauty says about who we are; in other words, does aesthetic experience make any unique contributions to that field of questions that traditionally refer to something like "selfhood" or "subjectivity"—a set of questions that Nietzsche called "the riddle that is assigned to each of us."

The second question is whether aesthetic experience is relevant for our understanding of ourselves as citizens of an ethical world; in other words, does beauty illuminate ethical life? Schelling once suggested that, when beauty is present, a "second empire" is opened to us. My questions then are whether entry into this second empire alters the axis of our self-understanding and opens new and productive avenues for speaking about the enigmas of ethical life.

Both questions emerge out of three arguments that frame Kant's *Critique of Judgment*. The first argument is that aesthetic experience is solely a matter of the subject, that in a judgment of taste we are not speaking about objects, but about who we are. Or, in Kant's words: "What is merely subjective in the presentation of an object, i.e. what constitutes its reference to the subject and not the object, is its aesthetic character."[1] In other words, in the decision that we recognize beauty we are not speaking about anything but ourselves, such that aesthetic experience must be understood as a form of pure self-confession. Furthermore, Kant's tacit claim is that the self of such confession is one that is unique, since the conditions of its appearance, the conditions of taste, outline a horizon of appearance that is unique and that renders possible the appearance of the subject in its subjectivity and these conditions of the appearance of the subject are not governed by the same laws of the appearance of objects in their possible objectivity.

The second argument is that aesthetic experience is thoroughly, rigorously, without relation to concepts. Taste and genius, beauty and sublimity alike not only avoid, they actively repel the language and rule of the concept. Though he does not thematize the question of language, not even his own overwhelmingly conceptual language, it is clear from what Kant says that aesthetic experience has a problematic relation to language in general. Consequently, the self-understanding that is disclosed in aesthetic experience problematizes the relation between language and the subject that confesses itself in such experience in an interesting way. In short, the subject that confesses itself in aesthetic experience is not one that understands itself according to its disclosure in either the "I think" or even in the "I speak,"[2] but differently—I will argue "lyrically." The lyrical subject is that form of the subject disclosed in relation to the realm of aesthetic experience.

The final argument of the third critique that provokes the questions I want to ask is Kant's contention that the grounds of aesthetic experience are unique in being simultaneously plural, yet non-empirical, and singular, yet universal. What Kant finds striking about these grounds of aesthetic experience is that they not only resonate with a profound sense of belonging, of a *senus communis*, but that these grounds present themselves as the symbol of a moral law that is the non-empirical coincidence of universality, plurality, and singularity. In the end, Kant suggests that the destiny of aesthetic experience, its truth, is the symbolic disclosure of an ethical subject and sensibility that is otherwise inconceivable. It is, in the end, literally beyond the concept. Apart from the logic of the concept, the disclosure of the aesthetic subject opens the subjectivity of the subject of this experience in a radically different manner, one that highlights the relation of the subject to both freedom and nature in a novel manner. This, in part, is what Kant means when he says that "beautiful things indicate that the human being belongs in the world."[3]

Such, in brief, are the claims of the *Critique of Judgment* that lead me to the questions concerning the achievement of aesthetic experience that follow. These Kantian claims compel me to follow through on my own conviction that without beauty life would be pointless and that the best way to understand the point that beauty makes about our lives is to say that it refers us to ourselves as ethical subjects. Beauty is the glimmer of an otherwise inconceivable ethical sense. The starting point for my comments comes from a series of remarks that Gadamer makes in a text that is dedicated chiefly to discussing the philosophical contribution of Kant's *Critique of Judgment*. My proposal is simply to elaborate on these questions and to do so by pursuing lines of interpretation opened by Gadamer in that essay, entitled "The Relevance of the Beautiful." Before turning to the details in Kant that I want to develop, a few remarks about Gadamer's relation to Kant and some subtle shifts in the focus of Gadamer's interpretation of Kant might help highlight both the originality of Gadamer's developments of Kant's achievements and the way in which both Gadamer and Kant make a contribution to the investigation of aesthetic experience that is apart from others—such as Schelling, Nietzsche, and Heidegger—who also find an original experience of truth in the work of art.

The importance of Kant's third critique for Gadamer's own philosophical project is clearly evidenced by the crucial role that he granted to it in the formulation of his sense of hermeneutics in *Truth and Method* in which Gadamer builds on and radicalizes Kant's disclosure of the insurmountable and unique form of finitude disclosed in aesthetic experience. But, despite the acknowledgment of Kant's insights, Kant is ultimately criticized for having unduly subjectivized aesthetics by virtue of having grounded his aesthetics on the concept of taste.[4] There Gadamer argues that, mired in the presumptions of the Enlightenment and its dream of the certifiable subject, Kant never finally broke out of the metaphysics of subjectivity, and consequently that the full force of aesthetic experience, though indicated, was never released into thinking. Gadamer grants that Kant understood, much to his own surprise, that the realm of the aesthetic belongs to the disclosure of truth and thus to the task of critique, that aesthetic experience performs a unique service in the project of taking experience to its limits. By granting the role of aesthetic experience for the critical project, Gadamer puts Kant in company with Nietzsche and Heidegger, both of whom find poetic practice fundamentally critical of the claims of conceptual knowledge. But in *Truth and Method*, Gadamer argues that Kant tamed the disruptive potential of the aesthetic insofar as he grounds aesthetic experience in a sense of taste that is allied with the normativity of a domesticated, metaphysical subject, rather than in the disruptive force and nondomesticizability of the figure of the genius that cannot be explained by reference to such a subject. Part of what I want to argue is that one can indeed find in Kant's conception of taste precisely what Gadamer says is lacking there; namely, a liberation of the subject from its modern constrictions

In "The Relevance of the Beautiful," the objections of *Truth and Method* do begin to fade in favor of a more elaborated analysis of some of the heuristic principles that Kant employs in his analysis of aesthetic experience, in particular those found in play, the symbol, and the celebration. It is these principles that raise some severe questions about the unity and nature of the aesthetic subject. In that text, written some fourteen years after *Truth and Method*, Gadamer is more intent on emphasizing that Kant's attempt to ground aesthetics in taste, that is, to thoroughly subjectivize aesthetics, is constructed on elements of taste that are not rooted in an Enlightenment sense of subjectivity. There one begins to see that Kant's analysis has the remarkable effect of undermining the very notion of a subject, at least the subject as defined by its relation to the possibility of discursive, that is, conceptual knowledge, such as one finds in the first critique in which we are defined by virtue of our capacity to conceptualize experience. More precisely, in "The Relevance of the Beautiful," Gadamer highlights aspects of Kant's sense of aesthetic subjectivity that define the subject precisely in its life *apart from* conceptuality. In doing this, Gadamer takes Kant to heart when Kant says that "Beauty is what universally pleases *without a concept*," and he calls attention to a dimension of aesthetic experience that is not inclined to a notion of subjectivity that possesses the appearance of an Enlightenment image of autonomy.

This slight shift in the central focus of Gadamer's treatment of Kant is significant. It is a move that operates precisely on the fault line of an important division in the history of aesthetic theory, and begins to show the extremity of Kant's place in that history by virtue of the priority he accords taste. In the history of discussions about the achievement of art in human life, one finds a wide range of arguments that the production of art is among the most profound manners in which we contemplate and experiment with possible answers to the riddle that we are for ourselves. From Aristotle, who in answer to the question that inaugurates his *Poetics*—"why do human beings make art?"—says that it is congenital (*symphyton*), up through Heidegger who speaks, with Hölderlin, of the poetic as our original form of dwelling, one finds frequent reference to poetic production as an original experience. That tradition seems to reach its peak in Nietzsche, who makes the astonishing observation that this *Kunsttrieb*, which so powerfully defines us, manifests itself in the remarkable phenomenon that in dreaming, when the mind is unfettered and free and left alone with itself, we produce images of light: in our sleep we make art. According to Nietzsche, at our most intimate and natural moment we are all producers of art, and so he writes lovingly of "The beautiful illusion of the dreamworld in the production of which every person is an artist."[5] Nietzsche's analysis of the *Kunsttrieb*, while decisive for the question of the role of genius in Kant's understanding of the realm of the aesthetic, is beyond the scope of my remarks, except to note that Nietzsche claims that there is an instinct that is both equiprimordial and incommensurate with this compulsion to make images. He claims that the struggle defining the alchemy of these original drives, the Apollinian and Dionysian, ultimately the struggle between the image and word, is the most powerful struggle that we can wage to know ourselves, and in the end it is a struggle that drives us beyond—or maybe it is better to say beneath—the language of concepts to the point of musical dissonance. In the end, for Nietzsche, like Kant, it is important to bear in mind that the limits of language are decisive in aesthetic experience.

But what is perhaps most interesting about Kant in this regard is that he is not simply claiming that the *production* of art is among the preeminent ways in which we explore possible answers to the riddle that we are for ourselves and so reveal ourselves to ourselves; rather, his claim is that the judgment of taste, *receptivity* for the experience of beauty—especially beauty that is unbidden, beauty that cannot be produced, namely the beauty of nature—"quickens"[6] and brings to life something of the subject that otherwise remains hidden. *Taste* rather than *genius* is the central concern for a critique of judgment. In it we find the secrets of free and finite judging. In other words, by centering his remarks on our capacity for the receptivity of the aesthetic, Kant is committed to the view that the grounds of aesthetic experience cannot be summoned by us and cannot be produced at will. He is also committed to the view that the experience of those grounds is felt most intensely in nature, in that about which Kant says that "In considering nature and the ability it displays in organized products, we say far too little if we call this an *analogue of art*" (AK, 374). The subject of aesthetic experience is quickened, not produced, and this difference is all important.

In *Truth and Method*, Gadamer seems to align himself with those whose interest is in aesthetic production since he criticizes Kant for grounding aesthetic disclosure on taste rather than genius. That is, there the production of art seems to define the question of the aesthetic, whereas Kant's interest is more directed to beauty as the rule of art, especially beauty understood as unbidden, since for Kant the real opacity, the finitude, of aesthetic experience in the work of art is exhibited in that which art inherits from nature. But, as the very title of "The Relevance of the Beautiful" indicates, that essay shifts the question of aesthetic experience from the issue of production of art to the question of our receptivity for a sense of beauty that is not thinkable according to the calculus of production. Before turning to these issues in Kant, one final point needs to be noted, namely, that in this shift in Gadamer's treatment of Kant there is also a narrowing of the field of aesthetic experience insofar as reference is made to beauty and not the sublime. In quietly moving away from the experience of sublimity, Gadamer follows the move that Kant makes as well when he says that "the concept of the sublime is not nearly so . . . important and rich in consequences as is that of the beautiful" (AK, 246). That is a delimitation of the aesthetic that needs to be challenged, but, for the moment, it is a challenge that I want to defer since the point that I want to pursue now is this claim that in the recognition of beauty one finds a new sense of subjectivity "quickened."

Let me return to my two questions: does the capacity for beauty say something about who we are? Does beauty illuminate another, otherwise inconceivable, ethical sensibility? Let me suggest that my remarks up to this point have been dedicated to trying to clarify the direction of Kant's investigations into these questions, and to indicate how the slight shift in Gadamer's treatment of Kant brings this direction into sharper focus. Two points in particular are worth emphasizing. The first is that Kant is concerned chiefly with the promises of beauty, not with the work of art as such; the second is that Kant is concerned with an experience that, while communicable, is independent of the concept. Some further comments on each of these points will help me move forward with my two questions.

It seems clear that, in the present historical juncture, art operates in horizons wide of that which one might call beautiful. The kinship between art and beauty, which in Kant's day was taken as natural, has been severed so cleanly that it now seems as if the real achievements of art are found outside of the orbit of the beautiful. Furthermore, it seems that aesthetic theory no longer treats of natural beauty either, but that it has dropped nature altogether from its agenda and now receives its directives from the production of works of art divorced from beauty.[7] As Gadamer points out, kitsch calls attentions to the vanities and pretension of beautiful art, mocking us when we forget our times; today it seems that art that pins itself to the claim of beauty has, at best, the air of an outmoded nostalgia surrounding it. Nietzsche put the point bluntly when he wrote that art "absolutely should not be measured according to the category of beauty" (GT, 104). But Nietzsche is not the first to make that claim, since only three decades after the third critique Hegel suggested that art, which he, like Kant, interpreted as the signature of beauty, was passé from the standpoint of truth.[8] I do not intend to ask about the possibility of beautiful art today, preferring instead to note, as Heidegger does in the Epilogue to "Origin of the Artwork," that perhaps the decision about Hegel's claim is yet to be made. The reason such an issue is not relevant at this point is that for Kant, as the title of Gadamer's essay indicates, *beauty* is relevant—art is relevant because it is, for Kant, one, but not the primordial, site in which beauty becomes possible. There is, however, a more original site of aesthetic experience.

In the quite prevalent tendency to regard Kant's third critique as centered on our experience of the work of art, the greatest insight of that text is fundamentally misplaced. Art simply is not the central issue in aesthetic experience, and that is the reason he does not ground his aesthetics in the figure of the genius; rather, what is at stake is the effort to speak both out of and to an experience of something fundamentally other and yet intimate, something so strange that it is completely apart from the calculus of human production.[9] In the end, the center of the experience analyzed in the third critique is found in nature, which is why Kant says that "genius is the favorite of nature" (AK, 318), and why he writes that "one who has taste enough to judge the products of fine art with the greatest correctness and refinement may still be glad to leave a room in which one finds those beauties . . . and to turn instead to the beautiful in nature in order to find there, as it were a voluptuousness for the mind in a train of thought that he can never fully unravel. If that is how one chooses we shall ourselves regard this choice with esteem and assume that this person has a beautiful soul." (AK, 299–300). What Kant praises here is the openness to something different, the effort to understand that which is not obedient to the laws of the human mind. In aesthetic experience as Kant understands it, something nonartefactual "speaks" and this means that a radically new, a nontechnomorphic, understanding of nature is demanded, one that is not the metaphysical representation of an already constituted region of causality and, furthermore, one whose concept does not stand in an antinomial relationship with freedom.[10]

This brings me to the second point that I wanted to emphasize: aesthetic experience is completely independent of the concept. Gadamer makes this point when, after asking what it was that led philosophy to turn its attention to the beautiful, he writes that "remembering ancient thought helps us to see more clearly that in the beautiful and in art we encounter a significance *that goes far beyond everything conceptual*" (GW, Bd. I, 107; emphasis added). He reminds us that this does not mean aesthetic experience should simply be defined as nonconceptual, saying that "the experience of [beauty] cannot be understood by reference to an abstract opposition to conceptual knowledge" (GW, Bd. I,192). Rather, the communicable thread of aesthetic experience is a different language from the "language" of the concept, and so it cannot be understood by means of any relation, especially a privative relation, to conceptuality.[11] In other words, aesthetic experience is our way of communicating what cannot be said in the concept. But rather than refer to the language of aesthetic experience as nonconceptual, it might be better to say that in it one finds the language of the secret, where the secret is not understood as something held back and jealously guarded, but as that which is a secret essentially because *it cannot be told*. In the end, the secret, that which weds us to language and simultaneously seals our lips, belongs very much to the aesthetic experience as Kant understands it. In this, Kant's views stand in sharp contrast with Hegel's, who, in tracing the migration of spirit in different works of art, begins with mute stone and finds the promise of beauty only redeeming itself in the arrival of the word.[12] It is no accident that Hegel chooses to give the final words of the *Phenomenology of Spirit* to a poet when he cites Schiller saying "aus dem Kelche dieses Geisterreiches / schäumt ihm seine Unendlichkeit."[13] The general tendency of philosophers to gravitate to the poem as the most philosophic expression of aesthetic experience is worth noting. Gadamer explains it by saying that "poetry, even the most incomprehensible, is conceivable and it is available for the conceptual. The close kinship between poetry and philosophy rests upon this" (GW, 62). This allure of the poem as that which seems to be able to capture even the incomprehensible in the word captivates Kant as well when he suggests that "among all the arts, poetry has the highest rank" (AK, 326). However, it should also be said that if we take Kant's remarks about the exclusion of the concept from the beautiful seriously, then this proximity between poetry and philosophy carries a risk; namely, the presumption that we who think from out of the language and logic of the concept speak its language. In truth, language must be learned anew in the poem, since in the poem it is precisely the language of the concept that falls silent so that another language might be spoken.

Kant tries to speak of this secret, this unknown language, in two ways, both rather baffling but crucial to my concerns. First, when asking about genius he speaks of *aesthetic ideas*; second, when speaking of the presentation of beauty in taste he speaks of *symbolic hypotyposis*. Though distinct, those two notions belong together. Both, from the vantage point of the concept, are lapses in the logic of the universe; both are impertinent.

Kant says that "an aesthetic idea cannot become cognition because it is an *intuition* (of the imagination) for which an adequate concept can never be found" (AK, 342). Gadamer puts his finger on the point of aesthetic ideas when he tells us that "an idea is not a concept" (GW, 196)—reminding us that the field of thinking is wider than the field of conceptuality—and when he argues that we should not try to think aesthetic ideas as the simple complement or confirmation of rational ideas. He further notes that aesthetic ideas are not given, but are "original" in the double sense that they are not replicas of something pregiven and that they themselves give a rule, taking on what Kant calls "exemplary validity." What is notable about this form of the self-validation of aesthetic ideas is that it is grounded in the curious "flaw" that no example is perfect—that is, the force of its validity comes from its own imperfection, the difference internal to the identity that it establishes. Exemplarity wears its finitude as its truth.

But this force of finitude in aesthetic experience is even more clearly evident in the symbol, the language of taste, that finds its truth in the fractured relationship it exposes. In his discussion of the symbol, Gadamer reminds us that it was originally a technical word for a broken token that served as a means of recognizing others in a secret affiliation. (A host would give the guest one half of a broken token that could then be used by descendants of the guest should they come to that house in some distant future.) In short, according to its original meaning, the symbol was what Gadamer describes as an "a passport of antiquity" (GW, 122); that is, it was the manner in which we recognized something that was not previously known. After alluding to the role of the symbol in Aristophanes' speech about the essence of love in Plato's *Symposium*, where a link is drawn between the erotic and the symbolic, with Aristophanes saying that each of us is but the *symbolon* of a human being and that each of us pursues a never-ending search for the *symbolon* of himself, Gadamer then says that "this profound image for the marriage of souls . . . can be transferred to our experience of the beautiful" (GW, 123). In the symbol, beauty communicates without concepts and becomes the manner in which something is recognized, something of ourselves, that was not previously known. In the symbol, the language of the secret gets spoken.

When Kant introduces the symbol he does so by contrasting it with the schema that is the form of presentation he analyzed in the chapter on schematism in the first critique. There the schema seems to have been offered as the sole form of presentation proper to experience. In the third critique, Kant sharpens the specificity of the notion of the symbol by setting it as a alternative form to the schema. However, when Gadamer sets out to discuss the symbol, he follows a long-standing tradition, one that seems to begin with Goethe, of fine-tuning its sense in conjunction with a discussion of allegory rather than contrasting it with the schema. The question of the relation of the symbol and allegory is an important and involved one, made all the more difficult because Kant's use of these words marks a shift in their meanings.[14] Moreover, Kant himself seems to be unclear about their differences. For instance, the example that he gives in the third critique of a symbol—the pepper grinder as the symbol of the despotic state (AK, 352)—is, even by his own definition, really an allegory since it is not given in nature, but rests on convention. But despite such confusions, some features of the symbol are indisputable and can be drawn upon in order to discuss how it plays a central role in aesthetic experience for Kant.

Foremost is that, however else it is characterized, the symbol is defined as beyond calculation or capture; it cannot be arrested, but, as Goethe put it, is infinitely active and inaccessible in the image [as which it appears] so that, even expressed in all languages, it remains inexpressible.[15] Fulfilling itself in the ideal of untranslatablity—as does the poem—into anything other than itself, the symbol infinitely eludes the language of the concept since it is, by definition, excessive. As an intuition, the symbol beckons language, but as arresting the move into another, already known language, the symbol appears as the persistent memento of the ineffability of what it communicates.[16] In the symbol that which cannot be told openly appears. Gadamer interprets this by saying that in the symbol "it is not particularities but the totality of the experiential world and of the place of human beings in the world, above all one's finitude before transcendence, that is brought to experience" (GW, 123). It is, he says, "a communique of the holy" (GW, 123). There is a surplus in the symbol, and that is why Gadamer suggests that it is tinged with the divine. That is, in part, what Kant means in the third critique when he says that "all our knowledge of God is merely symbolic" (AK, 353). But it is important to bear in mind that this is not a metaphysical surplus; rather, this surplus that qualifies the symbol as the bearer of the sacred, emerges paradoxically out of the impossibility of the appearance of anything beyond the symbol. In the *Anthropology*, Kant argues that the symbol is intrinsically theological, but he argues vigorously against any metaphysics of the symbol that would convert the symbol into the idol.[17] One is reminded here of Meister Eckhart, especially his sermons on the poverty and silence requisite for the appearance of the sacred in the image.[18] The symbol beckons what we cannot know otherwise.

Everything hinges on understanding how the symbol exhibits indirectly, not represents, this "secret." Everything hinges on not interpreting the symbol either metaphysically or speculatively; on remembering that the symbol can never be recuperated by the concept, and that its truth is found rather in its intransitive residue, which can never fully appear and never be overcome or sublated into a concept. Though the symbol is dialectical in the sense that it always entails production of an excess, it resists any dialectical act of sublation into something beyond itself. The symbol is, in this respect, rigorously insistent on remaining itself. Properly understood, the symbol arrests every effort to move beyond this density of the symbol itself, such that the symbol becomes a hieroglyph for which no code can ever exist. Here, at the apogee of aesthetic experience, a transformation in the language and conditions of intelligibility is imparted.

Before saying more about the nature of this transformation, one more point needs to be reinforced about Kant's sense of the symbol: unlike allegory, the symbol is natural. It is given, not invented, and has nothing random about it. Nothing of artifice, nothing of human invention, nothing of convention is found in the symbol. In the end, this naturalness of the symbol goes hand in glove with the priority of the natural in aesthetic experience—a priority that is borne out when aesthetic judgment yields to teleological judgment—and it is this naturalness of the symbol, the absence of artifice in it, that leads to the view that nature is the supreme symbol. But it is important that such remarks not be taken as promoting a sort of metaphysical symbolism such as one finds in the medieval world.[19] Rather, to speak of nature as the supreme experience of the symbol is to invite a new sense of nature, which is precisely what Kant attempts shortly after his discussion of the symbol. The result is a sense of nature so generous that it shatters the economy of the concept. There Kant says repeatedly that a "mere blade of grass ... infinitely outdistances" (AK, 371–372; 378; 400; 409).[20] There as well he argues that our experience of nature opens up upon ethical experience; in other words, to be open to nature, one needs, in the end, an understanding of ethical life.

So aesthetic experience, this pure experience of the subject not closed to a world but porous, results in an awareness of the symbol. In the symbol, which indexes us to what is other and indomitable in its strangeness, the radical alterity of nature is disclosed. At that point in the disclosure of the finitude of experience, Kant says that a sudden transformation takes place in the subject and that this experience of alterity, which is not the representation of otherness but the disclosure of alterity *in* and *as* one's own limits, imparts an alteration that is the "quickening" of an ethical sense. Much like the suddenness that Aristotle describes when speaking of *metabole*, the arrival of the ethical here is not a transition that can be grasped.[21] It is an alteration, a quickening, in what is to be understood, one that is quite similar to the one Kant describes when he speaks of the paradox of the end of time and our inability to conceive that thought in any other way than as the ethical meaning of the sublime.[22] Kant refers to this ethical sense as faith, saying of it simply that "*Faith* (as *habitus*, not as *actus*) is reason's ethical way of thinking in affirming that which is not accessible to theoretical knowledge" (AK, 471).

In aesthetic experience, we are poised on the axis of a paradox since it is the perfect incompleteness, the inaccessiblity of the symbol that becomes the axis of an extension of the realm within which we may come to understand ourselves and others. It is a paradox that replicates the central paradox of taste as Kant analyzes it; namely, that in it one finds a claim to subjective universality (AK, 212).[23] But it is a paradox of language as well, of the secret: this aporetic subject of aesthetic experience exhibits the same features that one finds in lyric poetry, where the solitude of the poet becomes the way in which the poet declares a solidarity with others who remain forever beyond knowing.[24]

More, much more, needs to be said once this paradox of aesthetic experience is identified. More needs to be said about how the ineffability of the individual hints at something more. More too about the coincidence of opposites that Kant calls subjective universality and that I propose to call lyrical subjectivity. The purpose of the chapters that follow is, in large measure, to address these themes. But I will end this stage of my reflections by making reference to two comments that I believe go far toward encapsulating what needs to be taken from this first step opened by Kant's investigation of taste.

The first comment is from Gadamer, who says that "the experience of limits that we encounter in our life with others . . . [is] the common interest bearing us along."[25] The second is from Kant, who summed up the conditions and horizon of our common interest when he said that "beautiful things indicate that human beings belong in the world." Together, these remarks remind us that in the capacity to recognize beauty we are faced with an experience of our own finitude that comes directly from our subjectivity; we face the secret that we are for ourselves. Impossible to know, and yet hinted at in that very same impossibility. Kant reminds us that in aesthetic experience we come to know ourselves and others apart from the representations of the language of the concept. Gadamer reminds us that in the finitude of our experience we open ourselves to that which exceeds us.

I will conclude by answering the second question I posed at the outset: does this illuminate our ethical situation? By now, it should be clear that the answer has to be both "yes" and "no." No, if ethics is understood as the domain of discursive practices and the rule of the concepts of law. But what must be learned is that we need a better definition of what is at stake in the question of ethical life. Once we come to this understanding, we must answer this question by saying yes, because then we can grant with Kant that in the play of the powers of the mind and in our openness to another sense of nature we are indeed free, and this experience of freedom is the real experience at the heart of the ethical.

CHAPTER TWO

WOZU HERMENEUTIK?: ON POETRY AND THE POLITICAL

The title of this chapter echoes the title of one of Heidegger's more celebrated texts on language, namely, his 1946 "Wozu Dichter?" [What are poets for?]. To further situate my own title within a lineage, let me note that the title of Heidegger's text is itself a citation of a passage from Hölderlin's Elegy "Bread and Wine," which reads "wozu Dichter in dürftiger Zeit?" [what are poets for in needy times?]. These resonances are worth noting because the theme that Heidegger takes up in those texts, inspired by the question that Hölderlin poses in his poem, shapes the concerns about the original kinship of poetic practice and political life that I would like to address here. Kant's analysis of aesthetic experience draws language—even if only tacitly—into the center of the question concerning the significance of aesthetic experience in its relation to ethical life. Heidegger's work thematizes this experience of language, but only tacitly brings this experience to bear on the question of ethical life.

In "Wozu Dichter," written immediately after the war, Heidegger investigates the idea that there is an essential relation between language and history, and that this relation might provide some cues as to how the terms of community, of our shared life in time, is to be grasped in thought. More precisely, the implication of Heidegger's reflections on the specific relation between the workings of language in the poem and a "needy time" is that this relation opens up the horizon within which the elements of something like a nonmetaphysical conception of community can be thought. It is admittedly an odd claim: that language in the poem bears upon the question of political life in an original manner, and furthermore in a manner that is progressive with regard to the task of political reflections. The hidden assumption here is twofold. First, it is assumed that the framework of thinking about community that has governed the Western world since its inception, a framework defined by a metaphysics founded on the notion of an "idea" of community, is no longer tenable; it has exhausted itself in the present historical crisis. Second, it is assumed that we might find avenues for a different way of addressing the riddles of communal life by starting out from a new understanding of the kinship of the poetic and the political. It is a suggestion that Heidegger had made before, always to startling effect (one thinks, for instance, of his remark, in the 1942 lecture course on Hölderlin's "Der Ister," that Sophocles is the true Greek thinker of the *polis*).[1] But, although he would frequently allude to this political promise of reflections on the experience of language, Heidegger would never fully develop this kinship between language and community in any satisfactory manner, and the question of politics would come to be the Achilles heel for anyone who wished to attack and dismiss Heidegger's thought as a whole.

Gadamer, on the other hand, has made this issue one of the central concerns of his life's work, and indeed I believe that we will one day come to see that one of Gadamer's greatest contributions to philosophy has been to take up this suggestion regarding the political insights exposed in a rethinking of language and opened up its productive possibilities. Indeed, one of Gadamer's first publications engages this theme. I am referring to "Plato and the Poets" (1934), an essay written during the first months of the Nazification of Germany, an essay that displays its own opposition to that movement not only in the special treatment of its political topic, but also in its epigram, taken from Goethe: "One who philosophize is at odds with the forms and types of representation of the surrounding world, that is why Plato's dialogues are not often not only directed *at* some point, but also *against*."[2] Gadamer's purpose in that essay is to ask about the real standards that animate Plato's critique of poetry. His answer—the most general form of which is announced when he says that "in truth, the sense of this critique of poetry is determined solely from out of its context: it arises in a text on the "state' "[3]—opens up themes that eventually show themselves to be the leading themes of Gadamer's career: tradition and culture, theory and praxis, language and limits. It will also provide real insight into how we might think about the strange relation between poetic language and the idea of community. This then is one of those essays that lets one begin to understand the aptness of Habermas's characterization of Gadamer's thought as "the urbanization of the Heideggerian provinces."[4] That characterization rings so true because Gadamer's trademark in this and other essays is to develop what always remains a lacuna in Heidegger's own work, namely, the real and effective power of language at work in culture and political practice.

My intention in the remarks that follow is to renew this theme of the relation of poetry and the political in light of the reflections on this theme that emerge from Gadamer's hermeneutics. More precisely, I want to ask whether Gadamer's insights into this matter contribute something toward resolving the riddle one faces in a so-called postmodern conception of political life: how are we to speak about the mandates and possibilities of political practice in a political world that is not understood as constituted according to the bourgeois illusion of free and equal judiciary subjects born with rights that are innate rather than won? I believe that this question is worth posing because speaking about the enigmas of political life is far more frustrating, less amenable to stabilization and solidity, than a view of the world constituted according to such assumptions founded in the notion of the subject can ever fully acknowledge. That is why I will follow the lines opened up by Gadamer's reading of Plato's conception of the relation of poetry and the state, and so I will start with language, rather than any conception of a subject, as the basic element of all political matters, as the real and phenomenal stuff of any polis. I begin my remarks with the assumption that we live in a world that, in the words of Hannah Arendt, is "overgrown with an . . . in-between which consists of deeds and words and owes its origin exclusively to our acting and speaking directly *to* one another."⁵ The task then is to speak of this "in-between," this prior community of our permeability out of which we may emerge for a while as subjects. The first point to be established then is, as Gadamer's reflections on the relation between poetry and the political have demonstrated, that the notion of the subject is not tenable as a *starting point* for reflections on political practice. But of course this means understanding language as more original than any possible subject and as that out of which the subject itself comes to be.

The suggestion that we turn to the force of language as the starting point for political reflections is rather new. It is a suggestion that accords quite well with the other recent suggestion that the notions of "subjectivity" and "intersubjectivity" are problematic for any understanding of political life. Foucault put it clearly when he said that:

> 'I speak' runs counter to 'I think.' 'I think' led to the indubitable certainty of the 'I' and its existence; 'I speak,' on the other hand, distances, disperses, effaces that existence and lets only its empty emplacement appear. Thought about thought . . . has taught us that thought leads us to the deepest interiority. Speech about speech leads us, by way of literature as well as perhaps by other paths, to the outside in which the speaking subject disappears. No doubt that is why Western thought took so long to think the being of language: as if it had a premonition of the danger that the naked experience of language poses for the self-evidence of the 'I think.'⁶

The point is that language—multiple in its grammars, spontaneous in its outreach, poor at articulating itself—refuses to be repatriated to any sense of the interiority of the subject. It is, Foucault says, "the repetition of what continually murmurs outside."[7] When we reflect on language, we find that it is not subject to the subject we take ourselves to be, but that we are subject to it. We sit within the folds of our grammars. That, of course, is what Heidegger means when he says that "the human being speaks insofar as he responds to language" and that "language speaks"[8] It is also Gadamer's point, when, with a slightly different emphasis, he says that "being that can be understood is language."[9]

Heidegger's remarks on language go as far as possible toward regarding language as a matter of this "in-between" that constitutes the polis and the possibilities of praxis in that polis. But while he speaks quite directly about the ontological possibilities of this mid-world of language, he avoids—persistently and at great effort—discussing its political and practical possibilities. Gadamer's contribution and advance over Heidegger is to respond to that challenge.

But both Gadamer and Heidegger suggest that it is to language in its preeminent sense, language that listens and speaks to itself at the moment of its greatest density and concentration—namely, language in the poem—that we must turn if the question of language is to show its own relation to political life. When we follow through on this suggestion, we soon arrive at the rather peculiar and disturbing topic of Gadamer's article on Plato: poetry and the political. The issue, of course, does not concern political poetry, not poetry about politics, nor the politics of poetry; rather, it concerns *the meaning of political life that is found at the site of poetry's own possibility*. This means that the starting point for reflections on political life is found in the character of language understood as that which is able to give rise to poetry.

But as soon as one does this, it must be acknowledged that to ask about poetry and the political seems forced. What indeed are poets for in times of desolation? It strikes one as somewhat absurd when one hears the poet Canetti reading from the diary of an unknown poet writing in 1939 that "It is all over. If I was really a poet, I would have been able prevent the war."[10] It seems the height of philosophical arrogance that during the war, and the period of his withdrawal from active political life, Heidegger was not preoccupied with matters of law and resistance, justice and the state, or with the responsibilities of intellectuals in times of brutality, but with poetry, especially the poetry of Hölderlin, the "poet of poetry." Famously, Adorno would even ask if one could write poetry at all after Auschwitz. And yet this is precisely the claim regarding the political force of poetic language, the claim Gadamer takes up in his text on Plato and the poets, that I believe merits serious attention.

To begin to grasp that claim, to take it seriously, one needs to recognize that here a fundamentally new sense of the relation between language, thinking, and action—one quite different from the traditional conception of that relation—is at work. Consequently, as long as we think within the framework of such a conception of the place of language and thinking in the question of praxis—as long as, for instance, we work with a metaphysical conception of a disjunctive relation between theory and praxis, discourse and deeds, a disjunction that language itself displaces, we will not be able to make sense of those apparently eccentric and irresponsible remarks that grant poetry real political power. Furthermore, so long as we think within such a framework we will never quite understand why that same framework has generated the otherwise unintelligible event that happens so frequently in times of repression—namely, the rounding up and jailing of poets and literary figures as enemies of the state—making, as Borges said, censorship the mother of metaphor.

The notion that poets pose a danger to the state is an ancient one that has repeatedly found confirmation throughout history (Václev Havel, a poet who headed a state, is a remarkable and important exception).[11] As Gadamer points out, the historically decisive text for understanding this phenomenon is Plato's *Republic*. In that meditation on the essence of political life, Plato seems, even if with some hesitation, to take sides in what he describes as the "ancient quarrel between philosophy and poetry."[12] He is, as he indicates, simply inserting himself into a by then already "ancient" and well-defined quarrel, since one already finds Heraclitus, for instance, suggesting that "Homer deserves to be expelled from the competition and beaten with a staff" [Fr., 42], and that "in taking poets as testimony for things unknown, they are citing authorities that cannot be trusted" [Fr., A23].

It is a peculiar quarrel, one that revolves largely around the paradigms of ethical discourse and the preservation of tradition. It is also a dispute that takes place before the entry of the force of disciplinariness into thinking about such matters, transferring the issue into one fought between disciplines carved by the academy. In short, the quarrel that Plato inherits is more a matter of temperament, rather than of disciplines; in the end, it is most of all a matter of language itself. But Plato does not simply inherit this ancient quarrel: he shifts its locus and ups its stakes. The decisive Platonic addition to this quarrel is to show how this feud is in truth over the relation between the possibilities of language and political action. He makes most of his significant remarks about this quarrel after having escorted some, but not all, poets to the city limits (where Socrates' story in the *Republic* begins). Lest this exile of the poets be regarded as an extreme act found only in the irony of the *Republic*, it should be recalled that in the *Laws* he sets up even more rigorous standards for censorship and for the punishment of those poets who remain in the polis yet do not adequately follow the lead of the state. The problem with the poets, says Plato, is that from the vantage point of truth (*aletheia*) and morality (*dike*) they are irresponsible and frauds. Ultimately, this tension between the poet and the polis is said to revolve around the poet's puerile relation to language. More precisely: the poet taps into and plays with that dimension of language that relates to the irrational side of the soul (one should note the telling choice of words at this point: Plato refers here to the *alogon*, the "unspeakable"). To put Plato in the language of Freud: the poets, working with the merely possible, cripple our capacity to face the actual and its real principles, and they distort the economy of the human psyche. As we grow more responsible, we outgrow the need for such playing with possibilities, and we realize that if such stories (*mythoi*) are held onto too long or taken too seriously, they can breed an unhealthy mind and soul.

But Plato is more specific about the risk of poetic language. He clarifies this when he describes that dimension of language with which the poet plays as its mimetic dimension, and while he notes that language is not alone in permitting such mimetic activity—painting, music, and dance are also discussed—the mimetic dimension of language is most threatening because its employment, more than the other mimetic arts, veils and doubles itself, dividing what should be harmonized. As Gadamer notes: "On the other hand, one who really only imitates, or 'mimes,' another is no longer really himself: he expresses himself in an alien form. However, if he only imitates the other, then he is no longer himself and he is not the other. Imitation thus entails a self-diremption."[13] A difference is introduced into that which, for Plato, must be defined as an identity. But this mimetic power of language is also dangerous since, simply because it is language, it will be picked up by all, and eventually this difference, this contradiction, will weave its way into every place in the community defined by that language. Plato wants to guarantee that the deceptive power of language is never underestimated. Even when Plato seems to overturn his earlier judgment by allowing some poets to return, they are never without fetters—thus they are forbidden to make what is rightly private public, since that is the sort of gesture that injects contradiction between the city and the soul. Furthermore, we soon discover that the real language of truth, philosophy, is not only not mimetic, it is explicitly *antimimetic*. Importantly for the tradition that follows, this is said with an eye to political stability, to control, and to the security of power. The expulsion of the poets, the practitioners of mimesis, is thus for Plato a matter of *dike* and *aletheia*, a matter of affirming the imperative of keeping things in their place. This is the imperative of placing, the imperative of finding a universal imperative that can serve as the agent of an ordering subsumption.

There is much that should be said about the irony in all of this. For instance, that in the Spartan nightmare of this republic, books, like the

Republic, that disclosed the dialectical character of dialogue through its own mimetic power would not be tolerated. There is also something noteworthy in the fact that nowhere in the *Republic* is the proper mode of philosophic discourse, the mimesis of ideas, explicitly addressed. One might even say that the whole of the Platonic corpus is haunted by this question: the question of diegesis and mimesis, of writing and speech. We know that the question of writing is problematic for Plato, that his teacher and hero of the dialogues never wrote, indeed refused to write lest his words betray him, and that Plato never appears in the dialogues and never speaks in his own voice, but we tend to ignore the way in which this problematic of speaking and writing links to his other concerns, especially his political concerns. For Plato, writing, any style of writing, the very *act* of writing, is mimetic of speech. Writing, like every mode of mimesis, hides a certain fraudulence and concealment in its essential nature. Most problematic is that written language is not alive, that in its rigidity and inflexibility it effaces the speech that is its own origin. It hides its own truth and the truth of which it speaks. Or, put in Heidegger's more graphic prose, "In what is written, the scream is easily smothered."[14] This question of the relation of language and writing will be addressed here in Chapter Ten.

But the essential political point concerns control and security, the stability and perfection of the polis, all of which, according to Plato, are undermined by the relation to language that animates certain forms of poetry. The claim is not simply that poetry can be put to dangerous use, that poets can manipulate culture, but that its very possibility is hostile to the ideals and security of any state. The stable polis must guard against the conditions that breed and are bred by such mimetic activity. While the philosopher-king is the expert, the one with the know-how (the *techne*) for securing the real moorage points for knowing and acting, the poet, on the other hand, has the capacity to rob those moorage points of their stability by fostering a relation to language that is divided within itself.

It is an odd claim that says that the soul and the city cannot be consolidated in the presence of such speech. Aristotle, himself no poet to match Plato, felt that such a claim was simply unwarranted. For him, and this is why Western liberal thought finds Aristotle so consoling, society not only can tolerate but positively benefits from the practitioners of mimesis. But Aristotle can only say this to the extent that, despite his high regard for poetry, he downplays the political originality and efficacy of poetic speech. For him one "is a poet by virtue of the mimetic element in one's work, and it is action that one imitates."[15] The speech of the poet is reactive, not culturally formative, not original and as radical as Plato takes it to be. Furthermore, the veiling and duplicity of the poet that Plato took as housing the pernicious possibilities of poetry are for Aristotle simply evidence of the immaturity of poetry, not of its mature threat. The duplicity of the poet is like that of the child who innocently "plays at" being a firefighter or philosopher. The poet is simply being playful and thereby exhibiting an underdeveloped stage of speech. Poetry, like all forms of play, is part of the process of education, part of the fabric of culture. There is nothing hostile to philosophy or culture in poetry, it contains no intrinsic threat, because for Aristotle, as, for instance, for Hegel, poetry is simply something surpassed. But, in the end, the experience of language from which it emerges has no real claim to originality.

The issue over which Plato and Aristotle divide in this case is not whether poetry has an impact on culture. Both knew quite well that, long before philosophical reflections on courage found their focus, Homer had already captured the Greek imagination and taught them that courage was like Achilles. Heidegger will make the same point when he speaks of "the sway of poetry in the existence of a people."[16] Both Plato and Aristotle knew what Hegel said so well when he confessed that "the owl of Minerva only begins its flight with the beginnings of twilight,"[17] namely, that philosophic reflection always has the character of an afterthought, whereas poetic speech tends to project in advance of itself, and so its claim on the formation of consciousness precedes the claims of philosophizing. Neither is wholly of its time. But it will not be until Hegel that we become clear that it is this disjunction, this not being solely of the moment, that defines the relation of both poetry and philosophy to time and history is at the root of their ancient quarrel.

The quarrel between poetizing and philosophizing is, in part, founded in the differing relations to history defining each. It will also be Hegel who is the first to show that this differing relation to history is definitive of how each understands itself as responding to the moral obligation to live in one's own time. The poetic and philosophic imperatives are indexed in countervalent directions. Nonetheless, long before Hegel, both Plato and Aristotle knew that poetry would always have its impact on every time, and they both agreed that such impact was, at least potentially, revolutionary. But they split over the need for philosophy to retrodictively control and stabilize that impact. Both more or less believed that language could and should be directed to affirming or completing contents that preexisted it; but, as Gadamer points out, Plato, unlike Aristotle, also believed that the mimetic dimension of speech—namely, poetic language—harbored the possibility of both creating and transforming that which it named, of stepping outside of the stable and domesticating world of ideas. In short, Plato knew, or at least sensed and reacted against, the strange and un-Greek insight, that *language could unfold in the presence of nothing*. That is why he says that the poet speaks to the side of the soul that is *alogon*; that is, the poet does not respect the margins of the logos that define the boundaries of the thinkable and the governable margins of the polis. In this regard, Plato's conception of the force of poetic language, and above all of its significance for the nature of a political community, is close to what one finds in Heidegger and Gadamer. But, contrary to the embrace of this element of poetic language in them, Plato's decision to exile the poets is an effort to tame the threat posed to a metaphysics of the community, and to the claim that the language of metaphysics—namely, the concept—should serve as the governing language of the perfected polis.

Nietzsche understood the depth and radicality of poetic practices too, and he was aware of the power of such practices in the formation of communities. That is why he must invert the Aristotlean–Hegelian hierarchy that defines the relation between poetry and philosophy: "we have art lest we perish of the truth."[18] The will to truth stifles. Art liberates. The real appreciation of the political force of mimetic practices, of the poetic experience of language, begins with Kant, whose third critique granted aesthetic experience dominion in a realm independent of the philosophical concept. Hegel and Schelling will struggle to advance Kant's great insight. But ultimately it is Nietzsche who will open the door to this point and who will be decisive for the further advance that Heidegger will make in this matter.

But while Nietzsche moves far toward appreciating the full depth and radicality of the claims of poetic language, two factors work to restrain Nietzsche's conception of the poetic urge interpreted as the highest expression of the will to power. First, for Nietzsche language in all of its modes is derivative: in the end, music defeats and debases poetry and the reach of the word. Language does not directly touch upon the fundamentally original, but traces itself back to music, to tones and gestures, rhythm, and glances. Mimetic activity is a relation to the fundamental audibility, not possible legibility, of the world, and so for Nietzsche it is music rather than poetry that would form the site out of which the true character of community can emerge. The second factor restraining Nietzsche's conception of the relation between poetry and the political is that for Nietzsche this mimetic element that refuses to be tamed in the agon of Dionysus and Apollo remains the production of the ultimate metaphysical *subject*: the pure will to power. It is the pure unfolding of the will in the presence of nothing, pure self-assertion and triumph of the will within the horizon of the subject's control. That insertion of the subject into the revolutionary moment of the poetic event distorts its promise and ultimately becomes the political liability of Nietzsche's thought. This hidden deferral to the subject is also the danger to which Heidegger succumbed when he gave his address on the "The Self-Assertion of the German University" and the danger that he acknowledged later in life when he repeatedly remarked that "Nietzsche did me in."

This is a point of difference between Gadamer and Heidegger: unlike Gadamer, Heidegger first learned about the mimetic possibilities of art from Nietzsche, not Plato, and so Gadamer does not import the subjective force latent in Nietzsche's thought into the matter as Heidegger does. But, in the end, both Heidegger and Gadamer will learn what will prove to be the most decisive point from Hölderlin, for whom art is not the transformation of the real under the power of the will, but the capacity we possess "to wander beneath the thinkable."[19] In other words, poetry for Hölderlin is the advance of that which Plato tried to ward off, and which could find no place in the polis. Pressing this point in Hölderlin, Gadamer and Heidegger eventually outstripped both Plato and Nietzsche in the extent to which Plato understood what it means to say that language always unfolds in the presence of nothing, in what Heidegger described as "the peal of Stillness."[20]

Summing up, let me simply say that the claim emerging out of the hermeneutic approach to the character of poetic language is that all language fights the empire of representation, but that escaping this empire only becomes visible with the release of thinking from the presumptions of the subject. Furthermore, this becomes most clearly visible in the special repetition and reflexivity of poetic language both upon itself and in its reiteration in culture. Such poetic language, as Gadamer persistently reminds us, is not the production of a subject, but a rejoinder to something prior, in the moment in which we are still permeated by speech and action, before either has ossified outside of us, congealing us into subjects. It is, he argues, a language that "exposes" us, not a language that is our communicative tool.

Gadamer's early text on Plato and the poets highlights Plato's sense that there was a political risk in the possibilities of poetic language; namely, the fissures it exposed, the *hexis* it cultivated, led away from the stability of the state. That risk was measured against the dominant imperatives of the stable polis: placing, universalizing, technologizing (the driving question in Plato is, after all, the question of a technics of knowing).[21] The poet refuses to hold language within those borders, to respect the legitimacy of the status quo and of the tradition upholding it. Such language refuses to live within the limits of our present domesticity, to affirm the stable. It seems clear that Plato would agree with Hölderlin's remark that "language is the most dangerous of all goods," but, because his sense of the polis was of a stable and rational place, it seems equally clear that he would not agree with Hölderlin's other judgment that poetry is the "the most innocent of all occupations."

Gadamer's intention in "Plato and the Poets" is to explore the hidden, the "dangerous" character of poetic language. When he does this, he will make a point remarkably similar to one that Adorno will make almost thirty years later, when he said that "the deep process, which every work of art marks, is buried in the irreconcilability of its moments; it is to be thought as the idea of art, as the image of reconciliation."[22] The point is simple: works of art, mimetic actions, as memoranda of things no longer and anticipations of what is not yet, as displaced from the discourse of the day, introduce a utopian and thus critical element in the life of the polis. As able to utter the unutterable, art is the medium of negative, the social antithesis of society, and art goes on living only through this antithesis. In the words of Adorno again: "Art is not only the placeholder of a better praxis than the one which rules in the present; it is also the critique of praxis as the domination of that which brutally preserves itself in the midst of what is."[23] Mimetic activity, which is but one name for the logic of the poetic event, is a groping after the still uncongealed and displaced potentials of an age. Opening possibilities, acting on behalf of the still fragmentary, mimetic activity, works as a reminder of the possibility of an integrated life, and of the real damages of every present life. It possesses a utopian and, as such, revolutionary character.

The sense of the political force of language that one finds in Gadamer and Heidegger merges easily with this sense of the utopian potential active in the mimetic arts in Adorno and other representatives of Critical Theory. But there is something that emerges from the hermeneutic conception of poetic language that is difficult to extract from any critical theorist, namely, the fundamentally *anarchic* potential of language, the capacity of language to unfold itself outside of the boundaries of the thinkable, to take leave even of itself. Language in the poem, both as heard and as spoken, refuses to cling to the present. It is, as Heidegger put it, "ready to renounce the old gods." Readiness for this renunciation and, at the same time, a founding of the new are what offer the poet language and, equally, what the language of the poet offers. Poetry speaks out of this hesitation between memory and hope—a hesitation that Heidegger called "sacred mourning,"[24] the hermeneutics of which take us out of the present place of the polis. Poetry, understood as a spirit that is nourished on such hesitation and waiting, reminds us of this authentic hesitation that should accompany every relation to the polis.

There is, of course, much more. Language is clearly a primary constituent of community. It is, as Gadamer has indicated, among the very few human possibilities that grows by being shared and divided among us. Property, food, material goods shrink when we share them; language, love, friendship, learning grow.[25] The "in-between" of the polis, the site of praxis, is defined as the perpetual and irreducible tension of that ineluctable shrinkage and growth, as the multiple dialectics of the material and immaterial, of excess and scarcity. Language, not with a capital "L," not "Language" as a sort of universalizing house, but what Bakhtin called the "heteroglossia" of languages, gives shape and form; it articulates and draws the lines of every polis. It belongs to the possibilities that enable the creative growth and openness of the polis. But, as Gadamer reminds us, what is needed is an understanding of language that begins by remembering that language is poorest at articulating itself. When those potentials emerge, when language comes to speak itself as it does in the poem, then the untenability of the philosophical discourse about the polis, which is governed by the grammar and univocal language of ideals, of security, self-preservation, of stability, comes into view. We discover the lability and mobility of the living polis when language is released from the fetters of our assumptions about it and ourselves. Naming the repressive—that is, the petrified remnants of every polis—calling things by their real and possible names, revealing them for what they are, discursively robbing them of their presumed constancy—that is the progressive potential of all speech. The being of language, which is what poetic language is most adept at exposing and releasing, has this potential because, as part of the formative and phenomenal stuff of the "in-between" on which the place and possibilities of praxis take place, *the being of language renders unthinkable the very notion of the polis as a stable place that might be the secure home of autonomous subjects*. In the end, the kinship of poetic language to the site out of which the true nature of political life is to be thought stands as a powerful memorandum of the need for every community to recognize that, if it is to be alive and responsive to its sources, then it must both open itself to differences and nourish itself on an openness to the anarchic potential of its own grounds.

I conclude with two further points that warrant attention. The first is a worry. The worry that no matter how much one might praise the potential for political life that is brought into view by thinking through the character of poetic language, it still must be conceded that poetry never did much good in the face of violence and misery or human degradation. The limits of understanding mark every theoretical, every nonmaterial reply to injustice, and the best of such replies are self-conscious about their own limitations in this matter and do not seek to overstep themselves. But to acknowledge this limit is not to undermine the great contribution to what can be learned here and what this might mean. The greatest hope will always reside in some form of understanding such as what might be opened here. One must always remember that unself-critical strategic action, unhesitating action uninformed and undisplaced by either memory or hope, does not do much good without understanding.

The second point is that in the present historical moment we have only begun to broach the question posed by the relation between poetry and the political, a question that, as Gadamer reminds us, obsessed Plato, but that we have lost. We have lost something of the capacity to open ourselves to the real force of language, especially at the moment of its greatest concentration, in the poem. The real meaning of poetry remains to be defetischized and questioned anew along the lines of its own special doubling and production. To do this, to continue this line of reflection, we would do well to think more about Gadamer's insight that "the poet makes herself into tool of her imaging: she forms things to the extent that she speaks. But what one forms is, more than the shape of things, the human being herself who expresses himself in his existence, and who knows herself in her actions."[26] Nonetheless, even if the question of poetry must be raised anew, and even if we must confront our worry about its efficacy in political life, one can say without worry that the meaning of poetry is more than that it adds to the world objects of contemplation and pleasure. Rather, such activities always remind us that all modes of discourse strain the borders of our world, that all forms of speech are potentially transformative and so risky, and that no one has sole authority on the questions of our political life. Finally—again a lesson from Gadamer's insights into the risks of authority—that in the conversation about such matters no one qualifies as an expert, and listening is as much an issue as is speaking.

One is tempted to ask if, after Auschwitz, any writing that is not poetry will suffice.

CHAPTER THREE

BETWEEN THE LINES: ON LANGUAGE, TRANSLATION, AND TRADITION

There is no muse of philosophy, nor is there one for translation.

—Walter Benjamin

The intention of this chapter is to address a tension in language, one not elective in our relation to language but made necessary by the nature of language itself. It is, I want to argue, a tension resonating in all speech as both its looseness and life. This unresolvable tension—which I would characterize preliminarily as the way in which every language, like every person, lives somewhere between uniqueness and universality, a between that renders both notions obsolete from the outset—this tension articulates a problematic, a fine and difficult line, around which a hermeneutic theory of language might grow and yet remain responsive to the original experience of language. It is a tension drawn most tightly in those relations to language in which we listen to language *as* language, as, for instance, in translation and poetry. My intention is to discuss translation and poetry in the context of hermeneutic concerns with this peculiar inner divide in language; in particular, I am interested in thinking through the impossibility of any intersection between these two attentive and articulate relations to language as language. Furthermore, I want to indicate some of the ways in which this tension proper to language shapes the formation of traditions and the very possibility of mediation so that, in the end, while we might want to speak with Gadamer of the "fusion of horizons" it is clear that we also need to recognize the process of the fission of horizons as well.

To speak of the intersection of the questions put to us by language in the poem and language in translation means that I will be concerned with the topic of translation and untranslatability, since as Gadamer, rightly I believe, remarks: "the ideal of poetic saying fulfills itself in untranslatability."[1] It is a rather striking remark, especially for one who believes that, whatever else it might be "about," all poetry is the discourse of language with itself and that in the poem the reflexive burden of language reaches its peak. Such a remark means then that the perfection of the poem is found at that moment when language in the poem begin to seal off its promises, refusing to yield itself beyond its own uniqueness, threatening instead to fall into silence. The summit of the poem arrives precisely at the moment silence begins to enter its possibilities. There are of course many elements of the poem that might lead one to that decision about its essential untranslatability, but it seems evident that the most important consideration here is the preeminent way in which sound pins language to sense in the poem. In other words, it is the relation between sound and sense, the way sound carries sense in the poem, that is experienced as a relation of mutual excess: sound and sense do not replicate one another, even as they reflect one another. This mutual excess of sound and sense is what opens the tension that drives language in the poem. One might make this point differently and say that in the poem we find the real carnality of every language; that is, we meet that point in language from which it shows itself as radically "there," as both more and less than its communicable "meaning." Thus, in the poem, language calls for voice, which is why poetry cannot be read without being sounded by some voice, and in the poem voice discloses itself as the bearer of a unique body. The task of poetry then is to return language to its body, to drive all language home to the point of its own uniqueness, to the impasse of the word to the point of the untranslatability of the word.

Strangely though, like poetry, translation must pay heed to the way in which rhythm, sound, and sense are welded together as the body of the word as its felt presence and particularity. The inevitable alienation of every translation is this displacement of the body of the text; the strangeness of speaking different languages is felt in the voice, at the intersection of language and body. Yet the task of translation is to lift language to the point of its real reciprocity with other languages, to the point of passage and universality in language. In that regard at least, poetry and translation mark countervalent modes in which language can be heard and answered as language. This is why Gadamer's remark on the perfection of the poem in its untranslatability must be heard as producing a tension when it is put together with other comments he makes about language. Here I would refer to a passage from *Truth and Method* in which the locus of concern is shifted from the possibility of poetry to the meaning and horizon of translation: "every translation . . . is the completion, the perfection, of the interpretation that the translator has made of the words given him. The example of translation, then, shows that language as the medium of understanding must be consciously created by an *explicit mediation*" (*WM*, 362, emphasis added). In short, while poetry stands as the pinnacle of the experience of the finitude of language, of its opacity and resistance, translation must be seen as the experience of the mediation possible in language, of its porosity and expansive character. Seen together, these two possibilities inherent in language expose the tension I want to address.

It should be clear that, for Gadamer, the task of thinking language as the hermeneutic and horizon of being that can be understood leads unswervingly to the question of the scope of the mediation it opens up. But one should not overstate the meaning of such mediation since Gadamer is quite clear that every such mediation is finite: "my own efforts were directed toward not forgetting the limit that is implicit in every hermeneutical experience. . . . When I wrote the sentence 'Being which can be understood is language,' what was implied thereby was that that which is can never be completely understood" (*TI*, 334). The task of those of us who work in Gadamer's wake is to trace the labile line that trails after that finite mediation. It is to ask how language makes such mediation possible and, at the same time, binds that possibility to itself in such a way as to render all mediation finite. Doing this means following the living exchange that is possible in language that can be translated. It is precisely this possibility of an exchange that lets speech belong and be vital in every present, but that just as much lifts every discourse out of the captivity of its times. It is a living exchange that fundamentally links language and history as effective, making one the question of the other. Putting the matter this way, one can see that this is what Hegel formulated as the process that discloses the identity of identity and difference; this is what Hegel speaks of in terms of mediation. For him, such an exchange is really no exchange at all, but rather the passage and communication, the real permeability, of difference. But one might also say that this exchange is a matter of what Hölderlin referred to as the question of "measure" in language—but such a measure is more akin to music than any set of calibers or counters. It is a measure attuned to the calculus of difference, more than to any production of identity, at work in language. But Hegel, more than Hölderlin, has defined the terms of the question as it is posed by Gadamer, and so mediation is the focus of his way of addressing the possibilities of language.

Of course, the question of mediation is but one of the ways—a way not without its own prejudices—of formulating the questions of otherness, of understanding and difference, ultimately even the political questions of consensus and community not founded on the notion of the autonomous subject. This concern with mediation is the question that guides Gadamer's rendering of tradition as the same always understood in different ways (cf. *WM*, 295) and it equally articulates the axis running through Gadamer's account of the experience of the work of art, the struggle for communication, the logic of question and answer, and the fusion of horizons. One might suggest that for Gadamer mediation is the axis binding the limits of every experience in the transmission of tradition. But, in the end, all those accounts and issues remain tributaries to the overarching concern with the possibility of mediation opened up by language, and this is a concern on which poetry and translation bear with a peculiar weight, since it is precisely at the impossible intersection of poetry and translation that the rough edges of the relation between language and mediation expose themselves. There we reach the limits of both language and mediation, and there we meet the first glimmer of the finitude appropriate to each, a finitude that shadows and renders problematic the full fusion of every horizon. At that intersection, that is "where language is disrupted, where understanding will not succeed, questions are asked about the [textuality] of the text, and only then can the reconstruction of the text become a task" (*TI*, 342). That is the point of the real emergence of language as language, of the limits of textuality—a turning point in language and that of course is the moment of its real arrival. It a point that, with a slightly different emphasis, Blanchot characterized as the relation of language and interruption, and to which Adorno drew attention in his plays with parataxis. That point of disruption in language is the moment in which it speaks out its own dissonance. But, as Gadamer, like Heraclitus, reminds us, dissonance is the real secret of every harmony. Speaking of the tension proper to language leads directly to the mystery of the relation of such dissonance and harmony.

Later in *Truth and Method*, after drawing this link between translation and the struggle for understanding in the fullness of mediation in language—in other words, precisely when mediation seems to win the truth of language—Gadamer provides a caveat that reopens the dissonant space in language, marking not only the possibility of poetry, but the essential relation of all language to poetry: "Where a translation is necessary, the gap between the spirit of the original words and that of their reproduction *must* be accepted. *It is a gap that can never be completely closed*" (*WM*, 346, emphasis added). It is this "must" that I would like to discuss since it inscribes in all language the impossibility of a final and full mediation. In other words, it names untranslatability at the heart of even the possibility of translation.

Poetry lives in the enigmatic gap of mediation, the rich space of untranslatability; it speaks from a certain open wound in language and must be thought from out of that site. Language in the poem—language at the moment of its greatest concentration, self-articulation, and repetition—speaks both out of and to this zone that falls silent as it speaks. That is why Celan claimed that language in the poem has "a strong tendency to become mute."[2] In poetry, the relation of language and silence is enclosed and trespassed at once, and in its untranslatability, the law governing the poem, that relation is reversed: trespass becomes captivity, enclosure becomes liberation. The translation and the poem become not polar opposites, since language has no poles, but photographic negatives of one another. Yet even at this point, where from different directions silence enters, speech happens. Even here the gates of language never completely slam shut and enclose us in final silence. But it is important to remember that silence belongs to language nonetheless. That is the aporia and fascination of all poetry, and it is this aporia that singles out both poetry and its fulfillment in untranslatability as radical challenges to the possibility of full mediation.

That large issue of mediation in the hermeneutic field forms the backdrop of my smaller topic: namely, I would like to speak to that infinite, yet easily obliterated gap in the horizon of translation, a dissonant site in language gathering poetry and translation—distant limit experiences of language turned back upon itself—into the point of their deep reciprocity and countervalence. This is the point at which language is pinned tightly to itself, the point at which silence and speechlessness most define the question of language *as* language. I propose then to speak to that point and pay special attention to the dynamic at work between this mid-world of mediation and such wounded sites in language opened up by the aporia of language in the poem. Yet in posing the question as a question of a "between," I do not want to betray the question by prohibiting the deep questionableness of that very notion itself. So I would like to ask the following: if it is the case that language belongs to the fabric of every mediation—even, perhaps especially, the mediation that is history—then how are we to think about those rips in that fabric that concentrate in the difficult nexus of translation and poetry? If language provides the continuity that establishes traditions, then how does the aporetic dimension, equally proper to language, disturb such formation of tradition? How can we speak of, or silently respond to, the place of silence in speech, and how does this silence work in the conversation that comes to define history and tradition?

Of course, Hegel traced the full and ultimately seamless sweep of mediation precisely insofar as he followed the route of such shatterings. Hegel poses such a challenge precisely because he does not shy away from the riddle of what shatters the possibility of tradition, but rather confronts such negativities head-on. But Hegel's decision is to think that route as the path of negativity: the agony of spirit confronting its own diremptions in the movement of time, the anxiety of the slave, the growth and dissolution of the family and state, the death of art for truth, the parousia of such agony turned back upon itself. The result of that decision is the revelation that, despite the essential relation of pain and negativity, it is a healing route, the route of the wholeness and wholesomeness of spirit giving voice to itself as absolute. Every impasse gives way and becomes passage. Or so it seems. In the end, no set of reflections on mediation can escape Hegel's claim that in the end, "the wounds of Spirit heal and leave no scars behind."[3] And if it is fair to characterize the intent of hermeneutics as the remembrance of both the necessity and failure, that is, the finitude, of all mediation, then it is clear that the radicalization of Hegelian thought belongs to the hermeneutic project as a finite discourse on the finite.

However, if this is to be done, then one must not let the claims of the Hegelian thought of "*Aufhebung*" define the riddle of mediation. Whereas Gadamer picks up on Hegel's transformation of the Platonic question of *methexis* as defining the question of language and meditation (and as displacing the force of the question of *mimesis*), he nonetheless does not frame mediation in a thoroughly dialectical manner. One of Gadamer's great achievements is to have pried the question of mediation away from the all-embracing empire of the movement of *Aufhebung*, and one of the ways in which he accomplished that is by drawing our attention to the finitude of the mediating potentials of language, to the claims and failures of translation. It is a shift in the hermeneutic motion that might be heard most clearly in the directionality of the two notions at stake: the move is from the dialectic of *Aufhebung* to the hermeneutic of *Übersetzung*, from the verticality of "*auf*" to the twofold verticality and horizonality of "*über,*" from the willfulness of "*heben*" to problematic of "*setzen*" without the subject. It is a move from what Hegel described as a circle of concentric circles[4] to the play of concealment and unconcealment, passage and impasse, that drives the heterocentricity of every hermeneutic circle that stands as the emblem of openness, not of final closure.

Yet that move is not without its own difficulties, particularly if it is not ready to abandon the claims of full mediation that are found at such moments as consensus in understanding and the formation of tradition as always the same singular. It is then important that we ask about permeability of the divides and differences that make the task of mediation necessary. To what extent does the untranslatability of the repetition at work in poetic speech mark an impenetrable moment, the point at which mediation becomes refusal? Put yet another way: what must be said about the largest mediating potential, ultimately the "fusion of horizons"—the most Hegelian moment in Gadamer—if we radicalize such fissures and fissions in language that are pried open in the interstices of language at the point of untranslatability? The reflections on translation that follow—reflections that attempt to nudge the thought of translation to its most problematic point, the point at which it most resists being thought under the idea of mediation—are a detour back to this point.

The following remarks begin with a comment made by Heidegger, who never underestimated the question of translation, but rather expands the riddle that it is when he says: "Sage mir, was du vom Übersetzen hältst, und ich sage dir, wer du bist."[5] Now listen to its translation by Derrida: "Dis-moi ce que tu penses de la traduction, je te dirai qui tu es."[6] And my translation compelled by English somewhere between Heidegger and Derrida: "Tell me what you think about translation, and I will tell you who you are."

It is a stunning remark that redoubles itself in every translation, especially when one faces the full force of the word "*Übersetzen*" and the extent to which it is not translated by "traduction" / "translation." What we find here is a relay of words arguing something about what one must think about "translation"—that is, if indeed the word "must" can ever be brought into reflections on language.

That comment was made by Heidegger in the course of a semester-long lecture on Hölderlin's poetry. It is a remark that occurs at the point Heidegger comes to discuss Hölderlin's translation of Sophocles' *Antigone*, and it is particularly directed to the translation of the passage that reads "*polla ta deina kouden anthropon deinoteron pelei.*" That passage is translated into English by Wyckoff as "Many the wonders but nothing walks stranger than man." But it is a passage and translation Heidegger would translate quite otherwise: "Vielfältig das Unheimliche, nichts doch / über den Menschen hinaus Unheimlicheres ragend sich regt." His translation would be better rendered as "Strangeness is multiple, but nothing / rages toward the strange more than the human being." Hearing those different translations and noticing the slippage between them, one is drawn to the play of abundance and poverty of the three languages crossing one another. At their disjunction, in the midst of the slippage that each translation signals, it seems as if the thought itself cannot be wrested free of any language yet remains up for grabs in that crossing. In that relay of passages, one senses the provisionality of every translation. One senses that the perfection of any translation is the arrival of that element that does not lend itself to translation. Translations only fulfill their promise once the possibility of translation comes to an end. So long as translation remains a possibility, it remains an infinite possibility. As with every translation of the same a dispute arises and it is felt as the truth of Benjamin's contention that true translations are, in the end, untranslatable.

But the dispute that should finally emerge here, the way in which the thought is not freed from language and so is up for grabs, is not simply one between the translators or even between the languages. Curiously, every such quarrel between translators and translations only testifies to the deep reciprocity between languages, providing proof for Benjamin's claim that "languages are not strangers to one another, but, even apart from all historical relationship, are related a priori in what they want to say."[7] What should emerge is not the contest of translations, but the struggle of language coming to word: it is the dispute of each language with itself that is found between that relay of translations. What emerges most clearly in the confrontation that each language faces in its encounter with what we curiously call a "foreign" language is that each and every language is unsettled within itself. It is precisely when a language is asked most pointedly to define itself by answering the question of what can and cannot be said that the inner limits of that language begin to become apparent. In translation, as in the poem, language is thrown back on itself and pushed to its own barriers. Here, at its own limits, language most affirms and asserts itself, insisting on remaining itself. But it is nonetheless equally the point at which every language as such must run aground. In Gadamer's words: "Thinking sets to work [and here that means: language comes to word] at the point where translation, that is the illusion of the option of some transport of a thought, meets its ruin" (HW, 116). At that point we discover that translations are not only called for by the plurality of languages, but that there is a need for translation proper to each language once that language arrives at its own limits. Likewise we discover that translation between the plurality of languages does not happen simply as a matter of connecting the "likenesses" between languages, but of asking language itself to speak. No equivalences between languages makes translation possible. In the mimetic element of translation we learn that mimesis is never a matter of representation and reproduction, but of an emergence, extension, and setting to work of the word. Mimesis, properly understood, is much better described as what Hölderlin called "the simple advance of the unthinkable."[8]

In his commentary on Hölderlin's translation of Sophocles, Heidegger suggests that what we come to understand in thinking though that translation and the demands to which it responds is what he calls the essential "translation-neediness" [*Übersetzungsbedürftigkeit*] (HH, 79) of language in the poem. It is an unusual word, naming an equally strange thought. What might most be needed to be gathered from this word is not that everything must be, or be able to be, translated, but rather that poetry is the answer of language to its own such neediness. Poetry, which fulfills itself in the ideal of untranslatability, is the perfection of the possibilities of the summons of language to its own possible translation, rooted in the kinship of languages with one another. But it also must be said that this neediness is the differential element in language, the fissure in being that is exposed in the experience of language *as* language. This is what is given to be understood by language in the poem and in translation. It is this neediness that, in a different arena of concerns, lets both Hegel and Heidegger say that being and nothing are the same, and that allows both to characterize thinking as the answer to the call of the neediness set free by this original difference.

This point from which we must acknowledge that the approach of language, the point at which language truly emerges as itself, is the point of its withdrawal. We find that the full experience of language includes the experience of its retreat from every experience. In other words, we begin from the fact that speech is marked by the same curious doubling motion we find in love; namely, that the nearer we approach the other the more clearly the distance, strangeness, and final otherness of the other become evident. But, as Gadamer reminds us, this doubling in language equally opens up the distance that we can take from ourselves insofar as language belongs to all thinking. The neediness opened up in this differential element of language— that is, the necessity and failure of language to return to itself—which defines all language is, according to Hölderlin, experienced in its most compressed form in the language of tragedy. Here we find the hint of the tragic relation binding language and ruin—a relation that Hölderlin located in the caesura of the word, "the pure word, the counter-rhythmic rupture."[9] This is the characteristic of language that Benjamin referred to as "the great longing of language for its complementation."[10] It is this longing that speaks in every effort at translation. And of course, this relation of language to ruin, rupture, and longing says much about who we are. It says much about who we are as tragic beings. And who we are not.

The revealing difficulty in translating the passage from Sophocles that Heidegger takes as the conducting wire of his remarks on the possibility of translation comes in the word "*to deinon*," and more interesting even than the word itself is our failure today to find the word again that names its truth. There is, he says, a lack of words, a shortage, one curiously instituted, then helped along, by the translation of Greek thought into Latin—a translation that Heidegger characterized as the most fateful moment in the formation of Western thought[11]—and this shortage in contemporary Western languages says much about who we are and can be today. Here translation as an essential need of language opens up onto the relation between language and history. This is the shortage and need around which speech lives and grows, around which horizons fuse and defuse.

Typically, the word that Heidegger claims we lack, *to deinon*, is translated as "strange" and, according to Heidegger, even in this flattened translation what is said in this word names the key that both opens and does not open the essence of being human. It is an opening that points toward the strangeness of speech, an opening that leads us equally to the point at which word both begins and breaks off altogether—that is, to its own birth as well as closure, to our speech and our speechlessness at once. It also provides an opening to the wound in language that keeps poetry and the full passage of translation apart, yet equally necessary and bound together.

The strangeness named in *to deinon*, in Heidegger's reading of Hölderlin's struggle to translate *Antigone*, is simply that human being finds itself marked by its essential relation to language, by the "resonance of the word." But it must be understood that this resonance is with that which itself is needy, conflicted, and living on the edge of ruin, and that it marks us as beings defined by such conflict. This link between the being of human being and the word is such a strange point that it lets Heidegger remark that "only a being who speaks, that is thinks, can have a hand and in that having a hand bring hand-works to completion."[12] In the end, even the shape of our body gets articulated along this resonance with the tension of language. The body becomes one of the ways in which language comes to elaborate itself as us, and language one of the ways the body moves beyond the borders of skin. One thinks here of Helen Keller who, before her first words, lived in an infinitely compressed universe of skin, but with the word instantly found an infinite universe of distance and inwardness. Both the gift and agony of our being "who we are" lead us back to language since even our death must be thought as a kind of silence, as finally the silence that shadows speech. This is the point at which we might glimpse the essential relation between language and mortality that, according to Heidegger, only "flashes" before us. It is also the point from which we might hear the meaning of his claim that the poet speaks from the basic mood of "sacred mourning."

So when we come to the hermeneutic question of translation, we come to the heart and limit of who we are and can be. Most important is to recognize that when we address the question of translation, we then move in fields far broader than those concerned with the technicalities of exchange between languages. The experience of translation clearly belongs to the special anxiety of always being only on the way to language, never quite there, of, as Canetti recalls, the imminence having one's tongue cut off. The passage from Canetti that I have in mind and find pertinent is from his autobiography, *The Tongue Set Free*:

> My earliest memory is dipped in red. I come out of a door . . . the floor in front of me is red, and to the left a staircase goes down, equally red. . . . A door opens, and a smiling man steps forth . . . steps right up to me and says: "Show me your tongue." I stick out my tongue, he pulls out a jackknife, opens it, and brings the blade to my tongue. He says: "Now we'll cut off his tongue." I don't dare pull back my tongue, he moves the blade closer. In the last moment he pulls the knife back, saying "Not today, tomorrow."
>
> Every morning I step into the red hallway, the door opens, and the smiling man appears. I know what he is going to say and I wait for the command to show my tongue. I know he's going to cut it off, and I get more scared each time. That's how the day starts, and it happens often.[13]

That threat of losing one's tongue is the threat of every translation, of every poem as well since both live with the wound, the finitude, of all mediation in language. Both the translation and the poem open the horizon of language, the horizon of possible experience, onto the impossibility of every such opening; that is, onto the ultimate untranslatability of ourselves. Yet it seems to me that Hölderlin is right when he says that "rigorous mediation, however, is the law."[14] Both poetry and translation then bear witness to the trespass we are. Hermeneutic theory sits neither on the side of the law, nor of trespass, but is sensitive to the countervalence of the two. In the end, the understanding of language opened here, an understanding necessarily committed to the possibility of translation, reaches so far that Heidegger can say: "Tell me what you think about translation, and I will tell you who you are."

Let me conclude with some comments directed toward the question of language and mediation, comments that I hope remain close to the wounded site in language marked by poetry and translation, but that are directed toward the larger issues that emerge in discussing the relation of language, culture, and history.

Language, in the words of Levinas, is contact. A contact on a threshold that moves in two directions—toward the inside and outside at once—a contact that effaces both the inside and outside as such, opening each to the distance of the other and the distance that opens onto ourselves as well. It clearly articulates the permeability of human beings with one another, with their worlds, and it gives shape to the borders of every culture. The struggle to speak and communicate is the struggle to come to language as a site of such permeation and crossing. The failure to communicate and the evanescence of every success both testify to the organic life of language, of its death as well. But, as if in compensation for such failures and evanescence, the mobility of cultures, the phenomenal stuff of their life and death, springs from that same lability of languages. As Gadamer puts the point: "language is like a field upon which the most varied things might grow" (*HW*, 116). But the darker side of that remark is that the horizon of language, the limits of speech, of having a voice, draw the limits of history and culture.

Those limits of language are set in motion in many ways, but no relations to language do so more than those named translation and poetry. Both belong to the same site, both have an essential relation to the edges of language, and both are governed by the same measure. Both push language beyond, at times beneath, itself, setting it on its way. Language grants a culture its place insofar as it yields its own; culture carries the organic life of a language in its dynamics both internal to itself and with other cultures. In this respect, it must be said that language and culture sacrifice themselves to one another. Gadamer makes this point when he reminds us that of all the human goods, language belongs to that select group that grows and enriches itself the more it is divided and shared (see *L*, 45).

But language is more than such self-sacrifice; it is just as much a stabilizing force: the vehicle whereby tradition is transmitted, the voice of law, the vessel of grace and grief as well. To some extent Hegel is right when he describes the mediating powers of language as limitless and when he says about the formation of tradition as history that it lives in the temple of *mnemnosyne*. But what Hegel overlooked, even if only by a glance, is that memory, like all else that we are, lives only as the self-concealing self-sacrifice of silence in language. Remembering that, knowing as well that language and history are, as both Benjamin and Celan rightly saw, the language and history of the victors not the victims, means that history lives just as much in the dark site of *lethe*. Hegel remarked that "history is the slaughterbench of the happiness of peoples,"[15] and he also noted that the periods of happiness are its blank pages. What he did not remember is that when history is written, it is written by those who have the power and place granting speech. That there are those who, by virtue of many forces, are left without a voice and at the margins of the discourse of history. But it is important to see that such overlooking is not simply a lapse on Hegel's part; it is rather at the invitation of the silence that belongs to language itself. *Every formation of tradition in language necessarily includes a certain marginalization in silence.* The very fact that we are, as Hölderlin put it, "a conversation" makes such exclusion perpetually possible. The dynamics of memory and forgetfulness, one axis along which history turns, must be understood as belonging to the experience of language as shadowed by silence. This means that history and tradition must be read and written as an effort to bring to voice those who have none. Like poetry, every sense of history and tradition must face the burden of being grounded in silence. But this implies that both the writing of history and the formation of tradition must be understood as governed by the imperative to recover what is lost and silenced. Both history and tradition must be not only the extension of the thinkable, but equally open to the "simple advance of the unthinkable." Without wishing to yield to the metaphysical demand for an imperative here, it seems clear that the deeper call of speech is to work against such marginalization and exclusion in history. Poetry and translation, each in their own way, are relations to language that argue with that marginalization, and that is the reason that both have such political importance. Plato's decision, so significant in the formation of Western culture, to send the poets over the limits of the polis is an acknowledgment of that import.

In the end, the life and death of culture and history, victors and victims, memory and forgetfulness, cannot be thought apart from the experience of language. Its possibilities trace the parameters of memory and hope; its limits only the outer edges of forgetfulness, edges we sense just as we sense a word not yet spoken. Hölderlin's remark about the sameness of the measure that governs poetry and translation bears out this sensibility. It is the measureless measure of language itself come to word. The measure of language, a measure found on the edges and gaps of language in the experiences and promises of language held by poetry and translation, resists the insistence on stability that so deeply attracted Western thought after Plato. This metaphysical demand and stability insist that the dominant discourse of the day take itself as *the* single discourse of the Western tradition. But language experienced and thought as language in its particularity and density, at the site of its crossings with other languages, shows itself as destabilizing the margins of history and culture. Oppressive governments have long known that: censorship, the otherwise perplexing punishment of poets and literary figures, is the tribute rigid powers pay to the destabilizing power and differential element of language.

Translation is a border-crossing, an activity that always lives by moving back and forth over the limits of the polis and every community. As such, it is an activity that meets resistance at every turn, resistance in both directions of its motions. Every translator lives with that resistance; it is felt as the failure, at least as the difference that defines the relation of every translated text to its own original. It is a material resistance, one that leads us to ask anew about the very possibility of any translation whatsoever. In the end, the question of translation leads to questions about this materiality and resistance in language, to questions about both the promise and refusal of all language and saying.

But then that is always the point to which the topic of translation leads: to the limits of its own possibility, to a point beneath / outside / beyond language as it presently stands, to the materiality of every language, the unity of sound and sense, the sense of its inviolable integrity. Translation pushes hard against that point and those limits. It lives in a between, a midworld of particulars, where the hard choices must be made, where such choices make every bit of difference, and where the measure of such choices is not an exchange of stable identities, but a calculus of differences always in motion. In translation, language is experienced with a peculiar intensity, an intensity that opens us up to ourselves anew: "Tell me what you think about translation and I will tell you who you are." And who you are not. In the end, what sharpens the question of translation and gives it a perpetually renewing relevance for hermeneutics is that no matter how it is set in motion, no matter what calculus serves as its measure, it cannot escape the fact that it is always concerned with language in its particularity. Not with language in the abstract, not with generalities about language, but with language grounded in silence, finally a "this" multiplied and impossibly at odds with itself.

CHAPTER FOUR

ON BLANK PAGES, STORMS, AND OTHER IMAGES OF HISTORY: SPEAKING AND IMAGINING HISTORY

> We speak of our hearts, our plans, as if they were our own, and yet there is a power outside of us that tosses us about as it pleases until it lays us in the grave, and of this power we know nothing, neither where it came from nor where it is going.
>
> —Hölderlin, *Hyperion*

"History" is one of the names whereby we refer to that which is larger than what we define or can know, but that nonetheless defines each of us. It is what exceeds me and my times, yet as defining the context and possibilities that circumscribe what can emerge from out of my times, it summons me to the infinite task of understanding what history itself might be said to be. Precisely this infinite task constitutes the finitude of human life. To take up the question of history is not only to ask about the context within which any time may be understood, it is equally—perhaps even most of all—to address this finitude and to ask about how it is about to be brought forward to the word.

But what is perhaps most striking to one who would ask about how history is spoken of in philosophical discussions that take it seriously is the great variety of the senses of history that one finds. While it is widely acknowledged that "history" belongs to what thinking is called to address, and while it is fair to say that a consciousness of the effective life of history is almost a given in philosophical discussions of the past two centuries, the meaning of "history" is itself in fundamental dispute and sorely in need of some clarity. Nietzsche's effort to this end in his *On the Use and Disadvantage of History for Life* makes a significant advance in that direction and is worthy of attention, even if it does not find it in the following remarks.

The ambition of this chapter is not so great that it would pretend to bring even a small degree of clarity into these disputes. Rather, the purpose of what follows is simply to call attention to some features of this mosaic we call history that I believe need to receive greater emphasis in discussions that dare to speak of history. If some sense of clarity emerges, then it should be a clarity about the limits of speaking of history at all. What is to be seen is how far the struggle to open a sense of history must reach beyond the limits of what is sayable. What I hope emerges here is a sense of the mystery that the experience of history awakens in us. All of the features of history to which I will refer need to be understood as mementos of the finitude that is exposed in the question of history. Sensitivity to the force of history awakens us to the point at which we find ourselves experiencing the radical limits on the power of the present to shed sufficient light to clarify even itself—to say nothing of other times.

More important still: though it is not immediately apparent in every instance, in what follows it is assumed that the question put to us by history is a question that can only receive answers that are ethical or political. The reason is simple and basic: the realm of history, the manner in which the finitude proper to it appears, is human freedom. The field of the question of history is freedom and practical life. This means that, in the end, history itself and the histories that are told cannot be understood conceptually or scientifically or as matters of fact. Every particular history, as well as the idea of history as such, needs to be regarded not only as expressing the self-understanding of those who would write it, but also the struggle to actualize freedom. Consequently, whatever its determinate content, history is one of the ways finite beings express, and struggle to respond to, the ethical and political riddles, riddles rooted in freedom, of shared life in time. Wedded to the past, the stakes of history are nonetheless firmly lodged in the future.[1] The difficulty of coming to terms with history is above all a moral difficulty.[2] But this moral difficulty is worked out in an arena in which the capacity of language to gather memory is tested.

> When one considers the discontinuities of the mind and the discontinuities of the world, it is amazing that anything true has been established at all.
>
> —Leon Wieseltier, *Kaddish*

History would seem to find its roots in the human inclination toward continuities and the sense of finding truth that emerges out of connectedness.

History always first appears as the workings of some sort of synthesis. Kant, whose sense of the force of history is underdeveloped by present standards, is nonetheless largely responsible for establishing the prominence of a concern with history in contemporary philosophy by virtue of the case he made for understanding human experience as a synthetic event through and through. By exposing the workings of synthesis in the very capillaries of human experience, and by demonstrating how this synthetic impulse repeats itself throughout every form of human experience and understanding, Kant opens the door to the view that synthesis needs to be understood as extended in time and beyond the life of the individual; in other words, experience continues itself in history.

Hegel's conception of history as the synthetic work of spirit announces such a viewpoint in perhaps its most extreme form: history is the achievement of "freedom in the form of the state"[3] and the "presentation of the divine."[4] A later version of Hegel's view of history, one tempered by an increased sensitivity to the failures of spirit to accomplish its self-defined mandate in history, is to be found in Gadamer's notion of history as the "fusion of horizons" in which the unresolved tensions of the past are not sublated, but serve rather as sites for radical historical reflection.[5] In the end, even those who take the matter of history to heart still owe the first debt to Kant and his analysis of the life of synthesis.

While it is true that the question and elementality of history demand an understanding of the role of synthesis in experience, it is equally true that the logic of synthesis does not tell the full story of the roots of history. As a form of devotion to what is absent, history must equally struggle against this very same mandate of synthesis so that the claims of what is rescued by such tales of continuities and connections do not overshadow and finally erase what is omitted, what is forgotten, by such rescue efforts of memory. This means that, though born of memory and its peculiar power of preservation, history that understands its true task is relentlessly indexed to the riddle of forgetting and the penumbra that announces it. It does not take much effort to see that forgetting is, as it were, if not "older" than memory, then at least contemporaneous with it. The inner limits of our historicizing belong equally to the sources of history. Consequently, history is what it is not by virtue of any claim to have fully preserved the past, but rather by creating a realm that preserves the possibilities for the appearance of that which exceeds the achievements of memory in its present historical form. To say this is to acknowledge something more than the sentiment animating Tacitus's remark that "one can only laugh at the foolishness of one who would extinguish the memory of future times by virtue of the power of the present." It is to say more than that memory is fluid. It is rather to say that forgetting, not memory, is the most original way in which history happens. Such is the point Heidegger makes the opening issue and leitmotif of *Being and Time* when he begins the project of unfolding the kinship of being and time by speaking first of all of forgetting. The deepest operations of history are not those outlined by the logics of capture and recovery, but by loss and elusivity.

It is the lacerating course of time that dissolves all things that belongs to the root of history: "only the gods never die. All else in the world almighty time obliterates, crushes all to nothing."[6] History concerns itself with the residue of what has become nothing, and as such it must be understood as belonging to a realm of corruptibility. This does not conflict with Hegel's claim that history must be grasped as belonging to the space opened up by the appearance of freedom in the world. Quite the contrary: history is the most potent reminder of the corruptibility of freedom itself.

> ... the important thing for the remembering author is not what he experienced, but the weaving of his memory, the Penelope work of recollection. Or should one call it, rather, a Penelope work of forgetting? Is not the involuntary recollection, Proust's *memoire involontaire*, much closer to forgetting than what is usually called memory?
>
> —Walter Benjamin, "The Image of Proust"

In antiquity, Cleo, the muse of history, was, like all of the nine muses, presented as a child of Zeus and Mnemosyne, of order and memory.[7] But the image of the muse is not the only symbolic representation of the ancient sense of our relation to what has been brought to nothing by time. More powerful images of the strangeness of the past and of the way in which what is dead and absent haunt the living are to be found in images of Hades, which is the true realm of memory. The claims of the past make themselves know in several ways. Beyond the obvious ways—the documents, laws, buildings, wars, and laws—there are other ways in which fugitive times and those who belonged to such times are remembered: grave markers, funeral orations, and celebrations are just some of the ways in which the living refer themselves to the dead. Such efforts are "intended to place [the historical present] *en representation*, beyond the reach of time."[8] Even if, in the end, such works were but an illusory mastery of time, they served the ends of establishing a continuity of the present with the past and, after a fashion, of turning what was into what continues to be.

But the image of Hades, dark and different from the world of the day and its creatures (as the subconscious is when compared with conscious life), served a different end, namely, of providing a visible representation of the now invisible past.[9] In thinking of Hades, we find ourselves asking about the nature of the past. One visited the dead for many reasons (though always to receive some sort of knowledge) and by means of a variety of routes (always somehow dangerous). Three images of the realm of the dead stand out in Greek literature: Odysseus's visit to Hades in Book XI of Homer's *Odyssey*, Dionysius's visit to the underworld in order to bring a worthy tragedian back to the city of Athens in Aristophanes' *The Frogs*, and Er's experiences on the other side of the river of Lethe in Book X of Plato's *Republic*.[10] But it is the passages in Homer found in the book of the *Odyssey* that have come to be called "The Gathering of the Shades" that best suit my purpose of calling attention to an image in which the relation of the living and the dead is presented as a sort of difficult memory.

"The Gathering of the Shades" is paradigmatic of how Hades represents both the realm of the past remembered and, at the same time, the way in which that past exceeds the understanding of the living. It presents a view of the living and the dead as both able and not able to communicate.[11] Odysseus travels with his crew to Hades in order to speak with the blind prophet Tireseus who has always been able to foresee the future and now, precisely because he is blind, is able to see in the darkness of the underworld.[12] The purpose of this trip is for Odysseus to locate himself and find his way home. To be able to communicate with the dead, a ritual involving blood obtained from a sacrifice is required. Odysseus meets many legendary heroes and old friends, but in the end so many of the dead will crowd around him that he will be overwhelmed and so flee Hades in terror. But one encounter stands out as particularly revealing of the real nature, and the paradox, of such a journey: the meeting with his mother. Odysseus had been gone a long time and did not know that his mother had died (of grief over his fate). He sees her among the shades of the dead and, of necessity, must delay speaking with her until Tireseus has first tasted the blood and said what must be said. When he finally does speak with his mother, the poignant conversation concludes with Odysseus "desperate to hold her."[13] He reaches out three times in an effort to embrace her, but each time she flutters through his fingers, "dissolving like a dream."[14] He eventually cries out in despair and frustration, asking her why he cannot embrace her one more time, and she answers simply that such is the *dike*—the justice—of mortal life. The limits engraved in time cannot be breached.

This journey to Hades is a journey both to the realm of a distant past beyond Odysseus's own times and to the past that he himself has known. While in this realm Odysseus learns not only the future he must follow to find his way home, but also something of the present lives of his distant loves. What he learns most of all, and this is the most painful knowledge, is that the past he visits is truly of a different order and that, in the end, it cannot be grasped. As the dead come flooding around him he is full of dread and knows that he no longer belongs among these memories and that he cannot learn all that they might have to tell him. He knows as well that it will not be long until he joins them as they are (part of what Tireseus tells him is what he must do if he is to die well). It is, in the end, a beautiful image of the mystery—of the fascination and pain coupled together—of visiting the realm of what remains only as a memory. Ultimately one suffers rather than knows one's relation to the past. That in part is what Hölderlin means when he writes that "time is always [more knowable] when it is counted in suffering."[15]

> Proust's method is actualization, not reflection. He is filled with the insight that none of us has time to live the true dramas of the life we are destined for. This is what ages us—this and nothing else. The wrinkles and creases on our faces are the registration of the great passions, vices, insights that called on us; but we, the masters, were not home.
>
> —Walter Benjamin, "The Image of Proust"

The Greek imagery of Hades, understood as the native land of memory, presents us not only with an image of the past from the point of view of the living, but also, so far as it is possible, from the perspective of the dead.[16] The dead do not visit the living ("the Greeks are not really good with ghosts"),[17] but, when the living do manage to visit the dead, what they inevitably find is the memory of what has been suffered. What lasts is what has been suffered, and in the ancient world the images of those who have suffered greatest are presented as the images of those whose memory will last. And in doing this the image of Hades reminds us that history is what we suffer rather than being something we simply make or produce. It is the record of human passions, of errors, and of failed and lost efforts and dreams. History is the search for the way such passions can be recorded, both in language and other ways.

Hegel, who Heidegger rightly called "the last Greek," is perhaps the one who has labored most persistently to make this point in the modern age and to demonstrate the relation of history to human passions. For Hegel, history is the "slaughterbench" of the happiness of peoples and periods of happiness and peace are merely its "blank pages"[18]: "nothing great in the world has been accomplished without passion," which is one element (the other is the idea) in the great fabric of human history.[19] But this passion works in the form of negation and must do so if it is to enter history since time itself is "sensible negativity."[20] Passion must destroy if it is to build. Like time, it is the constant annihilation of the present. That is why Hegel argues that the record of this passion driving history is the record of the negative at work. For Hegel, however, this is the record that is written on *all appearance*. It is the price of appearance at all in the space of history: indeed we even wear the meaning time on our faces and as our bodies.[21] It is a passion that we suffer, not one that we either control or fully grasp. In this we are reminded that there is nothing abstract about the question time poses for us:

the human scale of this question is found in the experience of ageing that we each, each in our own way, undergo.

Hegel's way of taking up this movement—of the individual who ages as well as the history of peoples in transition—charts it as the movement of negativity itself. It is a negativity constantly struggling with itself and confronting, negating, its own results; it is thus, as Hegel says everywhere and always of the dialectic, the "negation of a negation." Furthermore, this "monstrous power of the negative"[22] is, according to Hegel, only to be grasped in the confrontation with death. It is only in death that the full power of the negative is witnessed. Death thus ultimately forms the axis for the happening of history, and so nothing less than death, "the absolute master,"[23] will let us glimpse the full nature of experience as historical, as the concrete movement of time. In the anxious confrontation with death the deepest stakes of the question of historical experience are exposed.[24] Likewise, the limits of our ability to represent historical experience appear at this point.

But while Hegel goes to great lengths to take up the full force of the negative in time and history, and while he makes it clear that the course of history is the path of sacrifice,[25] it is still the case that for Hegel history takes place in the "temple of Mnemosyne"[26] and that, in the end, nothing essential is lost. What is lost, what returns to forgetfulness never to emerge, the blank pages of history, simply loses its claim on the future and, in losing this claim, secures its own annihilation. As a sort of safeguard against the possibility of an error regarding history, the "image of the phoenix"[27] reminds us that not even the appearance of annihilation can fully obliterate the governing idea of history that memory preserves. In this way history continually corrects itself and thereby confirms its own truth: history is thus a theodicy driven by "the impulse of perfectibility."[28] For Hegel, the destination of history, though initially hidden and frequently obscured, remains in place.

Despite its remarkable insights, Hegel's insistence on the view that history marks the triumph of memory must ultimately be read as forgetting the elemental force of forgetting in the operations of history. Since Nietzsche, Benjamin, and Heidegger, that view has come under rather sharp criticism for the way in which such "essential" history effaces those forces that were pushed to the margins of power. To suggest that nothing essential is lost in history is to say that the victims of history, those who suffered the fate of being silenced by history, have no place in history. But Hegel's legacy and contribution to the discussion of history are still very much alive, even if not adequately recognized—namely, his view that history needs to be thought of as the unfolding of a destiny. The view that the present age is ultimately only to be comprehended as the issue of a necessary evolution (even if the present age understands itself as the time of a revolution) is a common denominator in a wide variety of conceptions of history at work in contemporary discussions. It is common even to those—such as Nietzsche, Benjamin, Heidegger, and Derrida[29]—who have gone far to mark the space of the forgotten for the question of history. In the end, the seductions of the power of retrodiction, which is the mode of address proper to history, are so great that they project themselves into the future. The power of the present gives the hue of destiny to every history. The present age cannot seem to understand itself except as having had to be. Yet in such a view the place of freedom in history loses its claims.

> What conclusions can we draw? To invite the gods ruins our relationship with them but set history in motion. A life in which the gods are not invited isn't worth living. It will be quieter, but there won't be any stories. And you could suppose that these dangerous invitations were in fact contrived by the gods themselves, because the gods get bored with people who have no stories.
>
> —Roberto Calasso, *The Marriage of Cadmus and Harmony*

But how appropriate is it to think of the movement of history as the unfolding of a destiny, in particular a destiny that follows the trajectory of a tragedy? It is clear that such a strategy is widespread among philosophers who make two special assumptions: first, that the complexities and confusions of this historical present cannot be understood in isolation, but need to be grasped as having emerged out of the past; and, second, that the present age needs to be understood as the arrival of a time of fundamental, epochal, transformation and rupture. In Hegel one finds both the first and perhaps most extreme formulation of these twin assumptions. The preface to Hegel's *Phaenomenologie des Geistes* lays out, and operates with, precisely these assumptions: the present age, described as a time of the birth of the radically new, is presented as the result of the exhaustion of the past. History is now to be understood as the manufacture of a crisis that can only resolve itself by a "leap"[30] to the new. In short, the destiny of history is ready to be exposed and this destiny is interpreted as exhibiting a tragic logic.

The view that the present age reveals itself as a time of singular crisis, even of catastrophe, that must be grasped as having been unfolded in the inexorable epochal logic of a historical destiny underpinning metaphysics and modernity unites Marx, Nietzsche, Heidegger, and Derrida.[31] Likewise, attempts to come to terms with the Holocaust—attempts such as one finds in Adorno, Lyotard, and Lacoue-Labarthe—frequently confront this topic explicitly, ultimately even needing to pose the question of the singularity of the crisis of the historical present.[32] Furthermore, this tendency to turn to an image of tragic destiny to comprehend the troubles of the present is not restricted to philosophers, but seems to belong very much to the tendencies of the age itself. So, for instance, at the PEN conference held a few years ago in Bled in the former Yugoslavia, the writers who spoke and sought to understand the crisis in Bosnia did so according to the model of a Sophoclean tragedy.³³ *Antigone* seemed to be the tragedy of choice in this case (and the choice of one's tragedy is all important) since the questions of law, government, death, and resistance were the preeminent concerns.³⁴ Only one speaker cautioned against the assumptions that are borne along by the use of such an interpretive model, suggesting that to take this Greek, this supremely Western invention, as a hermeneutic model, is to invite a sort of Trojan horse for all sorts of Western values into the dialogue that ensues. A curious paradox seems to emerge from this project of thinking the historical present according to the model of a tragic destiny: in order to render intelligible the end of a long-standing tradition the logic of a literary genre, which Aristotle analyzed definitively at the outset of that same tradition, is enlisted. Of course, one must ask whether this turn to tragedy as a model for thinking history signals the ability to see a transformations at work in history or whether it is the residue of that very same history with which Hegel, Nietzsche, Heidegger, and others are struggling to overcome. To what extent is the specific form of the historical consciousness of the present age itself deeply embedded in the very history that it would analyze?

> They all yearn to make of themselves a beautiful sacrifice, a difficult sacrifice, to bring transformation, and to die shedding light within this life, setting the matter ready for their true beginnings to cry into being, scorched by the strange ecstacy of the will ascending to say yes to destiny and illumination.
>
> —Ben Okri, *The Famished Road*

Literature has frequently proven itself to be more agile than philosophy at unfolding a course of events as a sort of destiny without giving its story an overbearing stamp of teleology and theodicy. But this point has been a bone of contention for philosophers since Plato argued for the expulsion of the tragic poets from the city while reserving all the stories for the ones the philosophers would tell. Yet, along with the discovery of the question of history, post-Kantian thought has demonstrated its readiness to reverse that Platonic argument and to take to heart the insights of the work of art for truth. When philosophers do in fact turn to literature, or to literary models, in order to work out a conception of history, then it is worth noting that Greek works of art, in particular Greek tragedy, have a clear priority. Schelling is the first to argue for such a priority of tragedy as an interpretive model, but his argument, made in the final letter of the *Letters on Dogmatism and Criticism*, stays largely on the level of an announcement. It is left to Hegel to turn this prospect into a systematic philosophical reality.

But between Schelling and Hegel we find what might be the most nuanced and original effort to raise questions regarding the nature of the historical present in the context of such concerns and models. Though largely, and unjustly, neglected in philosophical debates about history, it must be acknowledged as one of the deepest sources of inspiration for the respective contributions of Benjamin and Heidegger to those debates. Hölderlin's treatment of the question of history—framed by the themes of destiny, suffering, memory, forgetting, tragedy, and ancient Greece—is developed in a variety of formats such as letters, translations, poems, theoretical texts, and a novel. All these works, whatever their format, are suffused with a powerful sense that the proper relation to the past is found in mourning, and so it is ultimately in reflecting on this tonality of mourning that one finds the fullest sense of Hölderlin's notion of the claim of history and of the proper response to that claim.

Though this tonality of mourning saturates his work, and though it is difficult to point to any single text in which a "theory" of history might be said to be advanced, the most direct statement of Hölderlin's conception of history is found in a letter that he writes to his friend Casimir Böhlendorf in December 1801.[35] It is one of few efforts we have in which the question of history is posed poetically rather than conceptually;[36] in other words, here history is taken up not according to the imperatives of synthesis and systematicity, but from out of the mood of a mourning that is keyed to what cannot be recovered. This is a vision of history that regards history as a form of destiny (it is neither accident nor error), but that nonetheless is not speculative. History does not fulfill itself in its own recuperation: "with the exception of what for the Greeks and us must be the highest, namely to have a ... destiny, we must not bear any resemblance to them." Here in this letter, as elsewhere, Hölderlin's work continually reminds us that separation in time, history, presents us with a difference that cannot be overcome (as separation in space at least potentially permits). Rather, separation in time, which is preserved in language and memory, can only be suffered. The space of history can be no larger than the space that is circumscribed by the realms of language and memory. But, as Hölderlin points out in the letter to Böhlendorf, this fact has a consequence for understanding the present age: insofar as it has its roots in what has passed away and translated itself into word and the image of memory, it must be said that its has its roots in what is foreign. Severance defines our relation to the past, the caseura is the only possible way in which this relation can be presented, and "the lack of destiny, the *dysmoron*, is [thus] our weakness."[37] History, according to Hölderlin, presents us with the legacy of such severance in time. If it is the case that all suffering feels ancient, that is because suffering is how the past presents itself to us. Suffering associates itself with the ancient.

But, because there is discontinuity at work in the operations of history for Hölderlin, there can be no grand catastrophe, or turning point, of history to be thought as there is in Hegel. The crisis of the present age is of a different order; namely, that it knows its own crisis to be that it lacks a destiny. The workings of history present us with a sort of constant wounding and dislocation that admit neither systematicity nor closure. In short, history permits no absolutes, even in the most extreme moments of its own distress and caesura. Of course, this also means that no grand narrative of history is possible either—the absences it has produced have scarred us too deeply to permit such a present fiction to legitimate itself. In the Böhlendorf letter, Hölderlin says that he is "full of [the feeling] of departure." While that remark is made in the special context of his own present plans, it is a phrase that perfectly announces the experience of history as Hölderlin understands it: it is the experience of departure. "Like a howling north wind, the present blows through the blossoms of our spirit and cuts them down just when they would bloom."[38]

> When the storm rages around the hut, then I think of 'our storm'—or I walk along the quiet path of the Lahn river—or I dream away a period of rest with the image of a young woman in a raincoat, with a hat pulled down over her large peaceful eyes, who came into my office for the first time and whose comportment and shyness gave a brief answer to every question—and then I transpose this image upon the final day of the semester—and just then I know *that life is history*.
>
> —Martin Heidegger to Hannah Arendt

One image of history that serves in many ways to gather together the complexity of the experience of history is the image of the storm. Perhaps the best known and most focused employment of this image for these ends is found in Benjamin's imaginative "reading" of the Klee painting, *Angelus Novus* in his "On the Concept of History." After one sees the painting itself, one is struck by the great interpretative leaps Benjamin must make to view this painting in this way. Benjamin sees in this painting the "angel of history," "turned toward the past," witnessing "one single catastrophe" that the angel "would like to make whole."[39] But this angel is not a comfortable spectator regarding this ever-growing catastrophe of the past from afar—it is rather wrestling with the winds of a storm that is blowing from somewhere else, a storm so "violent" that the angel can no longer even close its wings. We are reminded by the way in which Benjamin presents this image that history does not permit a neutral or objective standpoint from which we might address ourselves to its riddles—it catches everything up in itself. This means that one who would speak of history has always already been implicated in and by it, and so the hermeneutic situation into which we are placed by the question of history is not unproblematic. To speak of history while enlisting the image of a storm, of the turbulence of time and of force, is to say that nothing remains constant for us and that the sole constant is that history is "effective" and eventful. In this way history claims us and, if we are to grasp the nature of this claim, if we are to see some of the ways in which we are claimed by it, then we must "brush history against the grain,"[40] we must turn into the storm.

In his letter to Arendt, then a young student with whom he was having an affair, Heidegger refers to the "storm" that their relationship had set loose in both their lives. Though invoking an image of a storm, the letter exhibits a quiet calmness and ends with the affirmation that "life is history." Eight years later, at the beginning of the time of great upheavals in history that he foolishly regarded as a time of destiny, Heidegger will conclude the infamous Rectoral Address with an invocation of the image of the storm once again. This time the image is drawn from a translation of a passage in Plato's *Republic* and one that self-consciously draws itself into the question of the history at that moment: "everything great stands in the storm."[41] If Hades serves as an image of the force of the past and history and of its special enigmas, then this image of the storm, which Benjamin suggests is always "blowing from Paradise,"[42] provides us with an image of the power of the future in history. The "storms" of history happen because the past, present, and future do not "rhyme," because they are discordant. The storm reminds us that history is still, always, a matter of promises yet to come. The content of these "promises" is an open question—so much so that Heidegger could, at one time, believe that they were announced by the National Socialists—and so while the image that Hades provides is full of the shades of the dead, the storm of the future is an open matter. Both images speak, each in its own way, of both the continuities and discontinuities of shared life in time. Both images present us with a view of history as too unsettled to be sedimented into any canon or tradition, especially a sense of tradition that one would feel free to designate as "the" tradition (the "the" is always out of place in discussions of tradition). History is that which continually disturbs and disrupts itself. Understood properly, we must say that to speak of closure in history is not a possibility, and to speak of systematicity is only a fiction. Historical reflection knows itself to be the enemy of finality and every pretension to final solutions. It is, by virtue its own nature, inherently critical, inherently indexed to change.

In you the virus of time began.

—Tony Kushner, *Angels in America*, Part 2

History might be born of the human inclination to synthesis and the urge to establish continuities in time, but in the end the experience of history serves to remind us both of the discontinuities that we suffer and the ineradicable limits of our ability to reach across time. History is precisely the operation of this double bind between synthesis and limit. That is why history needs to be understood as one of the ways in which human finitude articulates itself. That, I believe, is a point that ultimately let itself be established without significant dispute.

But what might be more a matter of dispute is the point most important for the question of history; namely, that it poses questions that only permit answers that are ethical or political. Here I can only conclude with a suggestion that echoes Kant's deep insights in the third critique about why it is that aesthetic experience needs to be regarded as an ethical matter, a matter of educating judgment. There he suggests that, because it "quickens" my awareness of what exceeds that which I can define and grasp conceptually, such experience opens me to senses of purpose and of community that exceed my private interests. Likewise, I would suggest that the experience of history, real historical reflection, opens us in much the same manner.

But then it must also be said that the experience of history, like aesthetic experience, is, in these times, exceedingly rare.

CHAPTER FIVE

TIME MADE LOUD:
ON LANGUAGE AND MUSIC

> Understanding a sentence is much more akin to understanding a theme in music than one might think.
>
> —Ludwig Wittgenstein, *Philosophical Grammar*

In the eleventh hour of his lecture course dedicated to a thought that Heidegger calls one of the leitmotifs of modernity, namely, "der Satz vom Grund" (a thought only inadequately translated by the translations to which we have become habituated: "the principle of ground" and "the principle of reason"), Heidegger turns his attention to describing the emergence of the limits of that thought and so of modernity. It is a gesture dedicated to clearing a way for the appearance of what Heidegger takes to be the summons of thinking today, a call from the future that he always argued has only been heard as the faintest of echoes. But his particular concern at this point in the lecture is to establish the limits of the notion of the subject and to show how the notion of the subject loses the preeminent place it had won in the course of modernity as an account of the essence of human being. Once the notion of the subject is dislodged as both the principle and the ground for thinking, Heidegger claims that the principle of ground itself is called into question, thereby opening the way for another kind of thinking, one that does not submit in advance to either principles or grounds. Characterizing the culmination of modernity as the end of a thinking that followed the dual guidelines provided by the principle of reason and the notion of the certifiable subject, Heidegger then alludes to the different style of thinking that is heralded by history at a juncture such as ours: "Understanding being means that man stands in the open projection of being according to his essence.... Through the understanding of being that is experienced and thought in that manner, the representation of human being as a subject is, to speak with Hegel, set aside. Only insofar as man stands in the clearing of being, according to his essence, is he a thinking being."[1] The point of course is that history has now readied thinking for the end of the representation of human being and that, with the collapse of such representations, thinking needs to ready itself for a different, presumably more original, experience of human being as the being of history and language, the being exposed to the destiny of being itself. Almost casually, and with great rapidity, Heidegger then compresses the entire remaining difficulty of modernity, the congealed residue of all that is to be set aside and surmounted by thinking today, into one word: "dialectic." He then argues that a certain language of thinking is played out in the dialectic, a call [*Geheiss*] and countercall [*Entsprechung*] that he contends, with unswerving persistence, remains wooden, ultimately calcified and too frozen ever to touch on and speak out what is most alive. The dialectic stands, for Heidegger, as the last refuge of a thinking that lives, not from time and history (that is, from a response to the finite destiny of being), but from static images that prop up a system of representations, principles, and reasons. Against the dialectical conception of history, ever the foil for Heidegger from the final pages of *Being and Time* to the texts of his final years, Heidegger suggests that an appreciation of a certain "leap," one too agile for any dialectical movement, is requisite for a thinking that is capable of comprehending the present, culminating, juncture of history and so touching upon its own truth: "the history of western thinking shows itself first of all and only as the destiny of being when we look back upon the whole of western thinking *from out of the leap* and that whole is to be thoughtfully preserved as the destiny of being that has happened" (SG, 150). Finally, Heidegger advises his listeners that a new sensitivity to tone is requisite for the full appreciation of the leap to be made today, that leap that permits this "look back" and thoughtful preservation of "the destiny of being" as "whole" and that is to prepare for the arrival of "post"-modernity: "the leap out of the principle of reason ... concealed itself behind the change in tonality of that same principle" (SG, 151). Sharpening that point, and yet rendering it even more puzzling, Heidegger then says that "if we fully think through the polysemic word '*Satz*' not only as 'statement', not only as 'utterance', not only as 'leap', but at the same time *in the musical sense* of 'movement', then we arrive at the complete connection to the principle of reason" (SG, 151). The movement here is from "Satz" to "Satz," from, finally, language to music. Or so it seems.

The movement of Heidegger's text is especially difficult at this point, and the claim in which it culminates is quite curious; that "Satz"—sentence, statement, utterance, proposition, principle—a word that names all that inclines toward language and above all toward the syntax of the dialectic, when taken to its radical truth, its deepest moment, exposes its musical sense. Almost imperceptibly, Heidegger takes his distance from Hegel, who jeers at "musical thinking which is no more that the formless jingling of bells or a warm misty feeling that never arrives at the concept."[2] At the end of modernity then, at the limits of the dialectic, at the moment when we hear the "resonance between being and ground resounding" (SG, 151), music appears.

That is a claim that sounds more commensurate with what one might expect from Nietzsche than from Heidegger. There is, or so it seems, a striking absence of any serious reflection on music in Heidegger's work. One finds powerful images of painterly works—who does not associate Van Gogh's painting of peasant shoes with Heidegger's meditation on the work of art?— as well as images of architecture and sculpture. Above all, one cannot read Heidegger without taking to heart the key role that meditation on poetry and certain specific poems plays in his work. The recovery of the finite experience of language, especially language at the moment of its greatest concentration and density—namely, language in the poem—seems to command the movement aimed at overcoming the metaphysics of subjectivity that is the trademark of modernity. Heidegger is not alone in his dedication to this recovery; Foucault put the point of this turn to language clearly when he wrote that 'I speak' runs counter to 'I think.' 'I think' led to the indubitable certainty of the 'I' and its existence; 'I speak,' on the other hand, distances, disperses, effaces that existence and lets only its empty emplacement appear.[3] Language then, this "repetition of what continually murmurs outside,"[4] has been the leading theme of work that has followed in Heidegger's wake. It has finally earned its name as the "house of being" and so one reads—without interruption—that "being that can be understood is language."[5] And yet there remain these haunting references to music and the arresting fact that tonality and musicality play a keynote role in the move beyond modernity. Nonetheless, despite Heidegger's clear predilection for musical language ("ringing," "sounding," "pealing," "fugue," "tonality," "resonance," "song," "echo," "rhythm"—the list could easily be continued), one never, or so it seems, finds extended reflections on musical work in Heidegger.[6] While the Greek temple perches dramatically on a cliff overlooking the raging sea below, one finds Beethoven's quartets languishing "like potatoes in the cellar" (H, 9).

But then there is Nietzsche, who stands between those bookends of modernity—Hegel and Heidegger—and who speaks both on behalf of a thinking that listens to music and quite pointedly against that view of the privilege of language in experience so strongly held today by those working in a context shaped by Heidegger. So, for instance, Nietzsche claims in *Twilight of the Idols* that "[o]ur real experiences are anything but loquacious. . . . They don't have the power of speech. What we can express with words is what we have passed beyond. Whatever we have words for that we have already got beyond. In all talk there is a grain of contempt" (GD, 451). Or in *Birth of Tragedy* he says: "Language, as the organ and symbol of appearance, can never reach the deep interior of music from without, but . . . remains only in external contact with it" (GT, 44). Where word picks up, we have reached a second order of experience, the other side of an echo. For Nietzsche, the threshold of language is not, as it is for Heidegger, the threshold of all thresholds, the threshold without a before, an outside or other. Rather, language, for Nietzsche, is the afterthought or reproduction of the more original experience that is best characterized as musical. In language, the closest approximation to that experience is the language of tragedy, the highest expression that language can bear of the conflicted nature of the will. That is a decision about the relation of language and ruin that Heidegger also might make (his admirations for Hölderlin's translations of Sophocles provide ample testimony for that claim), but however close Heidegger might come to Nietzsche on this point, it remains the case for Nietzsche that even tragedy, born out of the spirit of music, does not embody the antagonisms and agonies of the will as well, as profoundly, as music. For Nietzsche, even the well-chosen word, the word that has poetic power, inevitably falls short of the power of the note in motion and relation. In the end, we speak at all only because ours is a world in which music is possible. One confesses then that "it may well be that man is man, and that man 'borders on' limitations of a peculiar and open 'otherness', because he can produce and be possessed by music."[7] Music makes language possible, and language that reaches beyond the limits of representation pays homage to that debt. At the outset of *Twilight of the Idols* we are reminded that this point is all important to our time of passage.

What about music then? What about this appeal to tonality and this leap ["*Satz*"] that is to be thought as a musical movement ["*Satz*"] and that Heidegger calls the requirement of thinking that still lives today? To ask about music in the context of a concern with following Heidegger's effort to push thinking beyond the presumptions it assumed in modernity is not a matter of posing a question intended to extend something like "Heidegger's aesthetics" into a delimited field of artistic performance. Far from it. Such a question is, it should be clear from the outset, thoroughly remote from any such project, especially since one of the guiding efforts of Heidegger's approach to the work of art is to remove it from its metaphysical ghettoization in what has come to be called "aesthetics"—a word that among the legacies of modernity has most thoroughly saturated thinking today. It is not a matter of presuming in advance to know what Heidegger means when he speaks of "tonality" and a "musical sense," but of asking what these words might mean today. To what degree can we say that the enigmas of thinking today, the obstacles it confronts and the topics it is consigned, are exposed and repeated in the enigmas of music? More precisely, it is a matter of asking a very simple, if initially bizarre, question: *is there music*? If there is music, then what might it take to hear music today?

I believe that, in the end, this question of music becomes massive, moving far beyond one's initial expectations and opening a tangle of issues one might never suspect on the basis of Heidegger's passing reference to the question. Lacoue-Labarthe has already indicated one of the largest dimensions on which it touches:

> The interesting thing about the phenomenon at which it aims, as we can easily see, is that it should make possible to return, by basing the analysis initially on the intraphilosophical distinction between the visible (the theoretical, the eidetic, and the scopic, etc.) and the audible (or the acoustic, and I do not say the verbal), to the *hither side* of the "theoretical threshold" itself. It should make it possible to return to the place where the *theory of the subject* (but perhaps also *the subject of theory*) would see itself, if I may say so, be obliged to put into question its privileged apparatus, its instrument, which, from Plato to Lacan, is a specular instrument, And a *speculative* apparatus.[8]

My intention in what follows is not to broach the largest significance of the question of music for the movement between modernity and postmodernity, nor even to deal with the full question of music as it might be pursued in either Heidegger or Nietzsche. Rather, my specific intention is simply to raise, and then try and formulate, the question of the relation of words and music in the context of that relation as it is thought by both Heidegger and Nietzsche, and to raise that question first of all as a question itself rendered problematic, perhaps even preempted, by virtue of the relation pertaining between music and technological reproducibility. How far can we speak of the "refusal of clarification and assimilation into frameworks of meaning"[9] that is the discovery of every reflected experience of language without being drawn into the question of the relation of language and music if for no other reason than the astonishing fact that tonality, tempo, and rhythm—the elements of music—belong to any possible clarification and meaning of language. Might one need to think the refusal of the word together with the refusal of music? How far can the question of poetry be put before it is compelled to confront its own truth as song (US, 182), eventually coming to ask about what Mendelssohn described as "songs without words"? But, even before that question can be asked today, we need to take seriously the difficulty of any talk of music, if not always, then at least for today. It is that difficulty of questioning today that Heidegger drove home so insistently, a difficulty that Nietzsche naively passed by. In other words, in what follows I propose to begin to pose a question that one finds recommended by both Heidegger and Nietzsche as a question of special urgency for this historical moment at the culmination of modernity, in order to ask whether that very same question has been closed off by virtue of precisely this historical moment. Has music made an appearance as an issue for thinking only in the mode of its disappearance?

Is there music then? Of course it still remains Nietzsche rather than Heidegger who is possessed by this question and it is Nietzsche who first links this question to the question put to us by our age, thereby rendering it ineluctable. It its striking just how deeply Nietzsche defines the question of history at the end of modernity as a question pinned to the thought of music. Equally striking is how remote the question of music has become even in our reading of Nietzsche.[10] His claim is clear: music is, he contends, "a woman"[11] and without it "life would be an error" (*GD*, 393).[12] At least that is what he says shortly before unmasking the "four great errors" (*GD*, 477f), those metaphysical delusions that first emerge and show their hitherto hidden truth against the cool blue backdrop of the peculiar historical twilight that marks our age. Nietzsche's own sense, never unshadowed by a certain "untimely" ambivalence, is that he comes, in the apt words of Hölderlin before him, both "too late" and "too early,"[13] but always "after" those errors have been unveiled as such. Like Heidegger, Nietzsche finds it both continually necessary and impossible to place himself with respect to history by virtue of a separation from what Nietzsche characterizes as the high philosophical noon of metaphysics, namely, the era of such errors. For Nietzsche, it is a separation announced with the approach of twilight and night. But, more than a mere separation, Nietzsche claims that thinking today can only be characterized by a radical transformation, a reversal and countermovement, since he claims that beginning with him the direction of thought will no longer be best described as an ascent to bright lights, such as the curious ascent described by Socrates in the seventh book of the *Republic*. It is rather to be experienced as a time of passage through dark times, one through which we need to negotiate our way by new means and without the old idols that were the stars by which thought once took its own measure. It is that need for a new measure for thinking to which Zarathustra is answering when he says that "[w]ith the approach of midnight things are heard that by day may not be made loud" (*Z*, IV,3). Consequently, in order to grope our way through these turbulent times that define us as "after" metaphysics (a notion that we now need to define in order to defy), we who think out of this time of passage—a "we" dislocated and thoroughly problematized along with the thought of "life," as "error" or otherwise—we need to move away from our habitual speculative reliance on seeing, on *theoria* as defined in the Greek world, to a new relation to listening. The passage from noon to midnight is, as Lacoue-Labarthe has claimed, equally the passage from the visual to the aural. Music then plays the keynote role in awakening of these times. Likewise, our historical place bears a special relation to music. To think our time, the passage and destiny that it marks, we need to listen to the music of the night. If not for such music, "life would be an error." More to the point: if life can be said to make a point, then we hear it in music; quite simply, without music life would be pointless. Understanding such a point, Bloch finds it possible to speak of "the good fortune of the blind."[14]

Some of Nietzsche's claims about music seem clear at first: "Music," he says, is "deeper than dreams" and the Apollinian world of the eye and its plastic arts (GT, 22); it is the real voice of, and answer to, the pain and contradiction of life that get plastered over by the comforting so-called truths of religion and philosophy. In music, like childbirth, "*pain* is pronounced holy" (GD, 477). That "great pain, that slow pain in which we are burned with green wood . . . pain which takes its time [and which I might add *is* the pain *of* time] pain that forces . . . us to descend into our darkest depths."[15] As such, music is the "language of the will in its immediacy" (GT, 91). It is the discourse of the will unconstrained by the limited discourse of words. In an aphorism Nietzsche claims that "[w]e have art lest we perish of the truth,"[16] but to think through that aphorism it must be acknowledged that music is art par excellence, its deepest, most articulate moment. It is the truth that dislodges the truth that is the error from which we would otherwise perish. Music, of course, is what metaphysics always lacked and failed to hear, and so it is music that forms the countermovement to the decadence of the tradition; it guides us in the dark passage between twilight and dawn, it primes us for the future. The old center could not hold, but now Nietzsche seems to be saying that the future is melocentric—that is, if it has a center at all. The stakes could not be higher since everything for Nietzsche—the body, will, time and return, language and tragedy, pain and violence, every countermovement to nihilism—unfolds along an axis that is articulated by what Nietzsche calls music.

But the most obvious remark one can make about music simultaneously draws it closer to Heidegger's avowed concerns and hammers home the difficulty of thinking it in the context of these large concerns: music itself, the key to our time, needs to be thought as a certain relation to time. Music not only marks our time in a special manner, but also raises the question of time itself as its own special question. So music is doubly important insofar as it raises the question of time as the preeminent question of our time (for Nietzsche it appears most sharply as the thought of the eternal return; for Heidegger, initially at least, as the finite time of Dasein), and insofar as it is emblematic of the tropological passage between the times that Nietzsche himself marks—the time between Hegel, and the claim of the perfection of metaphysics, and today as the time calling for the overcoming of metaphysics. Nietzsche's historical place, like the place opened up by music, is best thought as pure passage that destroys itself in the movement that is its own happening. It is this passage that Heidegger referred to as demanding a "leap."

But the question that Heidegger leads us to ask today is this: what about this possibility of being "without" music—how real is this subjunctive that says life "would be" an error? What does it mean that we must mark our time as a musical passage, and even as a catacoustic moment out of tune with what preceded it, as a time of noise? Even Nietzsche, ever confident in the potency of music, concedes the difficulty: "After the song of the wanderer and shadow, the cave all at once became full of noise and laughter" (Z, 544). The question is: how far can we go toward thinking music in our time at all? To what extent does music itself remain captive, even prohibited, by our time? According to Nietzsche, music should speak to our time just as it once spoke with a special excellence as the spirit of that time giving birth to tragedy. But does it? Or does the riddle of our time *as* a time of twilight and transformation preempt the question of music as Nietzsche thought it, as redemption from "error"? Are there elements of "our time" that displace the possibility of its own truth?

To raise that question one must focus on its political significance. I believe that this decision to politicize that the question of music, to draw it forward into the question of social practices and political economies, is not arbitrary, but covertly recommended by Nietzsche himself when he says that only through music can we understand the joy in the annihilation of the individual, and that this "dionysian dissolution of the chains of individuality is . . . the basis of every political instinct" and the "fabric of community" (GT, 114). To understand the stakes of the question of music one needs to bear in mind that for Nietzsche, music, properly thought, defines the possibility of the polis as well as the dissolution of its borders. Music, for Nietzsche, has the power to overcome the individuation of the body and the distance that lives in the visual world, it has the power to draw us instead into the deep community of reciprocity, to the point of our true, our mutual, permeability. The polis in the time of twilight and transition, at the site beyond good and evil, understands music and is guided by it.

If there is music, that is. If the polis is possible. It is the despair of that possibility, the impossibility of political life today that shadows Heidegger and to which he gives voice when he sighs that "only a god can save us." The question of music is not far removed.

Adorno raised a preemptive question in his essay "On the Fetish Character of Music";[17] namely, must all music today sound like *Parsifal* did to Nietzsche's ears? In other words: are we already too late for the truth of our time? Is it now the case that music has become one more vehicle of escape, not a path of revelation? Is Jacques Attali right when he claims that "music is illustrative of the evolution of our entire society: deritualize a social form, repress an activity of the body, specialize its practice, see it as a spectacle, generalize its consumption, then see to it that it is stockpiled until it loses its meaning. Today, music heralds . . . the establishment of a society of repetition in which nothing will happen any more."[18] Have "the times" overtaken music, obliterating its truth?

Of course, the idea that music generates feelings of community, that among the arts it is the most immediately political, is not a new idea. Plato already knew the political power of music and its relation to order and disorder; he was quite sensitive to this power when he made the question of musical harmony one of the first issues to be addressed in the formation of the polis.[19] Aristotle, who discusses music in the context of his politics, acknowledged that power as well.[20] But the contemporary question about the relation of music and political life adds a new twist to that idea. It is a serious, and to Nietzsche potentially devastating, charge that says that the potentials of music do not guide, but are undermined and guided by, its relation to political economy. More precisely, the claim is that the peculiarities of music's mode of reproducibility—its readiness to be frozen mathematically in the digital recording, and its capacity to have its violence on the vinyl of the analogue recording—that those mathematical and violent elements of music now exposed by the modes of its reproducibility have left the situation of music today in such a regressive state that it all now can only sound like *Parsifal*, the threat of our time praised and celebrated. Social dynamics have married the technological imperative and in the process swallowed the possibility of music. Today, "even the performance sounds like its own phono recording."[21]

This readiness for the recording reveals what Adorno calls the "Egyptian quality" of music—a quality Nietzsche, writing at the very moment that the first recordings were being made, does not acknowledge.[22] But we must acknowledge that in the recording, time on the move, time that denies the emptiness of eternal duration by being perpetual movement and arrest, time that again and again affirms the ephemeral and incandescent, is *immobilized and paralyzed*. Precisely at the point that history and time emerge as worthy of thought, the technological reproducibility of the musical work of art seems to have frozen and stockpiled time and set history adrift. Given that revelation, can we speak of music with innocence today? Can music speak to us any longer? Can "we" ask the question of music without asking about its relation to such reproduction? Benjamin has already raised the question: "the work of art is always fundamentally reproducible. What had been made by men could always be imitated by men. . . . But technical reproducibility of works of art is something new."[23] Benjamin defined that "something new" first of all as a "withering of the aura of the work of art."[24] If music severs itself from its own auratic character, if it severs its relation to ritual by lending itself to such immobilization, then what does that mean for Nietzsche's claims? If music is immune to that paralysis, then it seems that we must concede that "up to now, we have not really known what music itself is called and who music is."[25] This time of twilight is the time of music's approach. But it is also a time in which technology has sharpened the difficulty of any "musical sense" by challenging the very meaning and possibility of music.[26] Does the "leap" ["*Satz*"] that Heidegger contends is required by history today, a leap needing a "musical sense," go limp and lose its life in the age of technological reproducibility? Has modernity so sedimented itself in the form of modern technology, which, like aesthetics, is one of the enduring legacies of the modernity now said to be drawing to a close, and so invaded the times that music can only appear in muffled and mummified form today? Benjamin argued that the withering of the aura is the condition for the emancipation of the work of art from its "parasitical dependence upon ritual"; it is from that point of emancipation that one can begin to understand why Heidegger spoke of the movement between modernity and postmodernity as a musical movement, as a "*Satz*" that is equally a leap to a new social basis for the work of art.

The specific challenge to Nietzsche's claims about music is clear: what kind of music can Nietzsche point to that resists such Egyptian potentials? It is simply too easy, too vague, to answer "Dionysian." Is the Dionysian found in Beethoven's "Ode to Joy"—music with words—listened to on the stereo or rigid according to the etiquette of the concert hall? Or is it only for one who can play music or compose? Can we sit serenely listening to such music of the primal will? Can it be written? Or does Beethoven, deaf at the end, conducting but unable to hear the orchestra playing his Ninth Symphony, reading the score, conducting by his bones, have the perfect relation to music, the ideal set of ears? Mahler proposed an answer when he said that the most important part of the music is not in the notes.[27]

Or do such questions simply displace the real issue of music? Does Heidegger's suggestive remark about a requisite "musical sense" today move in some altogether other direction? Is it appropriate to try to localize, to identify, music in such ways? If not, then how are we to draw near to the inner secret of music as Nietzsche understands it. Especially when—in a passage that echoes Heidegger's most urgent claim about all art—he claims that "music is not at all to be judged according to the category of beauty" (GT, 89), and that it runs far deeper than the world of "feelings" and "effects" (W, 382/SM, 35). The enigma of music only deepens once we recognize that need to think it freed from the claims of beauty, if we are to think it at all. The summons of music today is a call to questions only begun to be asked. Simply put: what happens in music when we recover it from its ghettoization in "aesthetics"? If we can recover it that far at all. What does it take to develop this "musical sense" to which Heidegger refers thinking today?

In the *Twilight of the Idols* Nietzsche writes that "all rhythm still appeals to our muscles" (GD, 112). Significantly, that remark occurs in the context of criticizing that "kind" of music that no longer leads us back to the body, music that specializes itself "at the expense of those faculties which are most closely related to it," and which, when touched upon, allow us to "enter into any skin" (*GD*, 111). That is one of the many remarks that point us the direction music is to be thought; namely, that music shows itself "on the passionately moved human body" (*W*, 29/*SM*, 377). Music elaborates itself on, if not as, the human body.

But then that is ultimately no surprise, since the body is the locus of the self-elaboration of every truth in Nietzsche. Everything confesses itself in some relation to the body. Ones see, for instance, the work of metaphysics in the posture and gait of our bodies. One sees such confession too in the bodies of *Zarathustra*: dwarfs, cripples, eunuchs, hunchbacks, "eunuchs" before the "harem" of history, those who "hobble" and "limp" into the twilight. Bodies incapable of any sort of "leap."

Of course, nothing escapes our being a body, a *this* in the utmost. Or, as Heidegger put it when writing of Nietzsche: "wir leben insofern wir leiben."[28] Speech is too a bodily act. In *The Gay Science* Nietzsche claims that language emerged to protect the body that speaks it out. But its relation to the body not withstanding, language never reaches and unfolds in the deep and dark places of music, and the reason explains Nietzsche's insistence that the reach of music outstrips that of language. Nietzsche's contention is that languages—always found only in the plural, always only what Bakhtin named "heteroglossia"—differentiate and divide, working along the fault lines of the principle of individuation. But music, as having its essential, its tonal subsoil rooted in the body *that we are all said to share*, possesses the potential to dissolve and annihilate the principle that individuates. This means of course that Nietzsche regards the body in its truth as gender-neutral; it is not so much the sexual body, but the anatomical body that we share. The body in question is anybody's body. Everybody belongs to the body that Nietzsche speaks about.

Obviously, this is a problematic claim at best since, in the end, the link between the body and the annihilation of the individual can only be fully understood if we understand the body as the sexual body, as the body defined, not by the borders of the skin, but the ecstatic body, the body that affirms itself in the other of its skin. Death is always mine, it is always the mortality of *this* body, not "the" body, which give it its force. In *Being and Time* Heidegger tried to think the "Jemeinigkeit" into which death delivers each of us such that every act can only be understood as an act of putting one's ownmost singularity on the line; yet he did that without reference to the sexuality of body. But death cannot be understood as a matter of anybody's body. It is only in this regard that one can see why Nietzsche says that music has always had the body as its subject, and it does so by taking us out of ourselves and setting us into question with the possibility of any fundamental relation at all—either in love or death. Relationality then, like the body, belongs to the essence of music, and that is what sets music apart from all else, giving it a potency greater than that found in the word. The word alone can make sense—it can speak and lay claim to being language—but the isolated note can never be called musical since in every note there is the resonance of another. A great musical work is thus, in Attali's phrase, "always a model of amorous relations, a model of relations with the other, of eternally recommenceable exaltation and appeasement, an exceptional figure of represented or repeated sexual relations."[29] Once we begin to understand the darkness and thirst of music, we discover that music has special relations with the erotic, but it also bears an equally deep affinity with death: "what touches or moves me in music, then, is my own mourning."[30] When properly understood, music emerges as binding love and death, joy and mourning, and that is why "the more joyful the joy, the purer the mourning slumbering within it" (US, 235).

The point Nietzsche wants to make is that the body understood as universally shared unites, and that it is the basis of our belonging together, of our universality and communal life. But what Nietzsche tends to forget precisely at this politically all important point is that even when thought as the ecstatic sexual body, it also keeps us apart and names our distance. As the site of pain and death—something that along with pleasure and birth defines the sexual body in equal measure—the body radically ruptures and forever unravels the prior community of our lived permeability that Heidegger called the "with world." What Nietzsche understates is that the body, though it belongs to that community, though it too has and is a shared language, ultimately remains, along with our mortality, that which individuates us to the hilt. One might say that the body is the name and locus of our mortality. By *this* body, not by the idea of body, but by *this one*, I am pulled back, ambiguously placed in community, left mysterious, dark and hidden from all probing and uninterrupted union. Even the sexual body cannot escape or overcome its fundamental "thisness," its being torn between its thisness and ecstasy.

Taking the body—too often the anatomical body stripped of both gender and sexuality—as the basis of community, localizing and universalizing the political at the conflicted site of the body, but refusing to problematize that conflict, is the reason that Nietzsche's politics are finally marked by a basic apoliticism, as well as by an incapacity to cope with the radical divides that belong to the nature of any community. It is, I would argue, precisely this apolitical politicism that Heidegger latches onto in his Rektoral address, and it is this attachment that let him be haunted by the thought that "Nietzsche hat mich kaputt gemacht."[31]

But the full question of how Heidegger picks up and pushes themes emerging from his reading of Nietzsche is much more complex than I have indicated. What is important to note is that, in the end, Heidegger's sense of language in referring us to language in the poem moves within the same horizon of concerns that one finds Nietzsche's discussion of music moving. It would be thoroughly misguided—a double travesty—if one proposed the question of the relation between language and music, a question awkwardly raised by both Heidegger and Nietzsche, as a matter of privilege, hierarchy, or priority. It is not a matter of competition that emerges here, but of a peculiar difficulty, a yearning and a cry too easily forgotten and effaced—a matter of relations and community still without clear formulation. In turning to language that folds back on itself attentive to rhythm, time, tone, and gesture, Heidegger brings us always back to language that, like music, prevails in what Hölderlin described as "a mode of relation and thematics,"[32] to language as a mode of song.[33] In other words, language in Heidegger might have very much to do with the relationality that draws Nietzsche to music, singling it out, distinguishing it "as the most original manifestation, under which is to be understood all becoming" (W, 382/SM, 35).

That remark brings us back to the most obvious issue in music—one of the principle issues challenged and transformed by the special mode of capture at work in music's reproducibility—namely, music as a mode of time: of relation, return, repetition, even, one might argue, of the redemption and revenge of time against itself. Music, having the body as its subject, the will as its immediate object, remains nonetheless always time made loud. It is our mode of communication with the movement of time, with all the ambiguities hinted at by the word "with." But Nietzsche remains strangely silent on this point of the relation between time and music, tending to slip into the unproblematized remark that music is a matter of "becoming." Of course it is becoming, but it is also, equally, dissolution and the play of resolution and relentless dissolution. It is the struggle of the harmonic. The "becoming" that is heard in music is essentially dissonance, the inner secret and truth of harmony, and of this dissonance Nietzsche says:

> the primordial phenomenon of Dionysian art is difficult to grasp, and there is only *one direct way* to make it intelligible and grasp it immediately: through the wonderful significance of *musical dissonance*. . . . only music can give us an idea of what is meant by the justification of the world as an aesthetic phenomenon. . . . [in it] we recognize a Dionysian phenomenon: it reveals to us the playful construction and destruction of the individual world as the overflow of a primordial delight. Thus the dark Heraclitus compares the world-building force to a playing child placing stones here and there and building sand hills only to overthrow them again (GT, 131)

The reference to Heraclitus is crucial: all of the Heraclitean fragments speak from out of a riddle of dissonance understood as the truth about harmony, the fact that dissolution cannot be felt without union. The playfulness of play, the play-space of time from which music lives and thrives, is this infinitely compressed infinity between union and dissolution, the real locus of becoming and locality of music. At that point of tension and openness, the point of dissonance and harmony alike, the instant is most fully alive. Held in the grip of music, one relates to time as pure self-destruction and passage; the present is no longer infinitely compressed between a merely deferred memory or hope. In music there is no time for such deferral. In music we learn that dissonance is not a destructive force, but a mode of love and affirmation, a redemptive creative act.

Another way of making the same point is to say that the sort of music that Nietzsche wants to affirm, music that understands the struggle and secret dissonance of harmony, has nothing nostalgic about it. It suffers no "revenge" against time. In Dionysian music, music that moves with the uninhibited will, there is no time to bemoan paths not taken, there are no "meanwhiles" teleologically pegged to something still remote, no dead movements, no moments outside the play-space of becoming, no moments not rich enough to return eternally. Of course, saying that does not obliterate the full force of dissolution, of the loss that belongs to becoming. Such music is not the music of contentment, but always of joy and mourning *at once*, of fullness and loss *at once*. Baudelaire's remark will always remain true: "Nothing can restore to the world the fragrance it has lost." The struggle of harmony is the struggle of death itself, the pain of dissolution, and insofar as it is felt on the "passionately moved human body" it is felt as the body in pieces, the body torn and in spasm. Music moves us, and does so always with the power both to tear us apart and bring us to the point of real communion. The temporality of musical dissonance is as much about pain and mortality as it is love and affirmation. That is why music has an essential relation to mourning and lamentation as well as celebration. In the end, music stands as the most powerful reminder that time is not so much about the so-called moments of time, about the ossification of the confrontation with the course of time into past/present/future, as it is about *dissonance*. Heidegger, of course, is the one who dedicated himself to thinking precisely such dissonance.

Real participation in music draws us into the dissonant body, and into the full instant at once, and it does so, so says Nietzsche at least, more fully and profoundly than words can ever communicate. Music places us, body and soul, at the site of dissonance, the very site of the pain and contradiction of life that get plastered over by the so-called truths of religion and philosophy. Religion and philosophy, having effaced the body and denied time, are incapable of thinking and affirming the profound pain, equally the deep joy, that issues out of the contradiction of being at all. The "musical sense" that Heidegger finds requisite today carries with it a receptivity to precisely what has been effaced by a thinking guided by the images of ontotheology, a thinking modeled after an infinite and omnipresent mind that has no body and suffers neither pain nor death.

Nothing touches and binds time and the body more directly than music, and that is why Nietzsche says: "music never *can* become a means;

one may push, screw, torture it; as tone, as roll of the drum, in its crudest and simplest stages, it still defeats poetry and abases the later to its reflection" (W, 42). Nothing outstrips its potential as "the language of the will in its immediacy." Language, as Nietzsche understands it, has a liability, a tendency to objectify time that music, living as it does from dissonance, does not. One might argue with and for Nietzsche, as Blanchot does, that Nietzsche's conception of language does not match his practice, that in his fragmentary writing, his aphorisms and the perpetual recoil of interruptions in his texts, *Nietzsche writes dissonance*. That, to some extent, is quite true, but, as Nietzsche knew, the liability of language, its propensity to metaphysics, will never be lifted so long as language has its grammars: "I fear we will believe in God so long as we have grammar" (GD, 406). Dissonance can never be made obedient to grammar. Captured by grammar, speech risks paralyzing the temporality of radical dissonance. Frozen-on-the-page writing risks effacing dissonance, which is carried in gesture and tone, even further. Or, as Heidegger put it: "In script the scream is easily smothered."[34]

Heidegger's rather abrupt reference to a "musical sense" summoned by the end of the metaphysics of modernity might have the appearance of a casual gesture, but, like most such abrupt flashes in Heidegger's texts, it has nothing casual about it. But, even if deliberate and calculated in its appearance, the meaning of that gesture itself, which opens a cut to the heart of the issue of the lecture, remains opaque at best. My intention here has simply been to suggest some of the lines that need to be pursued if that cut is to be followed through on its own terms. It has also been to open up an avenue of inquiry into Nietzsche that Heidegger himself does not take, but that nonetheless exposes a productive line of issues for both Heidegger and Nietzsche. There is then a serious question put to us by the thought of music today, one that Adorno seems to have raised with more directness than either Heidegger or Nietzsche. It is a question that draws together the seemingly divergent concerns of language, body, and technology. A question, in the end perhaps, of what Heidegger called the *Gestell*.

Most of all, it is a question concerned with far more than drawing an inarticulate line marking the unmarkable limits of language. It is important that we widen our view of just what that question is asking. The point is that music, which has always raised and then redoubled the question of reproduction and repetition in the move from score to performance to recording, and in its internal relation to mathematics and violence disclosed by the possibility of recording, has today been drawn so essentially into contemporary mutations of the question of reproduction, into what Heidegger thought under the name *Gestell*—question of modern technology and its own peculiar political economies and imperatives, questions, as Benjamin has pointed to, of fascism—that we can no longer pose the question of music apart from such concerns. Linked to technological reproduction, it seems that in these times music is in danger of severing its roots in ritual, sacrifice, and celebration. Its original meaning, which Nietzsche believed would teach us about the transformations necessary in ourselves to meet the demands of our times, is in the process of being transformed.

CHAPTER SIX

WHAT WE CANNOT SAY: ON LANGUAGE AND FREEDOM

> Diese Erhebung des allertiefsten Centri in Licht geschieht in keiner der uns sichtbaren Creaturen ausser im Menschen. Im Menschen ist die ganze Macht des finstern Princips und in eben demselben zugleich die ganze Kraft des Lichts. In ihm ist der tiefste Abgrund und der höchste Himmel, oder beide Centra.... Der Mensch hat dadurch ... der Geist. Denn der ewige Geist spricht die Einheit oder das Wort aus in die Natur. Das ausgesprochene (reale) Wort aber ist nur in der Einheit von Licht und Dunkel.
>
> —Schelling, *Philosophische Untersuchungen über das Wesen der menschlichen Freiheit.*

Usually, the experiences of freedom and language are thought together only in the idea of "free speech." This notion is a way of referring to the right of each and every person to express openly and with impunity his or her opinions. Without wishing in any way to challenge this right, I want to propose that there is a more original relation uniting our experiences of language and of freedom. Furthermore, I want to suggest that out of this original relation something decisive and unique emerges about the being of freedom and language, the being that each of us is. To that end, my intention in what follows is to ask about the kinship of language and freedom. More precisely, it is to ask a two-part question. First, to what extent does the word open up the experience of freedom? And, second, is it possible to speak of freedom? As you will see, I am not interested in the question of "free speech" here. I am, however, interested in asking whether the "fact" of language illuminates something of the "fact" of freedom. As the title of this chapter indicates, I will suggest that it is in approaching the *limits* of language that this question of the bond between language and freedom becomes most interesting. One might say that the point most in need of being spoken about in the matter of freedom is the point at which we cannot speak. At the limits of language, at the point at which what we can say is exceeded, something about the nature of freedom steps forward. Or, put even more paradoxically: I want to suggest that the proper expression of freedom is the existence of language itself, but that freedom is not able to be expressed as a proposition in language. Finally, I want to suggest that this paradox of the kinship of language and freedom has some significant consequences for what it means for us to try to speak of moral life, that is, to speak of human freedom.

This question, at least as I want to pose it, has two distinct philosophical heritages inspiring it. The concern with the theme of freedom has its roots in Kant and German Idealism, Schelling most of all, while my interest in the theme of the limits of language is indebted chiefly to Heidegger and Gadamer. But the impulse driving this effort to unite these two themes belongs to the future of philosophy, not its past: I believe that it is necessary for those of us who work out of this tradition inaugurated by Heidegger and Gadamer to find a way to speak more directly to questions that are traditionally taken as matters of moral philosophy. Lest there be any confusion about this matter, let me say here that I take "moral philosophy" to be that form of thinking that is centered above all on the enigma of human freedom; it is *not*, at least as I understand it, a form of thinking bent on setting up prescriptions for human behavior. One begins to take up the question of the "moral" only beyond the realm defined by "good" and "evil," only at the point at which one confronts the abyss of human freedom. While I confess that the questions of moral life have not been central to the tradition of hermeneutics, which has been more identified with the question of truth than of freedom, I nonetheless believe that in the future hermeneutics will come to be seen as marking an original achievement in the field of moral philosophy. My hope is to begin to open up avenues for this achievement to become more visible. One way for this to come to pass is to begin to understand how it is that the relation of thinking and language that has formed the center of the tradition of hermeneutics speaks, quite directly, to the relation of thinking and moral life as it has been unfolded by Kant and his immediate successors.

To begin this project, I want to argue that Kant's moral philosophy, which operates by unpacking the relation between reason and freedom, assumes (without ever thematizing) a quite distinct conception of language. More precisely, it is the conceptualizing possibility of the word that underpins Kant's efforts to grant an essential place to freedom in any understanding of human experience. In short, Kant privileges what one might call a metaphysical conception of language or, even better, the *language of metaphysics itself*; this means simply that, though he never explicitly avows it,

Kant privileges the language of the concept. However, the reflections on language that we find in Heidegger and Gadamer, for instance, include a sharp, and, to my mind, persuasive critique of such a conception of language. This "hermeneutic theory" of language undermines the presumptions of privilege that might be said to belong to the language of metaphysics. It challenges the hegemony of the concept in the name of another possibility of the word. Here we see that it is this other sort of relation to the word, one that is more the province of poetry than of philosophy, that drives us to the deepest forms of the experience of language. And, so my argument runs, it exposes us to the deepest form of the experience of freedom.

But here my question begins. I find Kant's arguments about the kinship between thinking and freedom compelling and I believe that an effort to grant freedom a place in how we think human experience must be central to all philosophizing worthy of its name. I believe that Kant is simply right when he suggests that only by acknowledging this issue of freedom, of the unconditioned, do we come to understand the moral weight of experience. But I find the treatment of language in Heidegger and Gadamer equally compelling, and just as central to any possible conception of human experience; and yet, as I will argue, this conception of language undermines much of what Kant will come to conclude regarding the moral law. So my question is this: is there anything that we might say about the riddle of moral life, the enigma of freedom, in light of the remarks on language that have been so central to the hermeneutic tradition?

In what follows my remarks will be divided into two parts. In the first part, which focuses chiefly on Kant's *Grundlegung*, my intention is to outline what one might call a juridical answer to this question about the kinship of language and moral life. This answer has provided a justification in the history of philosophy for the authority of philosophic language in matters of moral life. But it is precisely this answer that I believe is no longer tenable in light of what has been learned about language from hermeneutics. In the second part, which takes Kant's third critique as a point of departure, my intention is to outline what I believe is a more interesting answer to this question, an answer that Gadamer has done much to open up. Because I am most interested in the progressive possibilities that emerge out of the "hermeneutic" approach to this question, the second part of this chapter will be given more attention.

To clarify what I am calling the juridical account of the moral significance of the fact of language, four points need to be established: first, that in the history of philosophy the governing consensus is that truth is what we most desire and what language is most in need of saying; second, that the proper language of philosophizing is, in some manner or other, conceptual, and that the concept marks the summit of the possibilities of the word; third, that by virtue of its relation to truth and to the conceptualizing power of language philosophy must understand itself as bearing a unique duty to the law; fourth, that the desire, language, and duty of philosophy are understood as needing to be secured by being grounded in the act whereby philosophizing takes possession of itself. While a thorough treatment of my question would need to elaborate on all four points, it is the second and third points here—namely, the claims that the concept is the preeminent possibility of language and that the relation between the language of philosophy and the foundations of law is a privileged one—that will serve as the center of my remarks since together they ground what has long been assumed to be the legislative function of philosophy. What is most notable here is that the moral meaning of the fact of language is understood in this juridical account to be found in the way language opens up the possibility of law. On the other hand, in the hermeneutic account of language the fact of language is found to be testimony to the actuality of freedom.

We already find the argument for the legislative function of philosophy more or less explicitly formulated by Plato and Aristotle. Each suggests that there is a fundamental authority that philosophy has in matters concerning human affairs. Plato expresses this in the contention that the philosopher must be king, while Aristotle says simply that the life of the philosopher is closest to the life of god. But it is Kant who first explicitly formulates and thematizes the reason that philosophizing needs to arrogate to itself this privilege of being the supreme arbiter of moral life. He does this in the arguments on behalf of the categorical imperative in which the link between the speaking and thinking of universals and the possibility of a moral law is formulated. Kant does not refer to language as such in making his arguments at this point, but perhaps this is because he simply takes for granted the role of language: what, if not this potential of language, could found and legitimate our relation to universalizability? A simple trope of a possibility belonging to the word grounds moral reason: the law of universalization is grounded in the universalizing potential that is retained in the kinship of thinking and language. Respect for law shows itself to emerge out of a possibility of language. Even the "imperative," the "force," of conceptual, categorical, reasoning is explained by noting that it, like the word, is able to maintain itself in a relation to what is external to it. Though Kant himself will not say so (it will be left to Hegel to make this point), the structure of the moral law has its foundation in the structure of human language, and the highest accomplishment of language is found in the language of philosophy. We are moral beings because we can philosophize, and because we can philosophize our moral life is necessarily to be thought according to law. In the end, when we speak we lay down the law: *jus dicere*.

But, of course, even if to speak is always, in some sense, to speak the law, not all speech qualifies as *true* to the law. Such speech (in Kant's language, such "willing") is defined solely by its relation to the idea proper to law, the idea of universality, and this idea is the province of the language of metaphysics, which is defined by its self-reflexive commitment to the universalizing potential of language. The task of philosophy is to speak in a manner that opens up this formal realm of the universal. The basis of any possible metaphysics of morals is rooted in the moral privilege of the metaphysical relation to the universalizing potential of language. Moral life is thoroughly committed to the dream of the universalizability of the law, and the "grounds" of this law show themselves to be an expression of what is understood as the preeminent possibility of the word, namely, the law of universalizability governing the formation of concepts. In the end, moral life is defined and determined by the jurisdiction of the language of metaphysics. One of the revealing ways in which this thoroughgoing commitment to the universal is evidenced for Kant is found in his treatment of the role of the "example" in moral questions. Though each of our acts carries the burden of being *exemplary*, namely, of being simultaneously unique and universal in character, Kant resists the notion that *individual examples* that do not carry the universalizable force of law could ever be enlisted as a means of grounding moral life.[1] In the end, thinking and speaking of moral life are rigorously submitted to the authority of the language of metaphysics, the language of the concept, which preserves the possibility of the universality requisite for the law. The idiom of philosophy, the concept, binds human freedom to its own nature in the form of the moral law. From this point of view, a different sort of language, the language, for instance, of stories told in the singularity of proper names, cannot serve a fundamental role in the task of negotiating freedom thought within the realm of law.

My purpose is not to rehearse the details of Kantian ethical theory. Rather, my intention is simply to suggest that a certain conception of language operates, however covertly, in Kantian moral philosophy (and I believe that it could be shown to be a widespread tendency in moral philosophy generally). That conception of language takes the summit of the possibilities of the word to be found in the capacity for universalization and conceptualization. While Kant will draw upon this assumption without ever naming or acknowledging it when he tries to understand what can be said philosophically about moral life, it is Hegel who will be the first to explicitly name this assumption as a truth when he speaks of the "divine nature" of language as "inherently universal" and when he claims that "what is called unutterable is nothing else than the untrue."[2] Hegel will see history as the process, even the progress, of freedom, but, in the end, freedom is submitted to the jurisdiction of the concept and the law of universalization that is proper to the concept. Furthermore, Hegel, like Kant, will see in this so-called truth of language a sort of moral vocation being expressed: this promotion to the universal is what Hegel refers to as *Bildung*. One who weds oneself to particularity, one who lacks the powers of abstraction and universalization, is *ungebildet* and such a failing can only be understood as a moral failing. This process of *Bildung*, which repeatedly requires the sacrifice of particularity,[3] is, Hegel reminds us, not only a theoretical process, but equally a practical one—and the path of this process is the path of philosophy. Gadamer's remarks on *Bildung* in the first part of *Truth and Method* emphasize the role of the concept of *Bildung* in the humanistic tradition, and he does this most of all by highlighting the conception of universality that governs that concept and the role of language in its formation.

Kant's efforts to ask what philosophy might say about the riddles of moral life struggle to keep freedom, the basic "fact" of reason, as the unassailable center of any possible theorization of moral life. But the moment we begin to speak of freedom, the instant it becomes a matter for theory, as soon as it enters the field of conceptuality, the law of this field—namely, that what belongs to it is bound to the imperative of law as such—is enforced. In this way the language that we enlist to speak of the presence of freedom converts the idiomatic riddle of freedom into a problem of the universal idiom of the law. Freedom ceases to be what *dispenses* relations, and becomes instead the problem of how we are to *regulate* those relations.

Such, in broad outline, is what I have referred to as the juridical account of the moral significance of the fact of language. It is a point of view that holds that the significance of language for moral life is found first and foremost in the capacity of language to universalize, to conceptualize. However, hermeneutics has shown that the understanding of the nature of language operating in this juridically indexed view of language is thoroughly problematic. Once one grants that language resists and exceeds, rather than founds, the process of universalization, the transformation of the question of moral life into the question of law becomes problematic. Once the ineluctable finitude of language, rather than its conceptualizing potential, is acknowledged, a different sense of the moral meaning of language begins to emerge.

One of the chief contributions of hermeneutics to contemporary philosophizing has been its ability to open thinking up to this finite being of the word. But while it seems relatively clear that a hermeneutic conception of language does not lend itself to the view that finds the greatest potential of the word in its capacity to lay down the law in its universality, it still remains to be seen just what a hermeneutic conception of language might mean for the task of understanding moral life. In what follows my intention is to indicate a few of the avenues down which such an understanding might be found. To do this, it will be necessary to emphasize the radical kinship between language and freedom.

The universalization constitutive of the formulation of the moral law operates on a conception of language that regards the concept as the highest achievement of the word and the language of metaphysics as the proper form of the language that addresses the life of free beings. Though it remains an unannounced assumption, for Kant the way we understand our freedom is shaped in an essential way by the way we understand the formal possibilities opened up by the language we speak. The form of the moral law is rooted in an understanding of those formal possibilities of language that culminate in the concept. But hermeneutics has demonstrated in several ways—here one thinks of themes such as translation, silence, the workings of language in the poem, metaphor—that the finitude of language cannot be held fast for the operations of such universalization and conceptualization. Consequently, once we grant the elemental sameness of thinking and language, we need to grant as well that the workings of the word do not permit such universalization, such a formalization in law, of the freedom that remains always as the unassailable fact of reason. I believe we have seen that Kant draws some important moral conclusions—conclusions about the nature of our freedom—from the fact that we are speakers of language and that this language permits conceptualization among its possibilities. The question remains whether we can still draw any meaningful conclusions about our moral being from this fact of language once we think language from a hermeneutic point of view, that is, once we abandon the notion that conceptuality is the deepest truth and highest possibility of the word.

The path to answering this question, at least as Gadamer has opened it for us, begins, curiously, with Kant. But with a "different Kant" than the Kant who formulates the categorical imperative; namely, with the Kant who interrogates the character of aesthetic judgment in the third critique. There Kant struggles to come to terms with an experience that is strictly untranslatable into the language of the concept. When Kant defines the judgment of taste, he notes that it is by nature without any relation to a concept and that it must retain this nonconceptuality in every moment of such judgment.[4] This resistance to the concept is the chief defining feature of aesthetic judgment, and it is the feature that most clearly distinguishes such judgment from moral judgment, which is ultimately guided by the concept, in two ways: lacking a relation to the concept, there is no possibility of formulating the law (here ethical life is a matter of "judgment"), and, lacking a relation to the concept, there is no possibility of formulating a notion of the good itself (ethical life is a matter of an indeterminate "freedom"). But Kant's investigations into aesthetic experience bring him two surprises: first, that this experience harbors an a priori—in other words, that there is a new, a different form of universality to be found here, one that is not attached to the concept; and second, that this experience is relevant for our understanding of our moral life even though it does not turn us to a notion of the moral law. When Gadamer takes up the achievement of Kant's third critique in the first part of *Truth and Method* he turns his attentions primarily to the first of these points which concerns the connection between aesthetic experience and truth. My intention in what follows is to trace in more detail the second of these discoveries, namely, the discovery of the way that the nonconceptualizable experience of the beautiful illuminates something of moral life. In doing this, I will depart from Gadamer's interpretation of Kant in two crucial ways: first, I will suggest that Kant's third critique does not mark the subjectivization of aesthetics, but that it goes far toward dislodging our understanding of experience from any conception of the subject and the human; and, second, I will argue that the chief ethical insight of the third critique emerges out of an understanding not of the work of art, but of the experience of nature and that in this way Kant's moral philosophy moves away from the humanistic tradition. But both points are seen most clearly by beginning with some remarks on the quiet, but decisive, role of language in the third critique.

Kant does not make the role of language a theme in the *Critique of Judgment*, but, as with the treatment of the categorical imperative in the *Grundlegung*, the question of language haunts all that is said here since the analysis of aesthetic experience shows it to be simultaneously communicable and nonconceptual.[5] This time, however, a different sort of language shapes the issues. In the strict sense, the language of aesthetic experience is the language proper to what withholds itself, to what we cannot say, to what cannot be told. It is, one might be tempted to say, the language of the secret. As I noted in Chapter One, Kant tries to speak of this strange language in two ways. First, when asking about the genius, he speaks of the *aesthetic ideas* that guide thinking for the genius; second, when speaking of the presentation of beauty he speaks of *symbolic hypotyposis*, which is the language of taste. It is in speaking of the language of the symbol that Kant begins to clarify how the moral weight of aesthetic experience is presented to us.

Despite its importance, Kant's discussion of the symbol is remarkably brief and so it does not easily carry the explanatory burden that this notion must bear in the work as a whole. However, Gadamer's discussion of the symbol in "The Relevance of the Beautiful"[6] helps clarify the meaning of the symbol. Beginning by noting that the word "symbol" is originally a Greek word that referred to a fragment that served as a reminder of a hidden or forgotten connection between individuals, Gadamer moves to a discussion of Aristophanes' speech in the *Symposium* in which a link is drawn between the symbolic and the erotic. In that lovely speech, Aristophanes suggests that each of us is but the *symbolon* of a human being, and that we each pursue the never-ending search for the *symbolon* of ourselves. What becomes especially clear in drawing these ancient Greek senses of the symbolic into the operations of the symbolic that Kant describes is that in the symbol we are presented simultaneously with a knowledge of ourselves and of what exceeds that which we define and can know (which is why Kant suggests that the symbolic is always tinged with a sense of the divine).[7] In other words, in the symbol I experience myself as finite and yet, by virtue of the way that finitude is presented to me, as belonging to what exceeds my finite being and the cognitive possibilities of such a being. In the symbol, the aporias of finite life are presented, not effaced. In the symbol, finite being is opened beyond itself.

What is significant here is that the symbolic ruptures the economy and the logic of identity governing the operations of the concept since in the symbol something both is and is not at the same moment. Furthermore, the symbol is not able to be deciphered, the symbolic cannot be removed out of this ruptured logic of identity, it infinitely eludes translation into any form other than itself. One might say simply that the symbol is a hieroglyph for which no code can be found since it only comes into its own nature in belonging to that which withholds itself from any direct presentation. Thus, though the form of the symbolic marks the summit of the knowledge won in aesthetic experience, the symbol simultaneously stands as a memento of the *limits* of what can be said, what can be known, conceptually. The significance of this shift from the concept to the symbol as the summit of the formal possibilities of the language that arises out of experience becomes most clear when we remember that while the truth of the concept expresses itself as *law*, the truth of the symbol finds itself in the *openness* of the mind that knows itself to be finite. Here we begin to see why Kant refers to beauty as the *symbol* of morality, and we begin to see how dramatic this shift in the form of the presentation proper to the moral—the shift from the conceptual to the symbolic—is.

But perhaps the most important element for any understanding of the symbolic, one might even say, the most original element of the third critique, has to do with the role of *nature* in grasping the truth and significance of the symbol. Unfortunately, this is also the least recognized and understood dimension of the third critique. There are two ways in which the central role of nature is effaced in most readings of Kant: first, the first part of the *Kritik der Urteilskraft* is taken as a text concerned with the work of art, rather than with a form in which nature is presented; and, second, the second part of the text—namely, the treatment of judgment with respect to nature—is simply ignored.[8] Missing the force of what nature means in the third critique, one misses the most original moment of that work with respect to its contribution to the questions of moral life since it is ultimately in our relation to nature that we truly understand ourselves as moral beings. The moral life of a finite being finds its truth and its greatest task in finding its place in the life of nature. Here we begin to see how far the third critique moves away from a view of moral life that thinks within the orbit of humanism. It is precisely the nonhuman, it is that which comes without human bidding, that orients the moral judgment outlined in the third critique. Furthermore, this disclosure of nature as a sort of magnetic north for our moral compass can only be understood according to the workings of the symbol. The true language of moral life is symbolic. It remains the original language of freedom. This is a decisive point whose importance can be made clear by remembering that the symbol itself, the form in which the supreme experience of nature is expressed, must be understood as natural; in other words, it must be understood as exceeding the conceptual, cognitive, reach of the finite mind. This is why, as Gadamer points out, the symbol must be distinguished from allegory, which is an invention of the human mind.[9] The symbol is the form in which we communicate with that which is not designed by human purposes. In the symbol something is given that cannot be known otherwise. In the end, nature, which is the site and the form of the symbolic, shows itself to be the supreme riddle for judgment, and we learn that it is only judgment that has indexed itself to the original experience of nature that earns the name of "good" judgment.

But my purpose is not to investigate the relation of nature and judgment for Kant (though I would like to suggest that this issue is central for any thorough reflection on the theme of human freedom). Rather, my purpose is to indicate what I take to be an original, and yet to be explored, avenue for thinking through the riddle that freedom poses for a finite being and to show how thinking about the possibilities of language can help us understand that riddle. This is the avenue opened by the analysis of judgment that we find in Kant's third critique. There, in the possibilities opened up by his reflections on nature and above all on the language of the symbol, I believe that Kant offers a genuine alternative to the manner of thinking human freedom that does so with reference to the law. I have tried to suggest as well that these alternative routes to understanding freedom each owes much to the differing conceptions of language operating in them: the lawfulness of the conception of moral life outlined in the second critique rests upon an understanding of the formal possibilities of the language of the concept, while the openness that characterizes moral life that is exposed in the third critique rests upon an understanding of the finite possibilities of the language of the symbolic. However, Kant never fully thinks through the way in which the relation of language and freedom shapes how it is that freedom is understood. In the end, the treatment of the workings of the symbolic are never fully explored in Kant and this, I believe, is the reason some of the richest implications of the relation of freedom and nature remain unexamined by him. Ultimately, Kant lacks an adequate conception of the dynamics of the finitude of the disclosure proper to the symbolic. His assumptions about language, rooted in a more classical metaphysics of language, are not sufficiently open to enable him to pick up on his own deep insights into how the real depth of freedom can be thought out of the kinship between language and freedom. But this is the point at which the hermeneutic conception of the finitude of language can advance the route that Kant begins in the third critique.

In the final part of this chapter, my intention is to indicate some of those dimensions of a hermeneutic theory of language that I believe can enrich the discussion of freedom that Kant outlines.

The *Critique of Judgment* plays a decisive role in the problematic that is outlined in *Truth and Method*; consequently, the range of issues broached in the third critique, especially the most original issues such as the manner in which the question of freedom is opened up anew in the formal possibilities of the symbol, can be wedded nicely with the wider insights of *Truth and Method*. In short, it is not difficult to turn Gadamer's investigations into language back into Kant's concern with freedom. However, in large measure because Gadamer focuses on the question of the work of art rather than of nature for Kant, the problem of freedom that Kant exposes in connection with the experience of nature is never given its full due in *Truth and Method*.[10] Despite this, the understanding of language that Gadamer develops there is especially helpful in advancing the question of freedom that Kant announces. The chief contribution in this regard of Gadamer's insights into language is that they give us a way of understanding the relation of thinking and language that preserves the original, even the abyssal, force of freedom for us. The finitude of the word, above all the poetic word, that Gadamer describes in great detail mirrors the logic of the symbol that Kant only describes in rough contour. We thus learn something about the paradox of trying to speak about the nature of human freedom. In this way a hermeneutic sense of the workings of the word can say much about how it is that we can begin to speak of freedom without thereby converting it, from the outset, into a question of law. From Gadamer we can come to understand that the deepest moral significance of the "fact" of language is that it is a witness to the special character of human freedom. Speech, rather than being the ground of the formation of the universal claim of law, is the preeminent form of the practice of the singularity of freedom. In the word, what Schelling described as "the most abyssal center,"[11] which is full of both light and dark, is brought into the world. When we constitute the world linguistically, we constitute it as saturated with freedom. With the word, freedom is set loose in the world.

My contention has been that conceptions of language that take language to have conceptualization as its highest possibility invariably ossify the openness of the experience of freedom by turning it into a question of law. By doing this, the real "ground" of moral life is displaced from its roots in freedom into the dominion and demands of law. The assumption about the nature of language underpinning this move, an assumption that refers every possibility of language to the language proper to metaphysics, leads to a different understanding of the moral weight of the word in the world insofar as it is assumed that, with the word, the maxim of lawfulness is grounded.

But the hermeneutic conception of language, which understands that the word is not able to be contained in the concept, deepens the experience of freedom by recognizing that in language we are reminded that we live in a world larger than what we can either define or control. In other words, that we live in a world defined first and foremost by the experience of radical openness and indeterminacy.

Most important here is understanding the *finitude* proper to the word since it is in the finite nature of language that freedom is preserved as this openness to a world. Above all, one ought not conceive of this finitude as a sort of shortcoming of language, as if it meant something like the nonsensical commonplace that suggests that words cannot say everything. The finitude of language is not even found in the fact that all language solicits itself, that our speech always asks for a counterword and so always appears in the world as incomplete, as a request.[12] Rather, the finitude of the word, like that of the symbol, is found in the capacity of the word to unfold itself beyond the boundaries of the thinkable and of what is present without itself disappearing *as* word. What Gadamer demonstrates is how we need to think the finitude of the word as a form of *excess*, and it is especially in this regard that the poetic word resembles the symbol. As Gadamer has shown, this self-surpassing capacity of language does not sublate, or efface, itself in a transcendence that ends up in the abstraction of a universal. Rather, the density of the word, its linguistic being, serves as an intransitive residue that weds the word to the mystery of its own being. This, in part, is what Schelling means when he says that "the reality of the expressed word is however only found in the unity of light and darkness."[13] Language in the poem—in which metaphor and symbolic language, even sound, are decisive—is most adept at presenting this finite character of the word, and so it is no surprise that poetic language has been the focus of some of Gadamer's most extensive and original reflections on the nature of the word. It is precisely because language possesses this finite nature, this double being, that we are able, with our words, to grope in the region of our ignorance and learn.

Let me conclude by bringing these remarks back to my original concern with the question about the relation of language and freedom. I have proposed that a hermeneutic theory of language such as we find in Gadamer offers original and productive avenues for thinking through the riddles of human freedom. While the central role of the notion of *phronesis* in Gadamer's work is well known and is one obvious way in which many of the concerns of moral philosophy enter into hermeneutic theory, the moral force of the being of language that is disclosed there is still to be explored. To that end, I have merely made the suggestion that Gadamer's sensitivities to the finite character of the word open up possibilities that escape the legislative impulses of a juridical conception of language. Such a hermeneutic conception of language does this insofar as it undermines the claims to conceptuality governing the language of metaphysics. In so doing we are reminded that in our words we "elevate the deepest center of life"—namely, freedom—into the light. Speech, above all speech that knows itself to be finite—namely, poetic speech—bears witness to this freedom. In this way, I believe that a hermeneutic theory of language helps us to find a way to preserve the fact of freedom, which needs to be a dominant concern all philosophizing. It also serves as a reminder that poetic language might well merit the claim to be the most original language of moral life—even more so than the language of metaphysics.

But the ethical possibilities opened up by hermeneutic theory can still be enriched by taking to heart Kant's insights into the kinship of moral life and the experience of nature, and this I believe is the line of questioning that the hermeneutic tradition would do well to pursue. The experience of nature, and the effort to speak of that which comes to us unbidden and without reference to human purposes, poses a crucial question for any possible understanding of moral life. But a new beginning toward understanding the roots of this moral life and especially its roots in freedom can be made if we take seriously the insight that perhaps nothing comes so directly into the world from out of the experience of freedom as the word. Properly heard, the word is the most faithful affirmation, the most intimate experience for us, of the freedom from which the word is born.[14] But what we learn from the hermeneutic conception of the finitude of language is that freedom, which dispenses the word, is itself not fully sayable. The meaning of this is still to be explored, but, once it is addressed, it will, I believe, place us before the paradoxical question of how we are to understand freedom simultaneously as absolute, as "the basis of all reality,"[15] and as shadowed always by its own unpresentability and unfreedom. This, of course, is the question of moral life.

CHAPTER SEVEN

"TWO MOUTHFULS OF SILENCE": ON LANGUAGE AND PAIN

For Beauty is nothing but the beginning of terror, which we still can bear, and we admire it so because it serenely disdains to destroy us.

—Rilke, "The First Dunio Elegy"

Addressing language, trying to speak of language from language, needs somehow to avoid the assumption that the field of language is covered by voice and script, by what we say and what we write. To address language is to move to the periphery of the sayable. But one quickly learns that the periphery of the word draws silence forward as a challenge for any reflection on language. Here matters become difficult, since speaking of silence has its own peculiar impossibility, even if it has its own imperative for one who would address language *as* language. In the light of claims, such as one finds in Heidegger, that language needs to be heard precisely as that which emerges out of the unsayability of silence, the need to "speak" of silence becomes all the more pressing. And yet no direct discourse on silence is possible, no word summons it as word. It only appears obliquely. Only at the margins of the word do we become sensible of it. This delicate line pinning language and silence together, a line so difficult to trace, stains all language that would pay homage to this debt of all language to silence. Language that does this, language that lives at the margins of the word, preserves this strained relation of the word to silence, earns the honor of the name "poetry."

That is why Celan, who more than most, has struggled with this kinship of language and silence, says that "two mouthfuls of silence"[1] mark the place of the poem, "two kinds of strangeness next to each other" (III, 195). Reading Celan, we soon come to understand that to think the poem means remembering that silence has its own contours, and that it is not to be confused with the merely quiet, but needs to be heard as the unvocalized voice of the poem. It should be noted at the outset that such listening to silence is rare, demanding and painful at once. This is the source of the peculiar difficulty found in reading poetry. But, if the poem is to be read, silence must be heard along the rhythmic axis of its own idiom, for the idiom of the poetic word emphasizes itself most of all in contact with what it cannot convert into its own. In that contact with the radically other idiom of silence the poetic word is brought to its own brink, and there language announces its own apartness and inconvertibility as well. In that regard, the poetic word is simply itself, for it is "language actualized, set free under the sign of radical individuation . . . as aware of the limits drawn by language as of the possibilities it opens" (III, 197). One only begins to read the poem from this strained and compressed point at which language makes contact with silence. My purpose in what follows is to discuss these strains and compressions of language in Celan's poetry, and to unfold as well his own efforts to articulate the nature of such poetic language in "The Meridian" speech. Doing that, especially against the backdrop, which is a quite prominent one for Celan, of Heidegger's efforts to think through language in the poem, calls attention to one matrix of concerns—a matrix uniting language, mortality, body, and catastrophic history—at work in Celan's poetic thinking.

Initially, it always will seem that the word in the poem stands out against silence, that the word has won its place by a sort of triumph over silence. Yet the enigma of the poem is that in it the word not only stands out against the silent space surrounding it, but that it bears the traces of silence within itself as well by confirming the inner conflict of poetic language that announces itself in an apartness that seems to encrypt the word in silence. Language in the poem has an essential capacity to throw itself into darkness and cannot be read apart from that capacity. Saying that only reaffirms the impossibility of every poem, and the special impossibility defining Celan's poetic impulse—namely, of writing not only from that darkness, but to it. More precisely, it is to say that every poem is the discovery that the "pure word," the "absolute poem" (III, 199), is not, and that every word only stands as a countercall, a call that is equally for its own other: "the poem has always hoped, for this very reason, to speak on behalf of the *strange*—no, I can no longer use this word here—*on behalf of the other*, who knows, perhaps of an *altogether other*" (III, 196). This Levinasian "altogether other" is perhaps best spoken of as what Blanchot described as "the silence of silence which by no means has any relation to language for it does not come from language but has already departed from it."[2] The difficulty in reading the poem comes in understanding that such departure does not lead away from the poem, but rather that it belongs to language in the poem, and that this departure of the word from itself by an opening to its other even marks the "place" of all poetry.[3] This means that language in the poem refuses to be domesticated;

it refuses to be made easy. What seems paradoxical about Celan's understanding of this "departure" of language in the poem is that he speaks of it as the true homecoming of language to its ownmost truth. Celan refers to this curious homecoming of language in the poem when he says: "I am again at the point of my departure, searching for my own place of origin" (III, 202).

In such departure, every poem is thus the simple advance of what is otherwise unspeakable. The measure of the poem, what Hölderlin referred to as "Mass," is the distance that language in the poem goes along the route of that advance. Here it should go without saying that such measure cannot be made by any ready-made calibers or calculus, especially those found in the linguistic economies of representation. Rather, it is the measureless measure of language itself, and its meaning is precisely and simply what the poem teaches its readers by educating their speech. Pioneering poets like Celan, those who for us today mark the distance language has been able to move from speech that finds the center of gravity of its language in its representational potential, will likely need quite some time to find and educate their readers. Of course, this doubled truth of language in the poem, that its homecoming is found precisely in its departure from itself, means that such language has an inexhaustible, impossible task as its truth.

But when we speak specifically of Celan's poetry, then we do well to remember that for him this poetic impossibility is redoubled, and that the remarkable compression of his language should be thought from that point. There is a double unspeakability for Celan writing in German—the language of his deferred death, a language he freshened against himself[4]—and between silences. That is to say that Celan's language is forced to nourish itself not only against the threat of its own other, but equally on "black milk" (I, 41), "ash" (I, 41), and "bitter almonds" (I, 78).[5] It is a language never far removed from the lacerations housed in its memory of pain and death. It is a language that speaks as an open wound even when it is the bearer of love and grace. In that regard, Celan's work gives new meaning to Bataille's remark that "love smells like death."[6] One learns of love when one knows its ineluctable relation to human fragility and mortality. The "pendulum of love swings" "at night" "between always and never" (I, 57). That is why it makes such sense to say that Celan wrote on "the terrain of death and mourning,"[7] and that will be why we might one day need to recognize the self-sacrifice that is an essential element of Celan's work.[8] Yet, speaking of such self-sacrifice of language in Celan's poetry is not only a matter of recognizing the fact that his language was the voice of treason and catastrophe, and that his tongue was the reminder of terror. The deepest meaning of sacrifice in the poem only comes "after" the "self" has "forgotten itself" (III, 193): "art creates a distance from the I" (III, 193). First and foremost, the place of sacrifice in the poem is a matter of recognizing the way silence belongs to Celan's poetry as the very life and renewal of its language. Ultimately, the deeper threat for the poet, the real risk of language in the poem, is of not finding one's voice at all, of having one's tongue cut off as it were, for "language is the tongue" (*US*, 203).⁹ Silence that overtakes the word is the risk of all poetry in every language. But one should not forget that, for Celan, the very achievement of speech bore the memory, the promise, of his own real silence: German remained always the language of his confrontation with death, the language of real annihilation. What Celan says of Danton applies with equal aptness to Celan himself: "we can only understand him through his death" (III, 188). A reminder that the dominion of the word includes always the possibility of death. "Art lives on" (III, 200), but for Celan only as the enduring confrontation with death.[10]

Being between two mouthfuls of silence, the poem is marked by a certain gasping for breath. "Poetry: that can mean a turn of breath" (III, 195). Yet it is precisely that struggle to breathe, that return of breath as the small effort of the body both to absorb its world and extend itself, that circumscribes the region and life of the poem as language that calls for voice, as language elaborating its relation to the body. Bearing in mind this relation of language and breath, of poems as works of breath, we can say that though it is impossibly—for the special case of Celan doubly—compressed, the poem should nonetheless be read as an advance and extension: the advance of the unspeakable and the slight extension of the body in the world.[11] The bond holding together this advance and extension, mutually of silence and the body, is all important, and is the topic toward which I intend my remarks to lead. But, for the present, the point to be noted is simply that the poem gathers these countervalent motions of compression and extension together and so stands as a "pause," as the place of "hope and thought" (III, 197). The poem lives at the site of this infinite and ambiguous compression and extension of the word and silence, breath and body, alike. "Poetry speaks out of an ambiguous ambiguity" (*US*, 74).

Celan repeatedly emphasizes the relation of the poem to silence in the "Meridian" speech when he asks about the meaning of the poem, about writing the poem (and that means as well about reading the poem since he understood that all reading is a rewriting and that every text becomes a palimpsest in being read). There Celan writes that "the poem shows a strong tendency toward becoming silent" (III, 197) and that it "asserts itself on its own margin" (III, 197). Living on this margin binding word and silence, language in Celan's poetry always threatens to close itself off, become airtight, and seal off its secrets. Calling Celan's poetry "hermetic"—a tag that Celan himself refused[12]—is a way of speaking to the difficulty of language at those margins.[13] It is also a way of naming our own difficulty of listening to that exquisitely compact and crystalline speech. But those margins are not, according to Celan, an option in the poem; they are rather the margins of every poem as language that folds back upon itself. Finally, they are margins that are to be thought specifically as articulating a meridian that is a conflicted unity, one Celan characterized with a remarkably Heraclitean phrase that says of that unity that it "rejoins itself via both poles" (III, 202).[14] That is a phrase that equally echoes Heidegger's description of the poem as "the point of a spear . . . gathering together the supreme and extreme" (*US*, 37).

However else we might characterize it, language in the poem is language at the moment of its greatest concentration and density, and whatever else it might be "about," the poem needs to be read as the discourse of language with itself. But to make such an assertion is equally to say that all language is poetic in its truth, since, as Novalis put the point, "the peculiar property of language [is] that it is solely concerned with itself" (quoted in *US*, 241; see the Appendix here). It is this fold and repetition of language, the moment in which language calls attention to itself *as* language, that hold the words of the poem together as a poem and intensify the experience of its language. Yet, in reading Celan, we discover as well that to the unity of the poem, this curious necessity at work in the poem that leaves us with the knowledge that no word in the poem could be otherwise—a necessity that means that the poem fulfills itself in its own untranslatability—to that unity of language in the poem belongs the countervalent idiom of silence. At the summit of its poetic moment, the coherence of the poem is not univocal: "Yes is not sheered from No" (I, 135). Thus, language in the poem refuses the goal of fluency that so deeply imprints itself on our everyday relation to language, a relation to language in which language trails continuously after its own unbroken reification. The line of the poem, on the other hand, the meridian, needs to be thought as a hiatus, as its own idiomatic caesura. Language that does not articulate itself, and language is always poorest at such self-articulation, plasters over that divided line defining the poem. Celan's own syntactic chiasms, his moebius-strip inversions, tropes, and sharp punctuation breaks are some of the markers of the divisions along the meridian.

But the poem should not only be read as a dialogue with the counterrhythms of silence and the word. It is not only this tension of countervalent idioms. Rather, for Celan, in these countervalent idioms, "the otherness gives voice to what is most its own: its time" (III, 199). To read the poem we need to understand as well that the meridian it articulates intersects another line as well, one that is temporal. History intervenes, and the poem cannot resist its entry. Indeed, it needs to be understood as an invitation to such intervention. Consequently, "we can read it in different ways, we can give it a variety of accents: the acute of the present, the grave of history . . . the circumflex . . . of eternity. . . . I give it—*I have no other choice*—I give it an acute accent" (III, 190; emphasis added). Celan has "no other choice" simply because he writes in German. It is language itself, not the choice of the poet, that dictates the dates. No language is immunized against the memory of what it has spoken or of the anticipations it has permitted. Whenever language comes to speak as language, a certain relation to history and culture works itself to the surface in the structures of memory and anticipation belonging to all language. Even if it is always more than the vessel of history and culture, language can never speak without marking its relation to both, as well as to the marginalization in silence that is peculiar to both. One must understand Celan's own struggle with German, his effort to break down and reconfigure all received sedimentations of the language, as the search for words that have no replication in memory, a memory cut loose from the economy of retribution and revenge, yet one that retains the dignity of the name of "memory." For Celan, then, the task is to stretch German beyond itself, to the point from which it can give voice to what risks annihilation otherwise.[15] Such a project means that Celan's work stands as a forceful argument against Hegel's claim that history takes place in the "temple of *mnenosyne*."[16] Celan's poetic impulse is driven by the awareness that history is just as much the site of annihilation as of memory, and that the task of memory is to fight the risk that history will finally fall into the dark, silent, site of *lethe*. "The poem becomes a conversation—often it is desperate conversation" (III, 198) between language and silence, memory and forgetfulness.

But while the poem "is mindful of and indebted to its dates" (III, 196), it is not governed by the calendar it commemorates.[17] The poem is not handed its dates ready-made; rather, it is the original writing and founding of a calendar: "poetic writing is dating through and through."[18] In this regard, the poet must be read as having a basic role in the political life of those who share a language, as well as in the decisions of history. The full significance of that act, as both shattering and founding at once,[19] is a topic that moves beyond my present concerns to the larger topic of the relation between language, history, and catastrophe. But to allude to the direction in which that topic takes us, I would merely indicate that such (re)writing of calendars is what Benjamin is discussing in the XVth of the "Theses on the Philosophy of History" where he calls such dating a revolutionary act that "blasts the continuum of history."[20] The deepest call of language in the poem is the call that argues against the tendency language to marginalize and forget silence. The task of the poem is found in the call to give voice to that which is still without voice. That call, heard on the plane of history and the cultural life sustained by a language, is the call to rewrite history, to find the new dates that mark the edges of silence and give voice to history's victims to those dispossessed of a language.

But, for the question at hand, the question of reading Celan by following his remarks on how we are to listen to language in the poem, that relation of the poem to dates means finally that the poetry rewrites itself as "an eternalization of nothing but mortality, and in vain" (III, 200). Its entanglement in history means that the poem contains a perpetual call for its own rewriting. In the end, every poem is marked by the date it bears as well as by the relation between language and silence. As such, it is doubly both compressed and strained at once: by both language itself and time.

But those remarks only hint at the beginning of several difficulties for the reader of Celan's poetry. My intent in what follows is to draw out some of these special difficulties that face the reader of Celan, and to do so in order to prepare the way for beginning to think through some of the questions they raise about language in Celan's poetry. Most especially, my attention is drawn to the real presence and pressure of silence in his work, and to the dilemma of reading what is certainly more than "wordlessness" in his poetry. As an opening onto the avenue whereby the riddles of Celan's work may be addressed, I would propose reading Celan's "Meridian" speech as a reply to Heidegger's own reflections on both language and time. The curious lack of comment on Celan's work by Heidegger notwithstanding, I believe that there are profound kinships between Heidegger and Celan as readers of language in the poem, and that those kinships, when set next to their equally profound differences (especially with regard to Celan's claim that language is obliged to answer its time), draw both into a productive dialogue. Furthermore, to understand Celan, it seems important to realize that "Heidegger" is a strange and difficult sort of raw material for Celan, and that Celan was deeply concerned with finding a way through Heidegger to what he spoke of as "a hope, today, of a coming word, thinking, in the heart" (II, 255). More precisely, Celan had a need to find a way to answer to Heidegger's own political engagement with the Nazis. It was, however, a need quite independent of Heidegger's person; rather, it was rooted in what Celan perceived as Heidegger's own relation to German ("I see in Heidegger one who has won back the 'limpidity' of language for language"),[21] as well as to Heidegger's own understanding of language in the poem. The source of Celan's need in this regard might simply be that he believed that his perceived kinship with Heidegger was on a point that is essentially a direct and unambiguous criticism of the very kind of political engagement about which Heidegger remained stubbornly silent after the war.[22] For Celan, poetry is a deeply political matter and cannot be understood as otherwise: "words are viewed as a means of changing the world, and the protest against its violence and injustice results in a critique of language,"[23] which in turn results in a critique of the world. The meridian is the axis of a sharp, double-edged, critique.

Read against the backdrop of Celan's persistent concern with both learning from and finding a reply to Heidegger, Celan's own concerns are simultaneously thrown into sharper relief and emerge as giving voice to a powerful reply to Heidegger, a reply that is best understood as a radicalization of Heidegger. In the "Meridian" text, Celan is concerned with redefining Heidegger's own effort to give a precise name to the line about which Heidegger himself writes in "On 'the line'" where he is answering Ernst Jünger's text diagnosing "our" time(s) as marking the date of nihilism (the genealogy of those texts are worth noting: Jünger's text, itself an answer to Nietzsche, was written for the occasion of Heidegger's birthday).[24] But when reading Celan it is important to bear in mind that it is not just in his prose, but also in his poems, that he is animated by a sense of language that is given a powerful articulation in Heidegger's work. To begin to speak to the way in which Heidegger sheds lights on Celan one must begin with the extraordinary sensibility that underpins every remark on language in both Celan and Heidegger; namely, that "language is grounded in silence. Silence is the most concealed holder of measure."²⁵ For both, *silence* is the secret from out of which language comes to be and be experienced *as* language.

Learn to think with pain.

—Blanchot, *The Writing of Disaster*

"He speaks truly, who speaks shadows" (I, 135): the difficulty comes in writing and reading silence according to its own idiom, voice, and dialect that make it known only obliquely and as something like the shadow of language. It is difficult because "too much of my speaking: besieges the small crystal in your share of silence" (I, 157). The warning here is obvious: talk about silence tends to relentlessly efface its presence; contact with its own concept only hides the fact of its hiding. Silence in Celan's work is not a strategy, but one of the felt pressures of language itself in the poem. It is rather a "fact" that belongs to the life of the language Celan writes. The self-articulation of language in the poem, the effort to bring "facts" of language forward, is not a matter of another discourse "about" such language; it is not gained by further speech, but is already there, already granted. The difficulty is learning how to listen to language at that point that is already there, especially insofar as silence belongs to the way language is granted. So a certain reversal is requisite if we are to read the poem; reading requires the reenacting of what made the writing possible. We are called on to listen back to the point from which the word becomes necessary and speaks itself in its own apartness, to the point at which the word arrives as a gift. When we do this, the word is loud and clear in the poem.

But, even as the clarity of the word is heard, Celan reminds us that silence exerts its own pressure in the poem, and the poem cannot be read apart from that pressure. The pressure is clear and palpable in Celan's own poetry, and is one of the distinguishing marks of his work. It is so clear that Adorno claimed that "Celan's poems articulate unspeakable horror by being silent, thus turning their truth content into a negative quality. They emulate a language below the helpless prattle of human beings—even below the level of organic life as such. It is the language of dead matter, of stones and stars. . . . Celan writes poetry without an aura."²⁶ Disabused of an aura, Celan's poetry resists the tendency of language to permit its own reification, and so is particularly demanding of its readers. In that poetry one finds a language "north of the future" in which even stones and stars speak, so that for the first time they too know silence (must it be said that only that can be silent which has the possibility of speech?): speaking untranslatably—nothing known to our language: "Schweigewütiges / sternt" (III, 76). Here "the Medusa's head" (III, 192) turns the human to stone and finds that it speaks a new language. In large measure, then Adorno's comment is well taken, and is a gesture in the direction of the task of hearing the place of silence in Celan's language, but it does not go far enough. In the end, what we need to remember is that silence confesses its presence wordlessly and according to the measure of its own uncanny ubiquity.

One of the most unexpected ways in which we experience this dimension of language is found in the deep unity of language and the body. This is a point to which Celan refers when he says that the poet writes "from the angle of his existence, the angle of reflection of his bodily life" (III, 197). Celan's characterization of the poem as a "turn of breath" had already pointed toward the relation of language and body in the poem. To the extent that we acknowledge that the voice is a kind of body, and to the extent that we understand that language in the poem calls for voice (one knows this simply in knowing that a poem cannot be read silently, but must be sounded by some voice, even a loudless one),[27] to that extent we have begun to approach the real carnality of language in the poem. It is that carnality that bears along the mutually excessive relation of sound and sense in the poem, rendering the poem a particular "this" that resists being taken up on to the plane of universality. Because it is defined by this resistance rooted in the relation of sound and sense, language in the poem defies translation and that equally resists being taken up as a matter of communication or "meaningful content." Heidegger makes this point when he says "that language sounds and rings and vibrates, that it hovers and trembles, belongs to it in the same measure as does the fact that what is said has a meaning" (US, 205). In the poem, sound and sense each pin the other to itself so radically that neither can be thought apart from the other. The self-insistence of the poem on its own language arises from this point. Every poem is to be read as a "way . . . on which language becomes vocal; they are paths upon which language becomes voice . . . paths of physical life, perhaps outlines of an existence, a self-projection upon itself into the search for itself. . . . A sort of homecoming" (III, 201).

But if the sounding voice is the achievement of language in the body, if that is the bearer of the poetic word and its idiom, then the countervalent idiom, the idiom in which the body robs language of voice, the "mouthfuls of silence," the moment in which the body robs us of words, that is, the moment in which pain interrupts language. The preliminary sense of that interruption is rather evident: pain not only actively resists expression in words, but when we are in profound pain we are unable to speak; we lose the capacity to speak at all. In pain, the human space is contracted and compressed to the point from which language is no longer possible. But, in the final analysis, this contraction of the human space that happens in pain, the moment in which the body silences language, must be understood as a mime of death. Pain is a reminder of the basic fact of our facticity and finitude, and that means that it is a reminder of the real and present presence of death for us and of our aloneness before that fact. So when Heidegger says that "all that lives is painful" (US, 62) that means of course that all that lives is en route to its death and must be understood as such. In pain, the body that is normally unmindful and mute about itself becomes a reminder of the death it makes possible, and that reminder speaks as the pressure of silence on language. Pain belongs to the poem just as do voice and breath. Here then is the otherwise hidden "essential relation between death and language flashes up" (US, 215).[28] The point is that in the silence of pain "the edges of the self become coterminous with the edges of the body it will die with."[29]

One worries that Heidegger's treatment of the relation of pain and language risks mortifying the body by turning it into the mere bearer of an idea or even of the word, and that worry seems to be confirmed when one reads that "every view that tries to represent pain from the perspective of physical sensation remains cut off from the essence of pain" (US, 62). There is even what seems to be a move to encode pain, a move that would need to be addressed in the full effort to think through Heidegger's understanding of the meaning of pain, the move that allows Heidegger to say that "pain, the great soul's basic trait, remains pure harmony with the holiness of blue" (US, 64).[30] One is drawn up abruptly and puzzled by the remark that "the 'infinite torment' is consummate, perfected pain, pain that comes to the fullness of its nature" (US, 72). But in order to hear the full force of his claims, one must understand that Heidegger is calling into question our sense of the body as a visible, anatomical object, and he does this precisely by means of the attempt to rethink the relation of language and the body.[31] In the end, "the sounding of the voice is no longer explained as something merely physiological-physical" (US, 208), and "the mouth is not merely a kind of organ of the body understood as an organism" (US, 205). Yet, although a rethinking of the body is called for here, there is something slightly misleading about asking simply about "the" body, about "this flesh I purchased with my pains."[32] It is true, as Kant citing Epicurus maintained, that pain is "ultimately always of the body,"[33] but it is not true that it is *only* a matter of the body. Pain is always also a matter of the unshareability of our own death. One might even say that the apartness of the word in the poem mimics our own final apartness. In the end, the presence of silence in the poem, the countervalent pressure exerted on language by the body in pain, means that language in the poem is not only a matter of that which we can share, but also, as bearing the traces of silence, that it is equally the reminder of the final failure to speak about our own apartness. "The poem is alone.... One who writes it stays with it" (III, 198).

The pressure of silence in the poem, the "pain of syllables" (I, 280), the realization that "pain itself has the word" (US, 63), is an intimation of the relation of language to death. Poetry, as the discourse of language with itself, always bears traces of that relation, is always a discourse with death. The poem becomes a testimony to the isolation it denies; it becomes the communication of apartness. That is why Heidegger could claim that all poetry is written from the single mood of "mourning": "The spirit which answers to pain, the spirit attuned by and to pain, is mourning" (US, 235).[34] But from this perspective Celan's poetry is distinctive in that it is not only written from the point of mourning, but to it as well: "over all of this your / mourning: no / second heaven" (I, 222). Mourning then marks the place between the silences: "quickly / fade the sounds / this side and that side of mourning" (II, 78).

I believe that Celan was drawn to Heidegger because he sensed in Heidegger this kindred set of concerns to which Heidegger claims we are led by listening to language in the poem. He sensed as well that Heidegger understood that language in the poem is not simply a matter of "poesy," but that such language is ultimately a "homage to the majesty of the absurd which bespeaks the presence of human beings" (III, 190). In Heidegger's attempts to unfold and think the relation between death and language, Celan found someone thinking through language along an axis of concerns that Celan himself sought to bring to voice. Celan wrote always as a survivor—that is, as one who has outlived his death for the moment. His work speaks from out of that deferral, and its language, the pressure of silence, the voice of pain, bears traces of that deferred death.

To say that, however, is not to restrict Celan's work to the categories that would have us read him as a German-Jewish poet writing about the Holocaust—unless of course one is willing to say that "there is in the world a holocaust for every date, and every hour."[35] One need not deny the truth of Celan's life, but one constricts its full force and scope if one regards him only as a poet of the Holocaust. Nonetheless, it is true that Celan's work is always a confrontation with death. In a remarkable way it must even be read as an argument with death since it is always a struggle to speak across the apartness that both marks language of the poem and is the meaning of our deaths. In the end, Celan's work must also be read as a declaration of hope and love, as bearing witness to our belonging together in our apartness: "having gone this impossible way, this way of impossibility in your presence, I find something that consoles me a little bit. I find the connective and how the poem leads to encounter" (III, 202). In the end, we can say that if language in the poem echoes a truth borne by the body in pain, then it must equally be thought as resonating with the truth of the body in love. The poem oscillates between those poles bent back on one another, and lives between silence and song as the achievement of both. "The more joyful the joy, the purer the mourning slumbering within it. The deeper the mourning, the deeper the call of joy resting within it" (US, 235). Valéry echoes that insight when he writes: "Isn't it true that each person will leave behind a formless mass of perceived fragments, pains broken against the world, years lived in a minute, unfinished and chilly constructions, immense labors embraced in a single glance and dead. But all these ruins have a certain rose."[36]

Of course, to find the connective in our apartness is to name the secret of the poem as an impasse. It is to say of language with Hölderlin that "language, most dangerous of possessions, is given man . . . so that he might bear witness to he is,"[37] and it is to say as well with Celan that "no-one bears witness for the witness" (II, 72).

CHAPTER EIGHT

ON THE DARK SIDE OF THE MOON: ON LANGUAGE AND DEAFNESS

Language is grounded in silence.

—Martin Heidegger

We speak and write of language with great ease and frequency, and in so doing we invoke and perform the experience of language in the very act of speaking or writing. Its self-evidence seems unproblematic. It seems to bear witness to itself every time it becomes a question. Likewise, its significance for everything, even for our self-understanding, has been affirmed in the most unqualified terms. So it is said that language is "the house of being" and that "being that can be understood is language." Nothing seems more evident, nothing a larger empire than what is called language. And yet if we pause a moment and try to articulate something of this phenomenon of language, we soon need to confess that it is not entirely clear just what we are speaking about when we invoke this experience of language. In other words, it is not always clear just what this word "language" wants to summon one to experience and to think. It is in light of this perplexity that I want to speak about the question of language as posing for us a question with a special difficulty; namely, that it puts us in an experience so elementally enigmatic *in itself* that it almost defies our efforts to identify the simple event of its occurrence. Though intimately wedded to the very possibility of thinking, language itself natively eludes thought. My premise in what follows is that we know so little of what is meant by language that we might first need to ask about its most basic phenomenal character. I propose that nothing about language, not even its phenomenal character, can be taken for granted. To try to get clearer about what this word might mean animates the most general form of the question that I want to address in this chapter: *where (or, perhaps better, when) do we find language?*

This sense that there is a cryptic quality belonging to the word is not entirely new. It has been well and convincingly demonstrated by Heidegger, Gadamer, Derrida, and others. They remind us repeatedly that language is poorest at articulating itself; in other words, that, whatever else might define it, self-effacement, not self-presentation, always accompanies the appearance of language. Furthermore, it is precisely this self-concealing character of the word that needs to be the starting point in any effort to think the phenomenon of language. But the more one takes this native elusivity of the phenomenon of language to heart, the more one has difficulties even being able to say when there is language. Giving real weight to this self-concealing tendency of the word makes coming to grips with language feel like the effort to grasp fog. Or it feels like the effort to watch a lightening strike: one sees it typically only obliquely, and often misses its event.

Heidegger is sensitive to this difficulty and so he repeatedly argues that above all we need to undergo an experience of language *as* language. In the same vein, he continually cautions us against presuming that such an experience is readily available, or even that we might know the original form of such an experience. Heidegger never ceases to remind us that the simple experience of language is difficult, even when it is language itself that tries to speak of the experience of language. Consequently, we must struggle simply to experience the word as word. We cannot take it as given, as itself. That is why the heightened forms of language—especially poetry and translation—become the centerpieces of reflection on the question of language in the wake of Heidegger. They mark an experience of language in which its tendency to self-effacement is counteracted because in them the word itself is put in question. Thus, turning to the poem and to the enigma of translation is a way of drawing forward a self-conscious experience of the word. Yet even in these cases of language intensified, this unreflected character, this elusivity that marks our experience of the word, is so severe that, as Heidegger contends, we do not even have a word for the word. The experience of the word has escaped us to such an extent that we do not even have a word for the word itself; it has eluded even itself. In the end, the resistance of language to every effort to have language articulate itself needs to be acknowledged as the premier character of language. Once this is done, it becomes abundantly clear that the phenomenon of language, the very fact of language seemingly so self-evident, is still in need of clarity about its elemental nature.

In light of this self-encrypting character of the word, it seems necessary to ask again and again about the manner in which language is most originally offered to thought. By saying that we must do this "again and again," I want to emphasize that this elusivity of language cannot be conquered; it cannot be extinguished. We can, however, pay tribute to its truth by relentlessly encouraging those experiences that summon the word to a presence as itself.

Because this must be done at such a basic, phenomenal level, I want to think about this task in this chapter not by asking once again about either language in the poem or about translatability, but by posing what might appear to be a remarkably naive question, namely, "when is the word?" Notice that I am not yet ready to ask "what is language?" My question is much simpler than that: when is the word, whatever it might be? When we speak of language, what is the phenomenon of which we speak? How can we identify, in its most basic character, this event of language? The question seems naive because one is immediately tempted to give the obvious answer that the word is when I speak and when I write. But it is precisely this answer that must lose its self-evidence if the word is to appear and we are to get at the heart of the question put to us by the sheer fact of language. Until we do this, until the sheer fact of language comes forward, the fact of being will not be able to be recognized as well. Wittgenstein put this point well when he said that "the right expression in language for the miracle of the existence of the world is not any proposition *in* language, it is the existence of language itself."[1] And so it is no surprise that we find Gadamer suggesting that *Sprachvergessenheit* and *Seinsvergessenheit* need to be thought together. The stakes of the question of the experience of language could not be greater. Overlooking language, we overlook being.

To take this task to heart we need to begin by letting go of the seemingly self-evident assumption that script and speech are the preeminent sites of the appearance of the word. We must begin, instead, with the suspicion that these apparently uncomplicated appearances of the word might in fact present us with the chief forms in which language conceals, as well as reveals, itself. In what follows I want to reflect on my hesitation regarding the wide spread prejudice that speech and script mark the event of language in an original manner. To what extent do acoustic and visual images, audible speech and legible script, define the original form of the word *as* word? To what extent is it necessary that we shed the presumption that the word as word is essentially something audible and/or legible? To what extent is listening not primarlily an acoustic phenomenon? To what extent does the image-character of language that appears in script belong to language in an original manner? But if it is the case that we must be able to find the word apart from its appearance in what I say and what I write, then again: when is the word?

Obviously, such a double question—on the one hand, concerned with the role of the icon, of the visual image in the word, on the other hand, concerned with the role of sound, of the voice in the word—is too large to be dealt with properly in our confines here, even if, in the end, these questions belong together (Gadamer points out in the 1981 text "Stimme und Sprache"

such matters "belong in [such] a distinctive entanglement with one another"[2] that the question of script is never able to be completely severed from the question of speech). Although the question of the relation of language and sound entails a question of the relation of language and image, the emphasis of my remarks will be chiefly on the role of sound in the word. The reason for this choice is simple: there seems to be an even greater reliance in philosophical conceptions of language generally (and even more so in hermeneutic theory in particular) on the prejudice that the word must be sounded than on the presumption that the word must be written. Since Aristotle opened *De Interpretatione* with the claim that "written words are the signs of spoken words [which are the original form of the word]" (16a), the prejudice that the word appears as sound has legitimated itself and become an assumption that is almost unquestioned. This has been taken as true far more readily than any claim that script is a self-showing of language. For these reasons, I will direct my reflections on this question—when is the word?—mostly to one side of the obvious answer, namely the answer that says that the word is when one speaks. I want to ask about this view by discussing the silent language of the deaf. However, before turning directly to the attempt to speak of this silent language, I will make a few remarks about the relation of the word to script, since the sign language of the deaf gives the appearance of being an iconic language. Thus, some preliminary clarity about how sign language also touches upon the image-character of language is needed.

The question about the relation of word and image asks how it is that the word belongs to the image that it lets itself become in being written. Put in its most immediate form, the question is: What do these abstract images, these letters of the alphabet, have to do with the fact of the word? Put even more elementally, how does language belongs to the realm of the visible and thus the legible? One of the essential possibilities of language is that it be able to be written; that, even if it is not in fact put into script, all language contains something like "writability" among its determining possibilities. So it seems clear that, yes, it is the case that script is one of the original ways in which language presents itself to us. One finds an illustration of this view in Heidegger's comment in the *Parmenides* lecture course that "Being, word . . . script name an original and essential matrix. . . . The relation of being to man, namely the word, is, in handwriting, inscribed in a being."[3] Here script is regarded as an inscription, an objectification of the word itself. However, I would like to qualify Heidegger's remark and suggest that the matter is not so simple. I prefer to say that in the end this move into the materiality of the written image must be understood as a form of the self-alienation of the ideality of the word, that script—whatever magical powers it exhibits—numbers among the ways in which language hides its ownmost nature, even as it inscribes itself in a being. The truth of the word does not require that the word bear anything other than a *possible* relation to the image. There is an iconographic potential proper to the word, but if we take the *realization* of this potential in script as the original form of the word, then we constrict the wider experience of the word unduly. That experience is contained neither in the iconographic, nor in the acoustic potential of the word alone. One can agree with Gadamer when he says that "the use of words always already contains something like an urge to being fixed in writing" and, at the same time, still acknowledge that the written word is, in the end, epiphenomenal.

My point might not be in full accord with Gadamer's view on this matter, but it is not my intention here to interpret Gadamer. I say this because in the section of *Truth and Method* entitled "Language and Verbum" he explicitly argues that the Christian idea of incarnation needs to be enlisted in these questions and that once that is done the "phenomenon of language [emerges] out of its immersion in the ideality of meaning . . . for, in contrast to the Greek logos, the incarnate word is pure event."[4] His contention, quite in line with Heidegger's, is that we learn the real miracle of the word only when we come to understand that what is written is still the word. However, the question remains: is the experience of the word as word fully appreciated by thinking the word from out of its iconographic potential?

The truth of the word will not be able to be thought if we begin with the assumption that the word is unproblematically found in the written word or in sign. Even if it is the case that it is the word that is written, whether on paper or by the movement of the hand through the air, even if this materialization of the ideality of the word is not a form of its alienation, it still remains the case that a recovery is required if the written is to appear as the word itself. This act of recovery—namely, reading—about which Gadamer has taught us so much, seems to be a form of translation back out of the materiality of script, out of the iconographic potential of the word. And, as Gadamer so frequently likes to remind us, in its original form, reading is an act that mimes spoken speech. In other words, the experience of the written word returns us to the spoken word. He does this by referring us to the "inner ear" in which the ideality proper to the word is first disclosed. In short, the task of appreciating the phenomenal character of the word needs to open up the word so its visibility can be thought as coequal with its audibility.

Such a conclusion is, of course, not new, but proves to be a decisive issue, a crossroads of sorts, at the outset of philosophy when Plato expresses his concerns about the written word as the "corpse of a thought."[5] Ultimately, his efforts to think language (as *logos*) under the signature of the idea requires that he vigorously reject any compromise to the possible ideality of the word such as that which is found in the written word. Plato's deep suspicions about the materiality of the written word spring from this point at which the image character of the word realizes itself. More precisely, and yet perhaps underestimated by Plato himself, the appearance of the word in its ideality is first and foremost found in *hearing* the spoken word. Despite its evanescence, its fidelity to time, its capacity to be and not be at the same time, the audible word comes to stand as the original paradigm of the ideal. Hegel's argument in the *Phenomenology of Spirit* that speech is the soul existing as soul, and the claim that it is in a sort of interior speech that I present myself to myself, both lend weight to the view that the spoken word does indeed also have a claim to priority, just as Aristotle once argued.

But have we understood this audibility of language properly? Indeed, can we understand it insofar as we excise the complicity of script, the image character of the word realized, in the constitution of the experience of language as language? Can we ever understand the possible audibility of the word insofar as we think it as a pure ideality. Can we understand it if we think this audibility as essentially coupled with sound and voice? Or is it the case that hearing has a character that might not be able to be interpreted in terms of sound?

With these brief reminders of how the experience of language is implicated in the entangled co-constitution of language by both its audible and its visible character, I will return to the question "when is the word?" and try to clarify more precisely what sound, what speech has to do with the event of the word. I want to begin taking up this question by confessing that, initially at least, I approach it with the prejudice epidemic throughout the history of philosophy, namely, that sound, even unvocalized sound, has everything to do with the word. I begin with the confession that I have long shared the widespread presumption—one that I no longer share—that the audibility of the word is primarily an acoustic phenomenon.

Heidegger too begins his rather complicated reflections on the essence of language with this point of view. In the text "Das Wesen der Sprache" he writes that "for a long time language has been experienced from out of the activity of speaking. The names which occidental languages have given themselves give evidence of this: *glossa, lingua, langue, language*. Language is the tongue."[6] He continues by citing the Bible and the passage that refers to speaking in several tongues. He reminds us that for Aristotle language is thought from out of the experience of its being heard. Ultimately, for Heidegger, this relation of the word to sound, which for him is requisite for any understanding of the crucial and essential kinship between song and word, is decisive for any attempt to experience the being of the word. Nothing demonstrates this more than the poetic word and the foreign word, the untranslated word. When we hear a language spoken about which we have no knowledge, we still can recognize it as a language. The sounds identify themselves as articulated according to possibilities that let us know, apart from any reliance on meaning, that this is indeed a language. In the foreign language, the resonance of the word, its sonic character, is the clear bearer of its being as a language. Like the poem, in the foreign language that we cannot speak it is the cadence of the sounds that come forward to announce that here is a language, and that lets us begin to experience the language *as* a language. In the poetic word and the foreign word, one cannot deny what Gadamer calls the "effective unity of sense and sound which . . . is already there in every word."[7] Here the privilege of the spoken word for an experience of the word as word seems undeniable.

But if we make such a claim and think the audibility of the word in relation to an unreflected concept of hearing drawn from the experience of those who hear with their ears, then how are we to understand the relation of the deaf to the word? If we suggest that voice belongs to the experience of language as language, what are we to make of the language of the deaf, of those who hear no voice with bodily ears? Clearly, sign language is a language, and while the possibility of the sign might indeed rely on the image-character of the word, does this mean that such a language is without voice, or that listening does not belong to it? Obviously, this means that, if we are to think the audibility of the word, we need to drop the natural assumption that the spoken word needs to be articulated by a real voice or that it actually needs to be heard by an ear. It is with this in mind that two of the more interesting paths toward an understanding of voice opened up by Heidegger and by Gadamer are to be thought. Heidegger does this in *Being and Time* when he speaks of "the voice of conscience," of the most immediate form taken by the event in which one announces oneself to oneself. This 'voice' is distinguished from the many competing 'voices' claiming to be 'conscience' (the voices of my parents, my friends, my religious leaders, public opinion) precisely by virtue of the *silence* of its speech. Likewise, Gadamer will urge us to answer the question "when is the word" by turning our attention to the "inner word." In that notion we find one of Gadamer's most original contributions to the philosophical project of summoning us to an experience of the word. But this notion of the inner word in not easily understood, even though two sources are clearly evident in Gadamer's account of it: one can be traced back to the Stoic and Augustinian conception of the move from a *logos prophorikos* to a *logos endiathetos*; the other is owing to Gadamer's quite nuanced reflections on his experience as a reader, especially as a reader of poetry.

In line with the dual sources of this notion for Gadamer, there are two interpretative models that he enlists to clarify the nature of the inner word: the Christian model of the trinity and the model provided by the relation of reading to the spoken word. I do not propose rehearsing the ways in which Gadamer deploys these models as a means of explaining how the experience of the word as word is found in something like the inner word. But I do want to indicate that there is a clear tendency to grasp the word in both of these interpretative approaches as somehow belonging to a voice. Even when this voice is described as silent, it nonetheless remains a silent *voice*, and it is difficult to think the voice independent of the tongue. Silence only serves to qualify the notion of voice that still takes its cues from and understanding of language that belongs to the vocalizations of the tongue. One is reminded of Aristotle's observations in the *History of Animals* that "language is the articulation of voice by the tongue" (535a33). So, as a way of sharpening this question "when is the word?"—and ideally thereby contributing something to what might be said of the inner word—I will call attention to the question of the possible contribution of sound to the word by speaking of the language of the deaf.

If we are to let the language of the deaf pose a genuine challenge to our understanding of the experience of the word as word, then it is imperative that two points be established at the outset. First, that sign language truly is a fully developed language; and, second, that it is not a language the "speaks" like other languages speak, but that it is a radically different mode of language simply because it *cannot be spoken*; it resists being said as itself. This is something that sets the question of voice apart from the question of script, since every language can be written, even if it, in fact, is not.

I believe that the first point that I need to establish is a rather simple one. Sign language exhibits all the features—with the sole exception of speakability—of what we can call language: it is systematic, has syntax and grammar, it is able to act on things across the distances of space and time, it can problematize abstract notions, and it can reflect upon itself. In short, sign language is not simply a means of communication in the absence of genuine speech. Perhaps most significant, we should not forget that it possesses it own forms of the self-conscious expressions of the word—namely, poetry and translation, which are the final hallmarks of true language. I take it then that unless we accept sign as a proper language we will not be in a position to pose the question of language in its fullest reach. This means that like Plato, who writes in the *Cratytus* that "if we had neither voice nor tongue and yet wished to manifest things to one another, should we not, like those who are at present mute, endeavor to signify our meaning by the hands, head and other parts of the body?,"[8] we need to stretch our reflections on language to include sign language as intelligible even under the understanding of the relation of language and voice. For that to happen, the basic character of "voice" needs clarification, especially with regard to the presumption that voice is to be thought according to the model of audible speech.

The assumption that sound belongs to the nature of the word is somehow so intuitively compelling that it is natural to think of sign language as a sort of compensation, an impoverished substitute for spoken language. Because of this assumption, those of us who can hear frequently regard the deaf as having a deficient or restrictive relation to language. But while we might need to say that there is a difference between the realm opened up by audible and inaudible languages that is in need of attention, we need to say that both the audible and inaudible word still remains fully word *as* word. Holding sign language into the question of language has an impact on the answer to the question "when is the word?" simply because sign language challenges a seemingly natural set of conceptions about the relation of language and sound. It is also worth noting that these conceptions have in turn produced a number of misconceptions about sign language that need to be debunked if we are to engage sign language in the task of thinking the full experience of language as language.

First, we need to get over the view that the prelingually deaf relation to language is essentially defined by the absence of sound. If, as seems natural, we assume that the bond between word and audible sound is so basic that it essentially defines the very experience of the word, then it is equally natural to assume that the deaf innately feel their own relation to the word as lacking, as an experience of the word essentially shortchanged by the absence of its audibility. As a corollary to this assumption, one then concludes that the deaf, and here as always I am referring to the prelingually deaf, when reading written words do so as those of us who hear do and silently sound the words. But this is not the case. The deaf no more feel the lack of the spoken word when they sign than the hearing feel the absence of signing when we speak. When the deaf do struggle to speak, it is simply for our benefit; it is not for their own benefit, not out of any deep-seated impulse of the voice struggling to bring the word to itself. As for reading, the deaf relationship to the scripted word turns out to be a rather alien experience for them. Our relation to Chinese ideograms or Egyptian hieroglyphs might well be just as foreign to us as scripted English is to a signer. That is because a sign is not like the word we speak and thus can write. Our alphabet is set up as an instruction for the voice. It is designed to instruct both the tongue (with consonants) and the breath (with vowels). The scripted word might well emerge out of the image character of the word, but it equally developed with reference to the needs of those who hear. One can only wonder about the specific character of the written word that would have developed had we not had ears that hear sound. It is clear just how much the scripted word is predicated on, and limited by, the audibility of the word. This, of course, also means that it is not true to say the "the deaf speak by writing and hear by reading."

This brings me to my second misconception about sign, namely, that it is parasitic of the spoken word. The logic animating this prejudice is easily identified. It is a typical assumption that sign language developed out of the dominant language of each culture, and that it has a parasitic relation to the majority culture. We concede that language is determinative of culture, but, since we typically do not understand that sign language is an independent form of language, we do not grasp the true independence of deaf culture. And so we reinforce the view that sign is dependent on speech. This misunderstanding is expressed in the view that American Sign Language bears an essential relation to American English, and so on. Or in the view that sign language is simply universal, existing in an undifferentiated form around the globe. Of course, this image of a universal sign language, this notion that all signers can "talk" with one another, contradicts the view that sign is dependent on spoken language. But both beliefs are evidence of basic misconceptions about sign language. First, it should be noted that sign has developed with only the slightest influence from spoken language; and, second, the large variety of sign languages are as varied as the different spoken languages are from one another: their languages are limited only by the possibility of the gesture of hands and body, ours by the movement of the mouth. Furthermore, the relation between the various cultural forms of the sign do not mirror the relation between the languages of those cultures. Thus, a signer of American Sign Language would have a very easy time speaking with a French signer. But an American signer would find an exchange with a British signer almost as difficult as I would find an exchange with a speaker of Chinese. In short, sign exists as a language quite independent of the actualization of language in sound, just as the possibilities of the spoken word, initially at least, are independent of the actualization of the image character of the word in script.

The final misconception about sign that I must be overcome if we are to take sign into the question of language is the impression that one who signs somehow thinks in words that are like the words we speak. This simply is not true. Until we learn what it is like to think in sign, we will not be able to freely appreciate the relation of language and thought at all. To imagine what it is like for the prelingually deaf to think in sign as something like seeing hands making gesture seems about as naive as suggesting that those who speak must think by seeing a mouth form words. We would be better off imaging something like a sense of movement: thinking in sign might well be better described as like a flutter, and, if it is this, then it is much more obviously a temporal form in itself than is the strange flow of confused, barely formed words that we typically take to be thinking. In the end though, trying to imagine what it is like to think in sign, for those of us who hear, is a bit like trying to see the dark side of the moon. So long as we hold fast to our own sense of the audibility of the word as, in the first instance, an acoustic phenomenon, the special audibility of the inner word will not be heard. If we are to understand what it means to speak of the word as word, then we need to be acknowledge that sign language has its own distinctive, not parasitical, relation to the "voice" of this inner word.

Before moving forward from this point, I should note that my own language, my manner of speaking of these issues that I have taken from Heidegger, who speaks of "the word as word" and from Gadamer who speaks of "the inner word," is highly problematic in this context. Signers insist that a sign is not just a word by another name. Nor, of course, is it a sign in the usual sense such as we find analyzed in Heidegger's treatment of the sign in *Being and Time* in which the instrumental structure of the sign is made evident. This difference between sign and the spoken word is confirmed most compellingly by the hearing children of deaf parents who were raised with sign as their native language (presenting us with situation similar to that described by Herodotus who tells of the seventh-century B.C.E. Egyptian king who had hearing two children raised by deaf shepherds to learn what language they would speak, only to find that sign became their native language). Such hearing children of deaf adults often claim that they find it easier to think in sign. In other words, sign is experienced as a full language, complete in every regard, even satisfying the urge to bring language to voice.

I do not propose to probe these and other mysteries of sign language. My intention is not to speak of sign in any detail. But I do want to introduce the *fact* of sign *as* a full language in order to ask whether our conception of language is large enough, radical enough, so as to unable us to answer the question "when is the word?" in a manner that lets sign be recognized as "word." Let me insert here that, for reasons I have set out already, I do not want to accept the alternative answer to the challenge of sign that Aristotle proposes when he disqualifies sign as a language; that decision also leads Aristotle to suggest that the deaf cannot be taught to think and that they are less intelligent than the blind. Quite in opposition to Aristotle, I would prefer suggesting that the language of the hand is older—in every sense of the word—than the language of the tongue. By this I simply mean that sign language is perhaps more immediately like the language of the inner word than spoken language is. I say this mostly because of the temporal character of sign. And it is this character that leads me to the admittedly very strange and even quite ironic suggestion that the kinship between language and music—a kinship that Heidegger frequently sought to establish—might be more vital in the language of sign that the language of speech. The language invented by the deaf, language that has shed its acoustic character, might give us the best evidence we have of the deep affinity between language and music that we do well to understand as time made loud. Both sign language and music grow out of a silence that gives rise to voice. Sign simply stays closer to this source. When we understand this, we come to wonder anew about the kinship of thinking and the spoken word, which lets itself be written in the letters of the alphabet, all but six of which are, as Plato points out in the *Cratylus, unspeakable*. Written language bears the trace of this silence in its own way.

My intention here has not been to exalt sign language, but to ask, in the light of its features, "when is the word?" and to do this without taking for granted that language arises from speech that is defined by its acoustic potential. My claim has been that, when we do this, some of our most cherished assumptions about the event of language are troubled and thrown into question. Above all, it seems clear that if we want to think the constitutive role of voice in the word, then we need to start an understanding of the curious silence proper to the original form of voice. This silent voice is the element in which the unity of language and thought is found. This does not mean that the enigma of the event of language can be thought completely independent of speech, which is why Gadamer finds the Christian conception of "incarnation" so interesting, or that the question of the word can be asked apart from the riddle of the spoken word. But it does mean that the spoken word does not encompass the truth that the word "is" and that we need to widen our conceptions of when the event of language happens. We do this when we start to think how it is that silence belongs to the word.

But to say that the word as word, the inner word, is not be grasped either by the image of script or by sound is not to drive the original experience of language deep into an interior world of a subject, thereby removing it from the realm of communicability. Even as the inner word, language still remains first and foremost an opening onto a world that is relentlessly transgressive. It is rather evidence of the manner in which the experience of the word is the experience that, even it its communicative actuality, escapes capture and so remains always an unthinkable finitude. Language, as it is spoken and written, exceeds itself not only in the direction of its conceptional possibilities, but equally by referring itself as itself to the inner word. Concept and inner word mark the limits of language, the forms in which it opens up a world and the space of speech. My speaking and writing exceed myself in ways that I cannot grasp. Gadamer likes to say that no word is a final word, and this is true simply because every word is excessive. Every word is experienced in countervalent directions and in this way language sets me into the world, extends me beyond the threshold of the self; every word is, in this regard, a poetic word that opens a world. But this also means that the word cannot say itself as word. The word can never bring itself to a concept, nor can it disclose itself to itself as such. So when Heidegger reminds us that we have no word for the word, he is really reminding us that it is the truth of the word that it remains like the dark side of the moon. It is, by definition, that which exceeds our reach. It is elusive even before its own disclosive reach.

We must say that the word is by nature cryptic, that, in the words of Heidegger, it is *diessig*, it shrouds itself in fog, and that it is what I am always, at best *unterwegs zu*. It is this finitude of the word that persistently draws us forward in search of language at the very same moment language itself hides. This is something we can learn from the language of hands in motion: that the word as word, language at its origins, is not formed by a reflective act, but by a poetic event. What we learn is that when we think, when we have something to do with the "inner word," there is an identity between the word and being that is not fully expressed in script or speech or sign. When we write or speak or sign, we enter into a second-order experience of language, still close to the source of the word, but nonetheless belonging to the logic of reflection where, as Hegel reminds us, everything, most of all language, becomes different. What this means is that when we try to come to terms with the original experience of language, we must be vigilant about the prejudices we bring to these reflections on the word. What is at stake in this search for the original event of the word is nothing less than our understanding of what might just be the preeminent, the definitive, event of being human.

CHAPTER NINE

SPEAKING OF NATURE: ON LANGUAGE AND THE UNBIDDEN WORLD

> The inner—what is that if not intensified sky, hurled through with birds and deep with the winds of homecoming.
>
> —Rilke

Though it is controversial that the realm of the poetic is a privileged site for reflection on language, it is not completely surprising: in the poetic we find the compressed experience of language. But to say further that language, especially poetic language, is a privileged site for how we think the being of nature is not only a matter of controversy, it is a great surprise far afield from expectations. Nonetheless, such is the claim one finds in Hölderlin.

This chapter, which is directed to unpacking this claim, is divided into three parts. In the first part, I want to speak somewhat programmatically about the relation between philosophizing and ethicality. I make these remarks to provide a context for the more detailed comments I make in the second part. I also make them as a sort of provocation. Here I argue that we would do well to index our thinking more originally to the question of ethical life, and that we need to understand the real concerns of ethicality as centered on the riddle of freedom, not on the production of rules of behavior. In the second part, I want to make some comments about Hölderlin's efforts to write a tragedy about Empedocles and to argue that in such poetic work, something of significance for the questions of ethical life becomes visible. More precisely, I want to suggest that there is an insight into the possibility of a different conception of ethicality formulated here in this failed and incomplete attempt at a tragedy. Furthermore, I want to argue that what we can learn from Hölderlin speaks quite directly to the points that I believe philosophizing today most needs to learn about the place of this riddle of freedom in ethical life. In particular, I will suggest that it is by setting the question of freedom in the horizon of the even larger question of nature, and that by presenting this horizon as necessarily exhibited in the form of a tragedy, in other words as a *poetic experience*, Hölderlin offers interesting possibilities for one who would make the effort to reorient reflection more originally toward a concern with ethical life. In the third part, I want to draw some tentative conclusions that link Hölderlin's special concerns developed in *The Death of Empedocles* with the issues I raise in the first part of this chapter. My argument here is that we can learn from Hölderlin what it means that we have lost the ability to pose the question of nature today. I also want to argue that addressing this lacuna is one way in which we can begin to open up anew the originary relation between philosophizing and ethicality, and that we can best accomplish this by beginning with the role of the poetic in the disclosure of this relation.

Let me begin by announcing, quite rapidly and without much explanation, three contentions that drive the following remarks.

First, I believe that the present age marks a time of exhaustion of the philosophical imagination. By this I simply mean that we live in an age in which forces and events are consolidating themselves rapidly, an age of significant changes, and yet the philosophical traditions we have inherited are unable to comprehend these changes (which, ironically, they have in many regards wrought), and the philosophical imaginations of our age lag behind the movement of history. Consequently, philosophizing has begun to lose its critical edge; it is simply struggling to comprehend its times. This, of course, is old news: Hegel had already made this theme the opening lament of his *Phenomenology of Spirit* when he wrote that "By the little which now satisfies Spirit, we can measure the extent of its loss."[1] But, our consciousness of this loss, and of its significance, takes a different form today than it did for Hegel, for whom it became the first moment in the rejuvenation of the philosophical form of Spirit. The complexity of this situation for us is captured wonderfully by Adorno's remark that "philosophy, which once seemed to be surpassed, keeps itself alive because it missed the moment of its realization."[2] For us, it seems that the lesson to be learned concerns the modesty of thinking in our age. Our's seems to be a time like the time Oedipus endured in "Oedipus at Colonus": the time after the time of collapse, but before the time of death.

Second, that technologies and technological reasoning, which clearly lack this modesty, are very much at the center of the transformations that we need to grasp in thought. This too comes as no surprise. Already in the late 1930s Heidegger had dedicated a great part of his energies in Beiträge to the analysis of Machenschaft as the central category according to which the historical present needs to be thought. What has become increasingly clear is that the human capacity for *producing* a world has come to saturate the lived world, and that it has also come to shape the forms of thinking with which we seek to comprehend that world. In other words, philosophizing has come to shape itself in a manner somehow affected by technological reasoning. Or, to use Heidegger's vocabulary here: Western thinking has imbued itself with the features of Machenschaft, and has thus come to be an expression what it needs to comprehend and critique. We thus stand before the problem of how we are to orient thinking in this historical juncture.

Third, that in order to live up to the task of reanimating the philosophical imagination, and uncovering a place from out of which issues of our day can be addressed critically, something like a new ethical understanding, a new understanding of what Hegel referred to as ethical life, is required. I believe that what is needed today is what Heidegger referred to as an "original ethic"—that is, a new understanding of the horizon out of which thinking is able to address the world lucidly and with respect. Unlike my first two contentions, this final point is, I suspect, a bit more controversial, and so, while all three claims will play a role in the following, it is this point that I would most like to address.

Put in a somewhat cruder form, I am suggesting that it is only out of something like a fresh relation to ethical life that philosophizing will be able to earn the honor of its name in the present historical juncture. My contention is that the ethical moment belongs to the origin of philosophizing, and it endures as its most far-reaching goal, but—due to the logic of its own history and its inability to separate itself from technological reasoning—this origin is obscured in important ways today. While the point of this chapter is to speak to this origin by speaking about Hölderlin's *The Death of Empedocles*, I believe that some preliminary and quite general remarks about this issue might help me orient the more detailed argument I want to make.

First, in order to understand this claim, it is essential that ethics here *not* be understood in a traditional sense, and that it *not* be understood as naming a determinate region of philosophizing. I do not, for instance, want to use this word "ethics" to refer to the effort to prescribe rules of behavior; rather I take it as centered on the enigma of human freedom. Ethics, as I understand it, is *manifestly not* something that could ever come to be "applied." Second, this means also that I begin with a sense of the ethical that does not take it as assuming the solidity of an autonomous subject; quite the contrary, I take the ethical moment in a sense akin to what Levinas means when he says that "it is the putting into question of my spontaneity by the presence of the other,"[3] and I take Heidegger's analysis of the porosity of Da-sein as equally a given in this matter. The ethical is simultaneous with the appearance of the point of alterity, and this alterity renders me a riddle to myself. So the ethical moment is the moment in which I am placed into radical question and in which I understand this question as wedded to freedom. Third, it should be clear from what I have just said that I also take the ethical as referring to a region that is beyond good and evil, indeed, that is perhaps antagonistic to the very economy of good and evil. Insofar as ethics is indeed about human life, it is not primarily defined by the spheres of guilt and responsibility (which are categories drawn from the realm of law, not of ethical life in the original sense), but is, as Spinoza (and the Greeks generally) knew, much more a matter of asking whether there can be a doctrine of the happy life. If we are ever to appreciate the ethical demands of philosophizing, then I believe we need to take to heart Nietzsche's criticisms of any sort of theologizing of ethical life, and we equally need to hold to Heidegger's criticisms of humanism as a form in which this question of the *ethos* of thinking can be opened up. In the end, what is necessary is that we come to understand "the ethical" in a new sense, and to understand how it is that this original sense of the ethical exerts a demand on thinking that can free it to its most far-reaching concerns. One of my chief intentions in this chapter is to address this need by trying to give some new sense of the force of the ethical, and to speak to the original relation of philosophizing and ethical life. As I have already said, I want to do this by means of a discussion of Hölderlin's tragedy *The Death of Empedocles*.

Before turning to Hölderlin's play, a few remarks about the context in which I want to read it are needed.

In 1795, twenty-one centuries after Aristotle had posed the question "why do human being make art?" in his *Poetics*, Schelling writes the *Letters on Dogmatism and Criticism* in which he argues that in the end, freedom will always "vanish from the light of reason," but that it is a "possibility preserved for art"—specifically, tragic art.[4] In short, Schelling not only argues that freedom is the great riddle for reflection, he also argues that, as Kant made evident as early as the first critique, reason will never be able to grasp the contradictions that freedom falls into in its relation to nature. It is, says Schelling, only art, which is not bound by the linear logic of conceptual reason and does not shy away from nature, that can preserve the light of freedom. Answering Aristotle's question, Schelling suggests that we make art as a way of objectifying and preserving freedom in the world. Art thus needs to be understood as the highest testimony of our freedom. With this claim, Schelling inaugurates a tradition that would ultimately struggle to recognize the achievement of art in human experience, and that would eventually set art in a privileged relation with truth (one sees this clearly in Nietzsche, Heidegger, Adorno, Benjamin, Gadamer, and Derrida, for instance). While this kinship between art and a new sense of truth has been well recognized since Schelling, the special relation between art and human freedom, a relationship that builds the heart of Kant's third critique, seems to have drifted by the wayside. But it is precisely this sense that art is both an *expression* of freedom, and that it is the only manner in which this freedom is *grasped*, that is decisive for Hölderlin in his efforts to write a specifically modern tragedy; that is, a tragedy that preserves the issue of freedom as it is proper to our times, not to the time of Greek tragedy. My claim is that because he lets himself be guided by this sense of freedom that exceeds reason, and because he presents this experience of freedom *performatively* in the work of art rather than conceptually, Hölderlin's tragedy opens up the question of freedom—and ultimately the questions of ethical life—in a unique and, for us, important manner. What is most unique here, and so worthy of our attention, is the way in which, by taking the question of freedom seriously and as "preserved for art," Hölderlin is led to the insight that freedom, the true horizon of ethical life, *is not defined by the realm of the human*. The Greek tragedies stand as a reminder of this—in them we find "monstrous couplings" of all sorts in which the realm of the human is breached—but for the Greeks the specific form of what we *suffer* as a result of this relation is different than it is for us. If we are to understand what is specifically *modern* about this tragedy, then it is necessary that we understand *why it is that one of the protagonists of a modern tragedy must be nature itself and it is necessary to understand why, in the face of this protagonist, the human hero must die a singular form of death, namely, suicide*. But, to understand these points, one must first open oneself to a different understanding of what is at play when we speak of nature. Obviously, it will mean that we cease to think of nature as a region of determined objects that are to be viewed primarily as belonging to a causal nexus. It is also necessary that we see how freedom too first becomes visible as itself once it is thought outside of the orbit of the human, and not as the doings of a subject. That is why the tragedy of Empedocles, the arc of strange reflections that ends in his death, unfolds in terms of the relation between the human and nature. In the end, I will suggest that it is only out of this strange relation—one perhaps better described as the relation between the human and the nonhuman, and one that Hölderlin suggests can only be presented tragically—that we find the first glimmer of the real stakes of the question of freedom and of ethical life.

The drama of the death of Empedocles has as its theme the same general theme that defined Holderlin's epistolary novel *Hyperion*, in which the hero, a modern German soldier living on a Greek island, struggles to overcome the feeling of separation from nature and from others that causes him so much anguish. *Hyperion* is the story of the longing for union, told from the point of the suffering that separation from that union produces. In the course of telling of his sufferings, Hyperion indicates that he believes the reason for this feeling of separation is rooted in the forms of modern life that have distanced us from the natural world. Our relation to nature is like the relation of the sick to health: we long for its return and, in the end, need no special reason to account for this longing. Separated from nature, we can only know separation as the rule of life since nature is the name of the origin site of belonging for us. Or, put in other words, Hyperion learns that one who does not live in harmony with the world does not live in harmony with oneself. Even if, as Kant reminds us so vividly, nature needs to be thought as the real meaning of the sublime, even if it is the name of the power that can destroy me, nature needs to be acknowledged as that which is not simply surrounding us, but *in* us. It is the name of what is most encompassing, and so to feel separated from it is to feel separated even from oneself. To be separated from nature, understood in this way, is a form of death. That, in part, is what he means when he says that "Fern und todt sind meine Geliebten" [distant and dead are my loved ones].

Hyperion's struggle is to bring his suffering into words and, in so doing, in giving a name and form to his suffering, to find a way not to overcome it, but to endure it. At the end of his reflections on the character of his sufferings Hyperion concludes that his best hope for enduring this agony is to be found in art. The reason is simple: art is not only an expression of what is most human—that is, freedom—but it is the way in which we are able to summon beauty in the world and, in this, find a glimmer of unity with the world. That is a viewpoint to which Hölderlin subscribes because he holds as true the claim that Kant made when he said that "Die schöne Dinge zeigen an, dass der Mensch in die Welt passe."[5] In other words, the pleasure we take in beauty is an indicator that we belong to that which is larger than what we can define, control, or know. To summon this pleasure, to remind us that we belong to the world, is the task of art. Hyperion also concludes that such an art form would have to be one that does not extinguish or sublate difference and the suffering it breeds, since to do that would be to extinguish his own singular being. To sublate suffering does not resolve it; it merely eradicates the one who suffers. So what is necessary is an art that shows the peculiar beauty of suffering. Of course, the form of art in which suffering is freely transfigured into beauty is tragedy. Hyperion suggests that it is no accident that the Athenians excelled at tragedy, since they were the last people—in the West at least—for whom such a unity with nature was possible. They understood what it means to say that nature is "*hen diapheron eauto*" [the one differentiated in itself].

While *Hyperion* ends on this note that refers us to art, and specifically to tragedy, as the form in which human freedom can address itself to the question of how we are able to find a home in the world, it does not take up its own suggestions in this regard. *Hyperion* does not adhere strictly to the form that it deems requisite for the task it announces. This, however, is precisely the effort of *The Death of Empedocles*. Here the story of the modern human relation to nature is told as a tragedy played out between Empedocles and nature itself. Here the sense of separation from nature is more acute, because now Hölderlin understands that death, which is the meaning of that separation for us, is a separation in time. And while I might be able to overcome a separation in space, separation in time is something we can only suffer. But here it becomes clear as well that Empedocles's need to die, rather than to simply suffer the death of separation from nature, his need to commit suicide—which, as the title indicates, is the destiny that this play struggles to present—must be thought from out of his failure to understand how his freedom, which shows itself both in his singularity and in his capacity for art, can find a home in nature, in that which is not defined by his own freedom and particularity.

The play is difficult to understand not simply because it remains incomplete; there is no "action" in the play to speak of, nothing "happens," even Empedocles' death is spoken of only obliquely. All the characters other than Empedocles focus all their speech on him: the priests of the old order fear him and plot a way of bringing about his "downfall" from the high esteem in which he is held by "the people"; Empedocles's close friends all confess that they do not understand him. Though he is at the center of everyone else's attention, Empedocles seems oblivious to every relation but one; namely, the relation in which he stands with nature. It is out of this relation that the possibility of every other relation will emerge. This becomes clear in Empedocles's long soliloquy, a beautiful speech that is really the effort of a poet to dialogue with nature itself. The speech, which Empedocles delivers standing alone, but longing for an answer to his words, is a lament and moves rapidly through a range of strong emotions: it begins with an expression of Empedocles's deep affection for nature (which he addresses as the unnamed "you" of the speech)—"In my stillness you came wandering softly, / You found me deep within the darkness of the hall, / You kindly one! You came not unhoped for and not from afar"—and it quickly moves to the expression of a deep sorrow—"O nature most intimate! You who are right before my eyes, do you still know your friend, who was profoundly loved, will you never know me again? The priest who brought the living song and life to you / Like sacrificial blood gladly shed?" As he speaks, Empedocles's sense of abandon deepens: "why do you push away this heart, which lovingly divined you, / And lock it up in tight chains / A heart which was born free, which came from itself and nothing else."

What we find here is Empedocles expressing a consciousness of his separation from nature, which he presents as a sort of unassimilable other. It is all-encompassing and sovereign, and, as such, resists Empedocles's efforts to draw it out. Simply put: nature shelters itself, or in Heraclitus's words "*physis krypthesthi phelei.*" It is larger than what the realm of the human can either contain or define, and yet it is that without which I cannot understand myself. It is also a speech in which the real locus of the reason we must stand in a specifically *tragic* relation with self-concealing nature is made clear. We first get a hint of this when Empedocles refers to himself as "The priest who brought the living song and life to you / *Like sacrificial blood gladly shed*." The point is this, that the human relation to nature must be thought in terms of how *language* belongs to this relation because it is in language that the real "fact of freedom" finds its most concrete expression, and it is in understanding the character of the sacrifice that is "demanded" by this situation that we first come to understand something of the original place we can find in our world. The question is, why is it that the effort to sing of nature, to speak the words that celebrate it and draw it into that which we can embrace, is like shedding blood sacrificially? Why is the activity of the poet experienced as a form of sacrifice? And why is this emblematic of the human relation to nature?

This is a difficult point, but it is the central point. That we speak, that there is language, is the greatest demonstration of our freedom—this is something we palpably feel in the *astonishing spontaneity of language*. And language is also the clearest reminder that freedom is always able to exceed reason since language has the capacity to unfold in the presence of nothing, to be *alogon*. Furthermore, Empedocles suggests that nature, which is "mute," needs language since it is in the word that the unity of nature is first attained. In language, the speculative meaning of nature appears—language is the one power that can embrace and give unity to all-embracing nature. Put in other words, nature is a poetic process and its unity is mirrored in the word. That is why Hölderlin refers to language as "die Blume des Mundes" [the flower of the mouth], because, like the flower that unites heaven and earth, the word draws together that which differentiates itself infinitely. The word is the self-reflection of nature, and it is the task of the poet (and Empedocles, says Hölderlin, was "born to be a poet") to bring this unity into being. That, in part, is what Empedocles means when he says that "In me, / In me, you sources of life, you once flowed out of the depths of the world and came together in me, and / The thirsty came to me." Earlier in the play he put the point more directly: "I companioned the estranged / My word names the unknown, / And the love of the living I carry / Up and down; what one of them lacks / I bring from another / And, soul inspiring, connect, / Rejuvenating, transform this hesitant world." He unites all things in love and in language. But, and this is the reason the human relation to nature demands a sacrifice and so can only be described as a tragedy, there is a double truth at work here since for this word of nature to be spoken the poet must separate himself from nature. This is because "in pure life, nature and art are only opposed harmoniously," but if this unity is to be exposed "it must be presented in the separateness" of the word. In "this moment, in the birth of the highest antagonism, the highest reconciliation appears." So, now Empedocles suffers from his love, that is, from his speculative longing for unity, and thus Empedocles is "a son of the monstrous oppositions of nature and art in which the world appeared before his eyes. A man within whom those oppositions are united so intimately that they become one within him."⁶ For this reason, he suffers the same malady as Oedipus: that is, he has an "eye too many, perhaps."

But why must Empedocles die? Why must he commit suicide (which seems to be a form of sacrifice quite different from what we find exhibited by Antigone, for example, who dies in the name of solidarity)? It is a peculiar death he chooses: he leaps into a volcano. In this death, it seems that all particularity is extinguished, no corpse remains, nothing remains of the body that is reabsorbed into nature; rather, the body is dispersed throughout the whole of nature. But this does not mean that it was the body that was the source of his separation from nature. Quite the contrary; the body is the way in which we most exhibit our belonging to nature. What his death means is simply that he *falls silent*. He dies to silence language. He abolishes the finitude proper to the human realm, but in doing this he abolishes as well the true form of his relation to nature.

But there is a obviously a deep paradox at the heart of such a way of thinking: the word is thought here as the divine in the human, and through the word nature is able to appear as a living totality. Yet it is precisely in the word that we find both the emblem of our finitude, of our separation from nature, and equally our way of embracing it. Hölderlin put this point compactly in an early version of *Hyperion* when he wrote as follows: "Let me speak humanly. When our original, infinite, being first began to suffer the full power of the first barriers, when poverty appeared coupled with abundance, love was there. You ask, when was that? Plato said: on the day Aphrodite was born. So then, when the beautiful world began for us, then we became conscious, then we were finite. Now we feel profoundly the limitation of our being, and there is something in us which gladly holds onto these chains—for if the divine in us was not limited by any resistance, we would know nothing outside of ourselves, and so also nothing of ourselves, and to know nothing of one's self, not to feel oneself, and to be annihilated, is for us the same thing."

In other words, the experience of limits, of being at the threshold, is the properly human experience. Language is perhaps the most intimate manner in which we confront ourselves at just such a threshold. And this word "nature" is the impoverished name of the threshold at which we dwell most ambiguously and in need of language.

Let me leave these rather detailed remarks about Hölderlin now and ask what they might have to do with the concerns I outlined at the beginning of my remarks. You will recall that my argument was as follows. First, that we need to understand our reflections as emerging out of, and as reaching toward, a deeper sense of freedom than the conception of freedom that regards it as the activity of a subject. I also suggested that this means granting that philosophizing emerges out of an ethical impulse. Second, I argued that, for this to come to pass, we need to restore the question of nature to the agenda of thinking and to do so in a manner that frees our conception of nature from the orbit of technological reasoning. Until philosophy recovers the question of nature and ceases to hand it over to the prerogatives of scientific and technological reasoning, we will not be in a position to recuperate that experience that can open us to a realm of being greater than that which bears the mark of the human subject. I also contended that Hölderlin had something to teach us in this regard. But now I must say more clearly what that is.

In the figure of Empedocles, Hölderlin presents us with someone who genuinely struggles to engage a realm of being that he has no hand in producing; in other words, the longing that defines him is the longing to find a home in a world not within his control, or even his knowledge. It is the longing to let the other present itself as fully other. He seeks a relation with that which he cannot subdue; better: he seeks that which embraces him and yet holds itself in reserve. And here, since the other that is at issue falls outside of the realm of the human, the return to a simple patronizing humanism in order to maintain this relation must fail. It will do no good, help in no fashion, for him to turn to human "values" to find what he seeks. So, like Oedipus, who faces two riddles, the riddle of the Sphinx and of his own identity, Empedocles too confronts a riddle: he must reach beyond himself—that is, the truth for one who possesses language; that is, for one who is finite and nonetheless exceeds the limitations of sheer finitude—and yet the riddle is how he is to do this without destroying himself in his own particularity. He tries to answer this riddle *as a poet*, that is, as one committed to language *as* language, and as one who dwells at the threshold of what is most human. This means as well that he takes up this riddle that he is for himself as one for whom the relation of language and freedom is central. Living at the threshold where language and nature intersect, Empedocles finds his life to be a continual death, he sees himself living in a condition of chronic sacrifice, and when he no longer finds comfort in the beauty of his words, a different kind of death, one that lets him fall silent, is necessary. In the second version of *The Death of Empedocles* Empedocles never comes to reconcile his condition; he never finds a way of affirming the mystery of his relation to that which he seeks, but cannot subdue.

Hölderlin rewrites *The Death of Empedocles* once more. In the third, and final, version Empedocles' death is given a new significance. He no longer longs to die, largely because he has come to accept, to affirm, the conditions of life at the threshold. What this means—in part at least—is that he accepts the truth that we cannot will union with what we love, and we cannot hold on to what we love forever. The experience of nature comes to be understood as a permanence that endures for us only fleetingly, like a fragrance. He still understands his condition as an impossible one, but now his capacity to *affirm* that condition has changed. It has changed insofar as the "saving power" of art has become clearer to him. This simply means that he has come to see more clearly just how the "real work" of art is found in the way it is one (perhaps "the") way in which we communicate with this riddle of nature that exceeds us. But, in the third version of the tragedy, Empedocles comes to believe that "we do not live in poetic times," in times when the force of language and the work art can find a place, and, because of this, he sadly says that he must die.

I do not intend to speak of the third version of *The Death of Empedocles*. I simply want to point out that what is different about Empedocles in this version, and what Hölderlin emphasizes in his commentary on the figure of Empedocles (written between the second and third versions), is that now the saving power of art has come more into focus. Now, at the center of this tragedy that depicts the relation of the human and the nonhuman, art appears as the form in which that relation is given its due.

What I would like to do by way of a conclusion is to try to generalize even further what it is that we can take away from Hölderlin's performance of this question of the relation of tragedy and ethical life in *The Death of Empedocles*. So, in the spirit of simply provocation, let me conclude with four theses about the question of ethical life, all of which have emerged for me out of the effort to follow Hölderlin's failed attempts to write a tragedy for these times. I opened this chapter with my apologies for the dogmatism of my beginning. Now I will conclude with more dogmatic remarks, and with the same apology.

The first thesis is that at the limits of that which is produced or defined by the realm of the human, at the point where our rules and our conceptualizing powers break off, the ethical moment begins. This is the experience at which we are put before the abyssal question of freedom, and this happens in such a way that we learn that this experience of freedom is both unpresentable and always shadowed by the risk of unfreedom. But this experience, in which we acknowledge that we cannot help but seek that which exceeds us, and which is very much at the heart of what Hölderlin's tragedy exposes, is one in which we open ourselves to the origins that breathe life into philosophizing. (Here, I might say as aside something that I fear could be misunderstood; namely, that it is imperative that this moment not be theologized or taken as an invitation to the move into religion. That, as Nietzsche reminds us, is invariably a Trojan horse in which we smuggle humanism back into the issue.)

Second, from Hölderlin we learn how difficult the experience of nature is and how this difficulty is amplified by the forms of modern life in which the humanly produced world is pervasive. We learn as well that for us, today, the question of nature begins with the recognition of the poverty of our experience in this matter. When Hölderlin refers to the Greek world as the last period in which such an experience was not marked by this impoverishment, he is reminding us of an important difference between our experience and the sort of experience that was fundamental in the eventual evolution of Western concepts of nature. Roberto Calasso named this difference well when wrote that "much was implicit in the Greek experience that has been lost to us today. When we look at the night sky, our first impression is one of amazement before a random profusion scattered across a dark background. Plato could still recognize 'the friezes in the sky.' And he maintained that those friezes were the 'most beautiful and exact' images in the visible order. But when we see a sash of fraying white, the Milky Way, girdle of some giantess, we are incapable of perceiving any order, let alone a movement within that order. No, we immediately start to think of distances, of the inconceivable light-years. We have lost the capacity, the optical capacity even, to place myths in the sky."[7] But recovering a new sense of the being of nature will require that we open ourselves to a different understanding of our place in the being of nature. It will require most of all overcoming the view that understands human freedom as in a basic conflict with nature.

Third, I believe that we need to recognize the achievements of art in disclosing the being of nature. Adorno put the point well when he said that "art accomplishes what nature strives for in vain: it opens its eyes."[8] But here too a sense of the limits of the human reach is important. To respect the difference between art and nature means both that we cease trying to understand nature as an analogue of art, and that we accept the limitations of art as a form of reflection on nature. Speaking of the ambiguity that defines the relation of art and nature is not an easy matter, and the reason for its difficulty is worthy of reflection. But rather than try to do that, let me simply cite a passage from Salman Rushdie's *The Ground Beneath Her Feet* that puts this point beautifully:

> Faced with the magnificence of nature, the artist is both humbled and provoked. There are photographs now of events on an unimaginable scale: the death of stars, the birth of galaxies, soupstirrings near the dawn of Time. Bright crowds of suns gather in the wilderness of the sky. . . . When we look at these images, there is, yes, legitimate wonderment at our own lengthening reach and grasp. But it would be vain indeed to praise our puny handiwork . . . when the universe is putting on so utterly unanswerable a show. Before the majesty of being, what is there to do but hang our heads?
>
> This is irksome. This, naturally, pisses us off.
>
> There is that within us which believes us worthy of the stars. . . . In our hearts we believe—we *know*—that our images are capable of being the equals of their subjects, that our creations can go the distance with Creation.[9]

But Hegel reminds us of the antidote to this hubris when he writes that "art cannot stand in competition with nature, and if it tries, it looks like a worm trying to crawl after an elephant."[10]

Finally, I believe that if we are to learn how to pose this question of nature, then we need to take seriously Kant's deep insight that the experience of nature is, first off and ultimately, an ethical matter, and not originally a question of cognition. This is the most difficult step and requires again that we cease to define the question of ethics as a human question, and that we begin to understand how it is that the question of freedom is the original question we face in thinking, one that even precedes the question of truth and that opens us to the being of that which comes to us unbidden. In the end, this might simply mean that we need to address ourselves to the lesson that Hölderlin's Empedocles, the one who is born to be a poet, continually struggles to learn: that I might need to love and affirm the being of that which forever exceeds every effort I might make to embrace it.

CHAPTER TEN

WORDS ON PAPER: ON LANGUAGE AND SCRIPT

> I ask that you pardon the script, since I have not acclimated myself to forming these letters.
>
> —Martin Heidegger to Elisabeth Blochmann

Throughout all its variations, hermeneutic theory remains committed to the remark that Gadamer makes in Part III of *Truth and Method*: "being that can be understood is language"[1] and consequently it readily finds itself in accord with Cratylus's claim that "language is perhaps the greatest topic of all."[2] Among the most distinctive trademarks of the hermeneutic approach to language is the effort to trace to the double force—both finitizing and fusing—of language in experience and do so in a manner that resists any abstraction that results in the construction of an artificial rational language. Attentive to the self-effacement of language, its capacity to throw itself ever anew into a darkness beyond the reach of its own reflexivity, hermeneutics has been first and foremost a theory alert to the finitude of all understanding. Guided by such convictions, hermeneutic theory has paid special attention to the conflicts and complexities of the struggle, ultimately—and I believe that this is important in the final analysis—an ethical struggle, to put oneself in words. This struggle to find words goes beyond the strategic problem of merely communicating information. Rather, it is a struggle that finally concerns the relation of language and being, and so this struggle to find oneself in words is among the most profound struggles in which one can engage. In a very real sense, the question of language always inevitably becomes a question of who one is—and is not. Hermeneutics pays homage to this relation of language and being insofar as it recognizes that when we understand something about the need for words, about how it is that we enter into relation with one another insofar as we put ourselves in words, we understand something important about ourselves.

In a letter to Gadamer dated February 29, 1972, Heidegger raises a question about this struggle in and with language to which hermeneutics addresses itself. Heidegger writes: "the more precise determination of hermeneutics presses forward to the question whether and in what manner the special universal claim of information, as an extreme case of the deficient mode of 'communication', can be recovered in hermeneutics.—Taking this task up [means suffering through and acknowledging] the *language-neediness of thinking*. . . . [It also means asking why] *thinking necessarily stays in the language-neediness of finding words?*"[3] After Gadamer cites this remark from Heidegger, he comments in return that "Of course Heidegger is right when he sees in information the extreme case that poses the most strenuous task for hermeneutics. But I must also ask myself here what the language-neediness of thinking really means."[4] The question about language, about putting oneself in words, that I want to take up ultimately concerns this question that Gadamer puts to Heidegger; that is, how are we to understand this notion of "language-neediness," this "need of language" with which one struggles in trying to put oneself in words? How does one "acknowledge" and "suffer through" the neediness of language? What might language "need"? Can we meaningfully speak about the need *of* words within our need *for* words?

Later in the same letter to Gadamer, Heidegger specifies his own understanding of this topic when he asks if there is a name for this need, a name for naming, a word for the need of the words into which one struggles to put oneself. As a sort of challenge, he asks Gadamer if there can be a "hermeneutic of such names," if, in other words, hermeneutics can acknowledge the finitude proper to the neediness of language itself. It is a perplexing question, one reminiscent of Heidegger's concern with arriving at an experience of language that is sufficiently radical to give a "word for word." But while this question that Heidegger asks is, as Gadamer suggests, puzzling, the direction in which Heidegger takes it is clear: this radicalization of the experience of language drives Heidegger to address the topic of language in the poem and to enlist Hölderlin's claim that such naming, which is the province of poetry, is so unique that it must be called holy. It is likewise this problematic of the neediness of language that leads Heidegger to speak of the "translation-neediness"of language[5] and to take up the issue of the relation of language and translation. A relation that in turn becomes of such fundamental importance that Heidegger is willing to say "tell me what you think about translation and I will tell you who you are."[6] Despite his hesitations regarding Heidegger's notion of the neediness of language, Gadamer's work moves in a direction congenial to Heidegger's on these themes and so Gadamer too is aware that language pays tribute to its own needs and limits in poetry and translation both of which stand as reminders that the guiding sentence of hermeneutics, "being that can be understood is language," means that "that which is can never be completely understood."[7]

It is then rather easy to see why poetry, which "fulfills itself in the ideal of untranslatability,"[8] and translation are decisive for every effort to think language *as* language and to do this outside of the orbit of metaphysical presumptions; that is, to think it independently of the empire of representation. When language is sharpened, when it is experienced "like the point of a spear,"[9] that is, when the finitude proper to it is experienced, then both poetry and translation come forward as questions, bringing language to the question of the idiom which is the point at which the question concerning the communicative character of language reaches its crisis.

I do not intend to take up the themes of either translation or poetry here, I do however want to note their proximity and final import for the special topic of my concern. Rather, my approach to this enigmatic question about the limits and "need of language" in the struggle to put oneself in words will pursue another, admittedly peculiar, angle. Nonetheless, I believe that it is a crucial question for those of us committed to the effort to solicit an understanding of language at its extremities. It is a question that Gadamer himself raises in his 1983 text entitled "Unterwegs zur Schrift" when he asks "Does not the use of words always already contain something like an urge to being fixed [in writing]?"[10] Posing such a question does not simply entail asking the question of the difference between orality and literacy. Nor is this question one that finds its stakes in determining some sort of hierarchy between speech and writing. In the end, I believe that Gadamer is quite right when he says that "there is no sharp division between orality and literacy."[11] The inner connection between speech and writing is a powerful one, so powerful that it seems a senseless practice to try to pull them apart in any fundamental way. But there is a question to be asked about what we must think about language if we pay heed to the idea that language not only lets itself be written, but—as Gadamer suggests—might even need to be written. What of this need of words to be fixed in script? Of course, this is the same question that Plato projects on every other question raised in the dialogues. One might even argue that Platonic texts can only be read if one understands that they have been written out of the logic of a worry about this urge to fix language in writing. Plato's concern is well known and put concisely when Socrates speaks to Phaedrus, who has fallen in love with a written text on love, about the peculiarly static character of the written word by saying that:

> Writing, Phaedrus, has this strange power, quite like painting in fact; for the creatures in paintings stand there like living beings, yet if you ask them anything they maintain a solemn silence. It is the same with written words. You might imagine they speak as if they were actually thinking about something but if you want to find out

about what they are saying and question them, they keep on giving the one and same message eternally. (275D–E)

Heidegger points out that there is a curious Parmenidean problem to be faced in the problematic of writing. Socrates suggests that a written text is like the corpse of thinking; mute and unresponsive, it captures nothing of the living eternity that the mind is capable of knowing, delivering instead only a 'now' immobilized for all time. It is not an accident that the subject of the text that provokes Socrates's remark is *eros* nor is it insignificant that the text arrives in the dialogue smuggled by Phaedrus under the cover of his cloak. Both desire and the secret belong to the full question of writing as Plato understands it. But I want to prescind from the full issue for now and simply make some remarks about what it means when language achieves the status of a written text.

One might argue against Plato that with the arrival of the written word what Schelling referred to as "a second empire of experience" opens up before us. Gadamer puts this point eloquently when he writes that

> there is nothing so strange and so demanding as the written word. Not even the encounter with speakers of a foreign tongue can be compared with this strangeness, since the language of gesture and of sound always contains an element of immediate understanding. Writing and what partakes of it—literature—is the intelligibility of mind transferred to the most alien medium. Nothing is so purely the trace of mind as writing. . . . The remnants of the life of the past, what is left of buildings, tools, the contents of graves, are weather-beaten by the storms of time, whereas a written tradition . . . is to such an extent pure mind that it speaks to us as if in the present.[12]

For the most part, hermeneutics has been focused on reading and the event of the realization of meaning in sound and voice; that is, it has pressed on the experience of language *as* language by means of attention to the reenactment and revitalization of "the living voice behind the writing."[13] That is why Gadamer can say that "I would define hermeneutics as the skill to let things speak which come to us in a fixed, petrified form, that of the text."[14] Or: "Writing, in all its spirituality, is only there when it is read. So words are what they are only as spoken discourse."[15] In other words, for the most part, hermeneutics has been directed to the recuperation of the already written word, to the recovery of voice in script, to the reanimation of already petrified language rather than the process whereby language becomes "petrified"—if indeed "petrified" is the appropriate word for what happens in writing.

But this seeming privilege of reading and the voice in hermeneutic reflections on language does not exclude the "other end" of language in the text, namely, the question of the transformation of word into writing. I should also note that this question about word become script does not deny that in the act of writing one might necessarily hear a sort of voice speaking. That language seeks voice and "asserts its creaturely rights in sound"[16] is clear, but there remains nonetheless a question of how this voice lets itself be recorded in writing. It is a question not of the semiological, but the iconographic, potential of language. Gadamer alludes to this in *Truth and Method* when he notes that "the legitimate question whether the word is nothing but a 'pure sign' or has something about it of the 'image' is thoroughly discredited by the *Cratylus* . . . ever since in all discussion on language the concept of the image (*eikon*) has been replaced by that of the sign (*semeion* or *semainon*). This is not just a terminological change, but it expresses an epoch-making decision about thought concerning language."[17] Against this, Gadamer argues that "the word is not just a sign. In a sense that is hard to grasp it is also something almost like an image. The word has an enigmatic bond with what it represents, a quality of belonging to its being."[18] It is, I believe, worth asking whether or not this sense in which the word is "almost like an image," this "bond with what it represents," is to be thought in trying to understand what it means that language lets itself be written. Can we imagine a language that *could not* be written?[19] What would have to happen in language for it to *refuse* the relation between speech and writing, voice and script? Certainly there are languages that can only be written in ways alien to our alphabetic writing, and, in the end, I believe that the unique aspects of the alphabet might be decisive for the issues I am trying to raise. It is worth noting that Plato, who confronted the alphabet as a relatively recent innovation, seems to find it worth remarking upon on several occasions.[20] In particular, he asks about the difference between noise and breath, between consonants and vowels as, for instance, in the following passage in the *Philebus* that draws that dialogue close to the story about the discovery of writing told in the *Phaedrus*: In the *Philebus*, Socrates speaks about the elements of writing and says:

> The unlimited variety of sound was discerned by some . . . godlike man . . . in Egypt called Theuth. He was the one who originally discerned the existence . . . of the vowels—not vowel in the singular but vowels in the plural—and then of other things which, though they could not be called articulate sounds, yet were noises of a kind. . . . in the end he found a number of such things and affixed to . . . each single member the name 'letter.' It was because he realized that none of us could ever get to know one of the collection by itself, in isolation from all the rest, that he conceived of 'letter' as a kind of bond of unity, uniting as it were all these sounds into one. (18B–D)

But Gadamer points to the *Cratylus* as the dialogue in which Socrates, who did not write, asks most directly about the relation of word and image. There, shortly after Hermogenes asks "what sort of imitation (*mimesis*) is a name (*onoma*)?" (423C), the often comic discussion moves through the question of the imitations found in sound (music) and image (painting) to the point at which Socrates introduces the topic of script: "That objects should be imitated in letters (*grammasi*) and syllables (*syllabais*), and so find expression, may appear ridiculous, Hermogenes, but it cannot be avoided" (425D). What follows this is a discussion of the relation between image (*eikon*) and word (*onoma*). It is a strange and difficult discussion about the shape of letters and the sounds of words. A discussion that, as Gadamer notes, takes the topic to the point of absurdity and ridicule, finally leading Socrates to say, "Do you not perceive that images are very far from having qualities which are the exact counterpart of the realities which they represent?" (432D). The ironic reason for this is that if an icon were perfect, its perfection would destroy the image-original relationship. An icon, says Socrates, "dares not reproduce every particular if it is to be an icon" (432B). He then suggests that it is important to stay alert to the necessary difference between icon and word—a suggestion that Walter Benjamin will make as well in his "Trauerspielbuch," only Benjamin, who is quite fascinated by the idea of handwriting, will say that in being alert to this difference, one is permitted a "gaze into the depths of language."

Plato's conclusion in the *Cratylus* notwithstanding, the topic of the relation of word and icon, and the possibility that such a relation is to be thought in the idea of script, is one that appears in several Platonic texts.[21] Nonetheless, it seems clear that the conclusion expressed in the *Cratylus* won the day and now what is most surprising is that we are no longer surprised by the conclusion that supersedes this one—namely, that number bears a deeper relation to the truth of words than icons. Leibniz becomes the true inheritor of that conclusion. Today, the prospect that the question of script, the iconography of language, might belong to the topic of language does strike one as somewhat ludicrous—and I must confess to my own trepidation about taking such a topic seriously, even though I am convinced that it is a topic needing to be addressed. I have come, much to my surprise, to take this topic seriously and have found a quite active concern with this topic of the iconographic potential of language in a number of texts with which I once believed myself to be familiar. An autobiographical note might help explain this.

When I broke the wrist of the hand that I write with, I found myself curiously tongue-tied, unable to put myself in words in all of the ways to which I was accustomed. Now, for an academic being cut off from writing poses special dilemmas in one's daily life. But my sense was that the experience of being unable to write, ultimately of being compelled to learn the rudiments of writing frustratingly slow with my other, untrained, hand, was not problematizing my relation to language so profoundly simply because of my special academic circumstances. If you want your empirical confirmation of this, simply try to write for some days with your untrained, other, hand. I came to realize that this was an experience that went beyond being an inconvenience to being something very much at the center of an experience of language that is bound up with the phenomena of alphabetization and the strange mimesis of script. It was an experience that gave new weight to claims such as the one that Hegel makes in the *Phenomenology of Spirit* when he writes that "the hand does not seem to be an external factor to fate; it seems rather to be related to it as something inner. . . . It is the living artificer of his fortune. . . . Thus the simple lines of the hand, the timbre and compass of the voice as the individual characteristic of speech—this too again as expressed in writing, where the hand gives it a more durable existence than the voice does, especially in the particular style of handwriting."[22] It also seemed to provide testimony that was a sort of photographic negative of Heidegger's celebrated claim that "only a being who can speak, that is think, can have a hand."[23] I discovered that I needed a hand to speak. But, in the end, what was surprising to me was that this broken wrist turned out to be not so much an experience "about" my hand as an experience "with" language. Heidegger again: "the hand has the essence of man within, because the word as the essential realm [*Wesensbereich*] of the hand is the essential realm of man."[24] Of course, this reciprocity between word and hand not only problematizes language, but should make us realize that the hand here is not simply to be understood according to an anatomical body that itself is profoundly shaped by a metaphysics that every hermeneutic sensitivity to language renders suspect.

Simply put: my problems with handwriting, my frustrations, drove me, with a strange ineluctibility, to take seriously the quite strange claim that Heidegger makes in his 1942/1943 lecture course on Parmenides that "Being, word, reading, script name an original and essential matrix in which the signing-writing hand belongs. The relation of being to man, namely, the word, is, in handwriting, inscribed in a being."[25] It is a baffling remark, one that I nonetheless found oddly compelling in light of my own experience, but it is neither as strange nor compelling as the remark that follows in which Heidegger writes that "when then writing is taken away from its essential origin, i.e. the hand . . . a transformation in the relation to being takes place."[26] Now Heidegger is interested in asking about "the 'invasion' of the typewriter into the realm of the word"[27] and though he speaks of the "destruction" and "degradation" of the typed word, he never quite explains his reasons for this judgment. He does, however, make two comments that lead one to suspect that the point to be made concerns the iconographic potential of language. First, he claims that the written word is language that is exposed to the eyes ["*dem Blick sich zeigende*"][28]; second, he claims that the essential belonging together of hand and word finds its summit in the image that is formed out of the sign ["*die . . . Zeichen zu Gebilden bildet*"].²⁹ That is why I have come to take the questions one finds in Plato about the icon and writing with a newfound seriousness. I do not want to overstate the issue. It should be clear that the role of the question of writing has concerns other than this: different types of writing, the relation of writing and the formation of traditions and disciplines, the relation of writing and desire, as well—and this is not far removed from the topic at hand—as the relation between writing and the body (a theme that even belongs to the subject of voice and breath as yet another manner in which the body extends itself into the world),³⁰ all these questions surround the question that I have taken up from Gadamer: what does it mean that there seems to be something like an "urge" in words to be fixed in writing. But it also seems clear that this question about the inner connection between word and script, the transformation of thought into its own hieroglyph, is one that cannot be dismissed as easily as Socrates seems to do in the *Cratylus*.

The point, as Gadamer notes in *Truth and Method*, is to ask how far we can think language independently of the sign and the representational conception of language that have governed metaphysics. When he develops this project in *Truth and Method*, he does so by noting how it moves beyond the Greek understanding of language. In the move from the section on "Language and *logos*" to the section on "Language and *verbum*," Gadamer notes that "there is an idea that is not Greek and that does more justice to the nature of language and prevented the forgetfulness of language in Western thought from being complete. It is the christian thought of *incarnation*."³¹ I want to note this move, and acknowledge—as Hegel and Benjamin also argue—that, in the end, it might be a move that cannot be avoided. But, for my present purposes, I want to try to pursue the question still in a Greek context because I believe that a crucial issue—the temporality of the iconographic potential of language—is found at the center of Plato's concerns and that it is precisely this issue that is erased in the Christianization of the matter. To that end, Gadamer makes a remark in "Unterwegs zur Schrift" that is especially helpful. There, citing the *Philebus* (39B), he notes that "It is '*mneme*' which "writes" *logoi* in our souls."³² According to Gadamer, this reference to memory marks "the entry of temporality and departure in time, which gives the finite being of man its stamp."³³

In the *Phaedrus*, Socrates contends that writing is a ruse that *must fail* since it is designated as *the illusory effort to outwit time by arresting it*. It is, he argues, only the semblance of eternity. At best it is the memento, the *aide memoire*, of a knowing that has already seen the idea and so, in truth, dispenses with writing in recollection; at worst it becomes the mechanism of the mortification of the dialectic. Two passages from the *Phaedrus* make this point. In the first, Socrates says that while "any discourse ought to be constructed like a living creature" Lysias's text, like every written text, is more like the "writing on a tomb" (264C–D). Interestingly he refers specifically to the tomb of Midas, one who immobilized all that his desire touched. In the second passage I have in mind, Socrates notes that the "inventor" of writing, the Egyptian King Theuth who thought that his discovery "provided a recipe for memory" (274D), eventually learned that "it implants forgetfulness in the soul [and] . . . is not a recipe for memory [*mneme*], but merely for reminder" [*hypomnema*] (275A), which is the semblance of memory, the illusion of time outwitted by the materiality of language as the icon.

The question is how far this temporal liability of language is to be understood as the trap of the icon. To what extent is the iconographic potential of the word the risk in all language that it will immobilize itself? Here the issues broaden and are driven to take up a complex of problems that include the relation between language, painting, and music.[34] Heidegger has taught us the insights that come with thinking works of art as modes of communication with time and history, and if we take that move seriously—especially with regard to the new directions in which that thought leads with respect to our understanding of the relation between painting and image—then it is necessary that we rethink the temporal meaning of the iconographic potential of language that lets itself become script. To do that means remembering as well Gadamer's insight that writing is completed only in reading; that the temporal arrest of writing finds its truth only in the temporal recovery of the act of reading. But Heidegger takes this temporal movement and need of writing even further when he says: "Writing, in its essential origin is hand-writing. We have named the disclosive taking up and taking notice of the written word 'reading,' i.e., gathering, in Greek *legein*, *logos*; but this word in originary thinking is the name for being itself."[35]

Let me conclude by returning this discussion to my opening remarks about the "neediness of language" to which Heidegger refers. I have limited my remarks to the way in which this "neediness" is to be thought in the relation of word and image in the iconographic character of language. I am aware that such a limitation is severe and poses serious problems, especially since even the special questions of writing can only be taken up by addressing the character of the transition between language that is spoken, written, and read. In that transition, in the moves between the ideality of meaning and the materiality of the word, language both completes and argues with itself at its limits.

But however it is that language becomes the bearer of ideality and the imaginary, it is important that we understand how language bears its truth as temporal possibilities: how, that is, writing—even if it is not able to outwit time and touch eternity—is the act of taking up a *temporal distance*, a distance that is found in the difference between word and icon. A distance that, as Gadamer has shown, is felt in the strangeness and authority of the text.

I conclude with a speculative question that I believe is important to ask, even if my remarks up to this point have not fully prepared for it. One of the basic claims of this book is that the questions of language are, at heart, ethical questions. If that is true then it is worth asking *just what sort of ethical act the taking up of this temporal distance in writing is*. Of course, that means asking as well about *the ethical meaning of the effort to cross that distance in reading*. Any understanding of Plato's contributions to these question must then ask: *what sort of ethical act is Socrates's refusal to write?*

Let me end by giving Plato's Socrates the last word. In the *Cratylus*, he offers a remarkable etymology of "*onoma*," he gives a word for word that establishes *word as the refusal of any final word*. He says simply that "word" is the word "for that reality for which we are still seeking" (421A).

CHAPTER ELEVEN

"LIKE A FIRE THAT
CONSUMES ALL BEFORE IT":
ON LANGUAGE AND IMAGE

> The phenomenon of fireworks can be viewed as the prototype of art.... Fireworks are apparitions par excellence.... They are a sign of heaven and yet artifactual; they are both a writing on the wall, rising and fading away in short order, and yet not a writing that has any meaning we can make sense of.
>
> —Adorno, *Aesthetic Theory*

The iconographic potential of language—its inherent capacity to wed itself to the image in script—poses a broader question about the relation of the disclosive power of the word to the disclosive power of images that do not, or at least not easily, let themselves be translated into language. So one comes to ask: how does the word relate to the image that makes no pretense to speech, no pretense to being script, but does nonetheless make a claim about the world? Do images that are not the written images of words *speak*? The intention of this chapter is to broach this question.

There are two quite discrete parts in what follows and, as I hope will become apparent, each part repeats in its own way the question that I want to address. One might restate that question in its broadest contours by asking about the claim and reach of *the word* in experience and truth and, equally, about the claim and reach of *the image* in experience and truth. How far do words and images go in their capacity to open up the truth of experience? Do the respective openings on experience engendered by words and by images yield genuinely different and discreet possibilities? Or is it the case that these possibilities let themselves be translated into one another? Such questions ask about the disclosive reach of words and of images, and—without wishing to set up a contest between these respective disclosive capacities—they also ask about the *relation* between the respective achievements of the word and of the image in experience. What I would like to believe is that the two parts of this chapter—as well as their relationship—*perform* something that words and images alike might, of necessity, betray. The *fidelity* of the word to itself, and of the image to itself, might, of necessity, undermine the capacity of each to address the other. It is the force of this fidelity that, in part at least, circumscribes the question I want to take up in what follows.

In the first part, I will make some observations about the history of philosophic efforts to speak of the image. Because I want to call attention to what I see as a widespread, perhaps endemic prejudice in the philosophic effort to appropriate the accomplishments of the image as it is unfolded by the work of art, I will refer in very condensed form to a range of philosophers who have made vital contributions to the effort to think the status of the image. While I risk oversimplifying matters, such a condensation has the advantage of calling attention to the enduring hallmarks characterizing philosophical treatments of the image.

Generally, my concern in the first part is to ask what the relation is between the seeing that is specific to the project of philosophy, namely, *theoria*, and the role that seeing plays in another project, namely that which the Greeks designated with the word *poeisis*, especially insofar as the poetic project involves the production of images. When Plato first thematizes the possibilities of truth that are opened up from the perspective of the imageless seeing proper to *theoria*, and when he traces the path whereby this is translated into the language of the idea, he frequently finds it necessary to go to great lengths to differentiate this theoretical look to ideas from the sort of seeing practiced by those concerned with the production of images in painting. Getting clear about *theoria* and about the nature of the idea meant seeing clearly how this form of seeing proper to the mind alone had to be distinguished from the painterly production of images.[1] Furthermore, Plato argues that the form of seeing that defines painting anticipates the seeing that defines all other forms of poetic practice, and so his criticisms of other art forms are rooted in a criticism of painting, which he sets up as the paradigm of poetic practice. Plato is following in the tradition established by Simonides, who made the celebrated claim that "painting is mute poetry while poetry is painting that talks."[2] Plato's argument is that so long as one thinks of what it means to "see" ideas according to the model of seeing practiced by the painter, one will never grasp the proper nature of seeing ideas. This is one reason Plato's criticisms of the arts are so relentless. The dispute between philosophy—which, it must be remembered, was just beginning to elaborate and legitimate its claims—and painting was, from the side of Plato, a bitter contest with the highest of stakes. It was also a contest crucial to the effort of philosophizing to legitimate the point of view from which it made claims to truth. Plato's legacy to philosophizing, enduring on so many scores, is inestimable in its silent power on this point, which privileges a specific form of seeing.

Recently, philosophers (one thinks of Benjamin, Merleau-Ponty, Foucault, Gadamer, Deleuze, and Derrida, for instance) have made significant efforts to appreciate the relation of thinking and images, thinking and painting. The question of the role of the image in thinking is no longer a question to be resisted, and the wide range of this question is now being explored. Even the centrality of painting for the interrogation of the poetic image no longer goes without saying in the technological age, since painting can no longer lay claim to being the sole preserve of images we make (an important caveat, but not one that fundamentally changes the structure of the issues). Today there seems to be a genuine mitigation of this former hostility to the poetic image from the side of philosophy, indeed at times one even has the sense that one can see the rudiments of some sort of rapprochement between philosophy and the form of seeing that is proper to painted images.[3] But despite the appearance of some advances in this matter, I believe that there might well be a constitutional opposition that philosophy has to the painted image. So I want to ask whether or not philosophy *as such*, perhaps even theory *as such*, can ever be in a position to grasp—without distorting, without betraying—images that find their visibility owing to a seeing other than that which belongs to theorizing and speculation. As an example of this prejudice that the work of art needs the discourse of theory, and that philosophy preserves for itself the final word about the work of art, I might refer to Heidegger's remark that "art as such is not a possible theme for artistic imaging."[4] In other words, the image lacks the self-reflexive capacity that defines philosophy. It soon becomes clear that even those who at first blush seem to be open to the possibilities of the image still betray residues of the Platonic decision about the image in their own thought; though the image can reflect something of the world, it cannot, *as image*, reflect on itself nor can it address the claims of language. So the question remains: can images address the disclosive claim of the word? Can images reflect on their own nature? This is the flip side of my earlier question: can the language of theory, the language of the concept, ever give due tribute to the disclosive power of the poetic image?

In the first part of this chapter, which addresses the question of the relation between art and philosophy from the perspective of philosophy, I simply want to make some observations about some of the prejudices that saturate efforts in philosophy to come to terms with painted images, even those efforts that are self-consciously trying to open a productive dialogue between theory and painting. While I have a tendency to share this prejudice, I confess that I have come to seriously question this presumption, which might well be inherent to the project of philosophy as such. In other words, its adherence to theoretical sight must lead it to understand its own project in some kind of *opposition* to the form of seeing proper to the poetic project. But to deny that there is an inevitable *contest* between philosophy and art, to suspect that this opposition might not be insurmountable, is not necessarily to conclude that the insights of each can be translated into the form of the other.

In the second part of this chapter, I will look at a series of ten paintings that I consider to be painterly rejoinders to this problematic of the relation between the word that has grown out of a discourse rooted in *theoria* and the image. These paintings constitute a remarkable engagement of the painter with the limits of language as well as being a meditation on the relation of word and image from the side of one committed to the efficacy of the images in such a relation. These paintings are from the Cy Twombly series entitled *Fifty Days at Ilium*, which is found in the Philadelphia Museum of Art. Painted in 1977–1978, this series of scribbles, rubbings, and scrapings, full of proper names—some only faintly visible beneath layers of paint—tries to present in the space of ten large canvases something decisive that Twombly sees in Homer's poem about the fall of Troy. These paintings are not best seen as aesthetic objects—they do not make a deliberate effort to be "beautiful"; rather, they need to be seen as painted meditations on the reach of language in the poem, the significance of the proper name, the force of translation, and the transition of words and images into one another. They are, in a sense, self-reflexive works as well as commentaries. I will also suggest that what is most decisive in these paintings is that they are specifically dedicated to the effort to say something about *death*. In the effort to disclose something of the ineluctable limit of death, we find the true acid test for the question of the respective reaches of words and images in experience.

In his *Lectures on Aesthetics*, Hegel notes that art only begins to emerge *as* art in Greece because it was in Greece that such works withdrew from their service to religion and the presentation of the divine.[5] The basic contours of Hegel's argument are simple and compelling: once art becomes conscious of itself by no longer regarding itself as serving the need to represent the divine that is external to itself—in other words, once it understands itself as form animated by spirit—art is freed to understand the enigma that it is. One could say that art no longer sees itself as a mere means, but becomes an end unto itself. With this change in the self-understanding of its own achievement, art becomes visible *as* art. When this happens, the power of *representation itself*, that is, the real *work* and the *form* animating and driving art, is able to appear. Art as an expression of spirit is now freed to become its own content.[6] The argument that in the Greek world a new artistic consciousness appears in the form of the plastic arts is, in many respects, a very old one. We already see something like this argument in Pliny who suggests that during the fifth century B.C. "the art of painting set itself apart," and that painters in Greece at that time were revolutionizing the idea of painting.[7] But despite the real transformation in the possibilities present in painting in his time, in most every respect, Plato's treatment of painting still largely interprets art insofar as it belongs to what we might loosely call religious life. While he does begin to broach the question of art as an independent form of practice, in the end, as one so clearly sees in the *Republic*, he never fully severs it from its relation to religious and ethical life. Although Plato's treatment of the work of art is indeed concerned with the work character of the work of art insofar as he regards it from the perspective of *mimesis*, which he takes to be the common root of the representational capacity of all the art, it also must be said that in the final analysis his concern with the work of art returns it to its "religious" service. In this regard, Plato's analysis of art remains rooted in an understanding of what happens in the work of art that does not yet understand art as freed to its own purposes. Nonetheless, his understanding of art, especially of painterly art, will prove to be decisive for the subsequent history of philosophy.

One needs to recognize that it is Aristotle who, when he writes his *Poetics*, composes the first text on art *as such*. Aristotle is the first to interrogate the essential character of the artwork without subordinating it to the purposes of religious life. That is why he is the first to attempt a genuine classification and separation of the arts: art, for Aristotle, is interesting in itself. As a result of this, Aristotle will significantly shift the horizon for philosophic approaches to art, even though many of the elements that structure Aristotle's analysis of the work of art are indebted to Plato. One way in which Aristotle's view departs from Plato's and yet has proven to having staying power in the history of philosophy is found in the fact that he privileges *poetry* over *painting* when indicating the summit of the possibilities of the work of art. He inaugurates a tradition that will eventually culminate in Heidegger's deep appreciation for the poetic word. But this shift from painting to poetry as the paradigm of the work of art does not fundamentally alter the judgment about images that Plato first articulated: seeing remains judged from the standpoint of *theoria*. Images still are said to fail to grasp the truth opened to theory. The word marks a higher achievement than the image even in the realm of art.

Aristotle opens the *Poetics* with the simple question: "why do human beings make art?"[8] The answer he gives grants the achievement of art in human life a dignity that is typically absent from the history of philosophy that follows in Aristotle's own wake. Answering his own question, Aristotle suggests three sets of reasons for our natural impulse to make art: first, it is thrilling, it is the source of a unique pleasure; second, it is educational, that is, it is a form of play of possibilities that enlarges our comprehension of the world; third, in the work of art we learn something of ourselves. Consequently, however else it might be understood, art needs to be understood as the self-presentation of our own nature. As Kant will later demonstrate, we see ourselves objectified in the work of art. Though the idea that art needs to be thought in some relation to its service to the divine is fundamentally absent in Aristotle—his treatment of art departs in a significant manner from what one finds in Plato—there are many important respects in which we find a real kinship between Plato and Aristotle on the question of the work of art. Most notable is the way in which each interprets the representational power of art in terms of *mimesis*. Both contend that the operations and work of art are best understood by thinking art as a form of *repetition*, that is, not as a fully originary form. But what is most important for my purposes is what happens when the shift from the primacy of painting (in Plato) to poetry (in Aristotle) enters into the interpretation of *mimesis*. The sense of *mimesis* that is thought from out of the experience of the *word*—above all, in the invisibility of the *spoken* word that Aristotle's attention to theater makes primary—is necessarily different from the conception of *mimesis* that is modeled after the silent *visibility* of the painted image. Without rehearsing the details of his investigation of the nature of the poetic word, let me simply indicate that Aristotle argues that *metaphor* stands as the peak of possibilities inherent in poetic speech. More than any other possibility of language, it speaks out and repeats the conflicted nature of what emerges from the conflicted roots of the impulse to art. For Aristotle then, metaphor, the stereoscopic capacity of language in which a sort of doubled thought is presented, marks the highpoint of the possibilities of language in the realm of art. Furthermore, it is in the light of metaphorical language that the mimetic heart of art is understood. Insofar as the roots of art are understood as lodged within the realm of language, and insofar as language is ultimately understood with reference to its conceptualizing capacities, art, which is not destined for the concept, is taken as somehow inferior to the achievements of philosophizing.

Despite his deep appreciation for the achievements of art—especially art that takes the shape of art's highest form, its true destiny, namely, the art of tragic theater—despite this real admiration for art, Aristotle, in the end, measures art against a standard defined by what he takes to be the superior possibilities opened in the horizon of philosophy. Whereas art operates in the element of the ideal of the idiom and so needs to be developed with reference to the proper name or the particularity of the image, philosophy elaborates itself in the more extensive, the all-inclusive idiom of the ideal. In its relation to ideality, in other words, insofar as it operates under the sign of the idea, of the concept, philosophy, according to Aristotle, is able to overtop the achievements of art. It does not, however, obliterate those achievements. In saying this, Aristotle mitigates and softens the sharp criticism that Plato directed at artistic practices. At the risk of a gross oversimplification, one might argue that in the history of philosophy, Plato and Aristotle define the two poles within which art finds its philosophic determination: either art is regarded with great suspicion and thus ghettoized in aesthetics where it can be regulated by the court of philosophy; or it is simply regarded as a puerile, a somewhat immature, form in which we explore ourselves and our world. But, in the end, under both scenarios, the work of art gets evaluated by the possibilities of conceptual reason and of the ideality specific to the concept, which still remains, despite every revolution, the mother tongue of philosophizing. In the end, both take the idealizing, conceptualizing capacity of language to be its supreme achievement, and both find the mute image to be inferior to the reach of the theoretical word when measured according to the demands of the truth of the idea. This assumption will saturate thinking in the subsequent history of philosophy.

There are, of course, serious efforts to reappraise the contribution of the image to human experience in that history; or, better, one might say that there are at least efforts to genuinely appreciate how problematic it is for philosophy to think the image. Many of the most penetrating of these attempts follow in the wake of Kant, and their most dramatic advance will be ushered in by Nietzsche. Above all, it is in the "schematism" of pure concepts outlined in the *Critique of Pure Reason* when Kant attempts to find a *homogeneity* of the image with both experience and the concept that some new possibility is opened with regard to the how we might think the status of the image in experience. Granted, the schema presents us with a rather rarified sense of what might constitute its "image-character" (it is in the end a modification of time that we find here); nonetheless, a door is opened by this thought. The imagination wins a new and original presence in this analysis, and even the sensible world is lent a new sense of possibility and essentiality. However, in the end, even in Kant's readiness to enlist the image into how it is that we must understand the deepest nature of human experience, it is the essential superiority of the concept to the image that is demonstrated.[9]

Nietzsche on the other hand, grants the image as its own, original, place in human experience. He does this by reminding us that when the mind is purely with itself, when it is free and unfettered, it produces images of light—it dreams. And in the dream, in this image-governed conversation that the soul has with itself, one of the roots of our impulse to make art is disclosed (his word, borrowed from Schelling via Hölderlin is "*Kunsttrieb*"). These roots of art are not supplemental to human nature, but its very definition. However, what is decisive for Nietzsche is that the image is not the sole root of this artistic drive: it stands rather in a countervalent relation with an impulse that fundamentally resists being taken up in the image. The Apollinian impulse to produce images must struggle with the Dionysian impulse to rapture. Because the impulse to art is a doublet, and a contradictory one at that, the true nature of art, art that reflects itself, is the art of contradiction—namely, *tragedy*. And the tragic, as such, cannot, for Nietzsche, find its way into images; it remains too static, too remote from the agility of time to say all at once the full force of contradiction at the heart of life. In this way, even though he grants it a primordial place in experience, Nietzsche retreats from the image. So, despite every advance of philosophic efforts to grant the image its proper dignity in the end, the return to a view such as the one Heidegger expresses in the Nietzsche volume when he writes that "thinkers are founders of that which never becomes visible in images"[10]—a sensibility quite contrary to that expressed by Leonardo da Vinci who said that one should "avoid words unless speaking with the blind."

Already at this point, after only indicating some key elements of what will prove to be enduring and largely unexamined assumptions guiding the appraisal of art in the history of philosophy, one can begin to see four pervasive prejudices of philosophers that are significant for the concerns of my question about the respective reaches of words and of images.

First, there is a prejudice that takes *the linguistic work of art* as the supreme form of the possibilities of art. Even if the language of poetry is not rigorously conceptual, it does, as a language, bear something of the life of the idea within itself and this proximity of the language of poetry to the language of the concept exerts a sort of magnetic pull of philosophic treatments of art to poetry. We see this view first formulated in Aristotle's *Poetics* (a text that might well have been entitled "Sophocles und das Wesen der Dichtung" since the essence of the poetic word is thought so directly out of the model provided by Sophocles). This privileging of the linguistic work of art remains a powerful force in philosophic treatments of art, so powerful that there is a clear tendency to interpret every form of art from out of a certain experience with the word. Hegel is one of the first to own up to this prejudice when, in the *Phenomenology of Spirit*, he traces the migration of Spirit as art through various forms of materiality that only finally fulfill their destiny in becoming word. Indeed, it is no accident that every citation in the *Phenomenology of Spirit*, as well as its final words, are drawn from poetic texts. Of course, Heidegger does not seriously problematize his own willing subscription to his prejudice in favor of the linguistic work of art and the effort to understand the realm of the artwork generally from out of an experience with the linguistic work. And yet for Heidegger this claim of the primacy of the word is paramount.

There are, of course, real, and apparent, exceptions to this tendency. Nietzsche is among the first to wager a new view of art that does not submit itself to the presumed dominance of the word. For Nietzsche, it is music more than either the power of the word or image that reaches furthest into the heart of life and repeats something of its own beat. Music and its relation to time far outstrip any potential of either the static image or the conceptualized word with regard to their disclosive powers. But Nietzsche finds the greatest challenge of his own effort to escape the claim of language to primacy in the recoil of this critique of language on his own efforts to speak at all. Himself limited to language, Nietzsche can only pound against the limits that restrain him so powerfully. It is this railing against the limits of language, of which he was so acutely conscious, that led to Nietzsche's own great experiments with the style of his own language, experiments that he himself found insufficient since as he writes, poignantly, and harshly, of his own language: "It should have *sung*, this "new soul"—and not spoken!"[11]

Second, this prejudice in favor of the linguistic work of art serves as a sort of Trojan horse that smuggles in the second enduring characterization of the philosophic assessment of the work of art; namely, a deep suspicion of the *participation of the image in works of art*. The philosophic assessment of the possibility of art finds art to be hierarchized and works that belong to the image invariably fall to a level in this hierarchy beneath those that belong to the word. So, in the end, it is not really surprising that Plato contends that the luminosity of the visible, which was so prized in Greece, cannot be captured or repeated in any relation to an image. Strangely, against expectation, the luminosity of the visible is, according to Plato, best repeated and captured in the word and its participation in the idea. Thus, Plato believes he must argue that to paint is to refuse to think; it is to miss the point of visibility itself. More: he even contends that, to the extent that we wed ourselves to images, we become the very image of those who are held captive and blind. Ironically (and the irony here makes all the difference once it is genuinely acknowledged), Plato presents this thought in one of the most celebrated literary images in the history of philosophy, namely, in the "Allegory of the Cave." This mistrust of images is so great, so all-embracing, that it even drives much of Plato's critique of the written word. The argument is that the written word, which is transferred and thus alienated into the image, becomes only "the corpse of a thought" (*Phaedo*, 264). Insofar as it is placed into the image in script, even language falls victim to its essential limitations from the perspective of theory.

Third, it is crucial to note that the claim that art, as Nietzsche argued, is *destined to be tragic* is a claim already evident in the Platonic and Aristotlean treatments of art. Likewise, it is a view subscribed to almost unanimously in the post-Kantian tradition. Understanding why this kinship of all art to tragedy is inherent in the Platonic–Aristotlean tradition is crucial for any understanding of the relation of philosophizing to art. Of course, there is widespread dispute over just what constitutes the tragic and over what works exemplifying this destiny (for instance, Plato finds its most crystallized form in Homer, while Aristotle finds it in Sophocles, more precisely in *Oedipus Rex*). But, whatever its precise configurations might be, the claim is basically this: that art is rooted not only in a contradictory impulse and so destined to be the elaboration of contradiction as such, but also that, in the end, works of art operate in the sphere of $\pi\alpha\varphi\omega\varsigma$ and that as a consequence of this attention to what we can only suffer, works of art naturally exhibit a distinctive and debilitating concern with death. We do not need to wait for

Hölderlin's profound reflections on the essential bond between poetic practices and mourning for this relation to be noted—it is, as Plato argued, the native tendency of poetizing to mourn.[12] And when Heidegger says that at its most reflexive moment, when language is "bent back upon itself like to point of a spear," the essential relation of language and death "flashes before us" he is not departing from Plato's own exploration of language in the poem in the *Republic* and *Phaedrus*. Operating on that dimension of the soul that suffers rather than theorizes what is presented to it, poetic works—both as they appear in images and in the language of the poem—work with the idiom of the idiom with that which can only be suffered, but not understood, with that which we can *only* mourn and affirm—but that remains literally inconceivable. Aristotle reaffirms this in the *Poetics* when he describes the supreme form of art as "the presentation of death and suffering on stage" (1452b10).

Fourth, this kinship of the work of art to mourning helps us understand why the philosophic treatment of *the work of art needs to be understood first and foremost as an ethico-politico matter, since mourning is among the preeminent forms that both preserve and limit the bonds of community*. Plato knew that such works, by their very nature, gave voice to the ultimate impossibility of community insofar as they bear this essential relation to death, to what separates us. He knew as well that mourning is a form in which that impossible community is also preserved after a fashion, but—and this is the important point for Plato—it is preserved as limited with respect to the sway of the law of reason. One sees this, for instance, in noting how deeply the *Republic* is concerned with the question of death. Plato, like Sophocles in *Antigone*, knew well that the question of the limits of the *polis* appears with the enigma of death. But, like Creon, Plato's concern is to take this enigma into the law of the idea and its imperative, not to hand it over to the realm of mourning. Without tracing all the elements of this argument, what needs to be noted for my purposes now is the simple fact that the stakes in the philosophic treatment of the work of art are ethical and political in character. The later degeneration of the approach to the work of art in "aesthetics" obliterates this ethical and political potential of such works. Both Plato and Aristotle knew that the work of art is displaced—misplaced really—when it is thought as the signature of "the aesthetic." Beauty and the pleasure proper to it are not the foremost categories for addressing what is at work in the work of art. Kant, who will unpack the ethical nature of the experience of the beauty in his analysis of the judgment of taste, will be the one who breaks the notion of the aesthetic wide open and returns the question of the work of art to its own nature.

But more needs to be said about this issue of the ethical stakes of the work of art as Plato understood it since my contention is that losing this sense of the ethical dimension of the work of art is one of the most fateful moments in the history of philosophy. What must be recalled is that Plato's concern is to elaborate the possibilities of the *polis*, as it can be thought under the signature of the idea that is disclosed to a theorizing that does not suffer death. Socrates' fearlessness before death is simply the dramatic confirmation of this conviction. The philosophic conception of the just community gets articulated in the idiom of the ideal. But, the work of art, bound to the particularity of the image and the individuality of the proper name, belongs to the realm of the idiom of the idiom. As such, the artwork arrives as a threat to the universal, which defines the bonds of the *polis* (which is why Adorno could contend that there is more revolutionary potential in a single volume of poetry than in the collected works of Marx). In other words, art grants a place to particularly and individuality—to the image and the proper name—absent from speculative thought, and in doing this it leaves a place for that which we cannot fully grasp, but which, in the end, one can only mourn.

This, as Plato well knew, cultivates a sensibility with regard to justice, to how life is shared, quite distinct from that approach that presents justice as an idea. The most powerful image I know that quite clearly expresses precisely this point—namely, that the relation of the work of art to the idiom, ultimately to death, is a relation that speaks of justice—is found in Homer. The passage I have in mind is found in the eleventh book of the *Odyssey*, which is the book that Plato rewrites in the "Myth of Er." Odysseus has gone to the realm of the dead to speak with the prophet Teiresias, who, precisely because he is blind, is able to see in the darkness of that realm. Odysseus learns that there is a ritual that must be observed for the living and the dead to converse, but, if it is followed properly, the dead will only speak the truth. After learning what he must know from Teiresias about the route home and about his own fate, Odysseus comes to speak to the shade of his mother. Having been gone many years, he had not known of her death and so he grieves what he now knows about her fate. He said that he longs to embrace her one more time, to "touch with love and taste the relief of salty tears." But since she is dead, that can no longer happen, and so her answer to his heartbroken entreaty is to remind him that the finality of death, and our ultimate apartness, is "the *dike* of mortal life" (225). In other words, Homer here presents the view that the justice mortals can give one another comes ultimately in the form of mourning. What we witness here is the manner in which death becomes the memento of our separation, our solitude, and the preserve of that which we can suffer, but cannot know. In this criticism of the work of art, Socrates makes it clear that such a lesson undermines the project of the *Republic*, which is to institute and preserve the law of the common that is itself disclosed in the idea.

In the end, the tension between the claims of philosophy and those of the work of art must be seen as emerging out of this contest about justice and the idiom proper to it. This argument about the idiom proper to political and ethical life is mitigated somewhat when Aristotle shifts the understanding of the mimetic basis of the work of art from the idea of painting, as Plato understood it, to the idea of the linguistic work. It is mitigated because in the word there always remains the possibility of conceptualization. But in the image we find a very real recalcitrance before the concept. The image weds itself to the particular, to the singular, in a way matched in language only by the proper name. And in this, the image stands as a sort of outside to the law of the common that philosophizing has so long sought. There are, of course, exceptions to this "rule." One thinks here of the extent to which Kant's *Critique of Judgment* is an attempt to recuperate—better: to expand—the philosophic appreciation of the idiom of the good and to open up an approach to the work of art as an experience that must be defined in the first instance *as radically apart from the horizon of the concept and the law proper to it.*

My sense is that Kant's argument is yet to be fully appreciated, and that, in part at least, is what motivates me in the second part of this chapter in which I want to look at how we find many of these very same issues to which I have just alluded being addressed, not conceptually, but in some other manner that, for lack of a better work, I will call painterly. What is so striking about much contemporary painting is that it exhibits—*in its own way*—a deep awareness and concern with so many of the questions that have long haunted the philosophic effort to comprehend the achievement of art in human experience and knowledge. What is especially interesting about many contemporary artists is the degree of philosophical sophistication that animates their artistic sensibility. Without necessarily sacrificing fidelity to the nature and possibilities proper to the image, painters now respond in their own way to many of the issues raised by philosophers. Let me say at the outset that I absolutely do not want to take up these paintings in order to simply illustrate or confirm some set of philosophic views, thereby turning the painterly work into a sort of handmaiden of philosophy. Rather I want to take seriously the possibility that in these works we find some real argument with what might be learned of art from even the most sympathetic philosophic appreciations of such works.

One reason I have chosen to look at this series by Twombly is that I find it directly engaged in questions about the nature of painting and its relation to the linguistic work, and so clearly concerned with the idiom of the idiom, and the possibility of the passage of the idiom into yet another. It presents us with a reply from the side of painting to Plato's critique of painting. Twombly does this by "taking the side" of Homer "against" Plato as it were. Here then we have the alliance of a painter with a poet against the claims of a philosopher. What I find especially exciting about these specific works by Twombly is that he is reimagining and repeating Homer in an acknowledged dialogue with Alexander Pope's own remarkable repetition of Homer in Pope's effort to bring something like Homer's Greek into English. Twombly is acutely aware that translation mediates every issue here. The question of language, of the limits and between of language in the plural, experienced in translation, belongs to what these images seek to address. But in the end, I have chosen these paintings because I have come to love them more than I understand them and so need, somehow, to affirm them. I should also add that I am intrigued by three further facts about Twombly. First, that he frequently practices drawing at night in the dark as a deliberate strategy to defeat his eye and hand, and as the systematic effort to undo his skill as a draftsman. In other words, his relation to the images he produces is not guided by some conception of accuracy of reproduction or repetition. Second, he lives much of his life in Italy, as an expatriot for whom the question of the possibility of translation is a daily, lived question. Finally, I am fascinated by the fact that he suffers from mild aphasia and has trouble writing something as simple as his address. In short, his work and his life are situated in several betweens and on many borders. This sense of dwelling at a border shines through his work.

In order to appreciate these ten canvases it is important that we take seriously Twombly's own insistence that these paintings be viewed as a single work, a single painting spread across the canvases in large rooms. We also need to understand them as emerging out of his reading of the Alexander Pope translation of the *Iliad*. That translation, in iambic pentameter, which was published serially between the years 1715 and 1720 along with Pope's own commentary on the text, clearly serves as a second inspiration, a double text, for Twombly. So here we have a painter (Twombly) taking up in images a question about the relation of words and images posed by a philosophy (Plato) and offering a reply in paint by making images that repeat a story told by a poet (Homer), who never wrote. Even more, the work of this poet is read through the translation and reflections of another poet (Pope). It is from Pope's introduction to this translation that Twombly takes both the title and an image for one of the most striking of these paintings and that I have cited as the title of this chapter: "Like a fire that consumes all before it." That line, slightly modified by Twombly, is drawn from Pope's translation of Homer's line: "*hoi d'ar isan, hōs ei te pyri chthon pasa nemoito.*" Pope himself singles out these words as the most apt description of Homer's own poetic language which he has spent years struggling to appreciate, and so Pope writes that "the course of Homer's verses *pour along like a fire that sweeps the whole earth before it.*"[13] Citing these words, turning the words themselves into an element of an image, pushing the words back into their image-character as *written* language, Twombly repeats Pope's homage to the power of Homer's poetic language. But this fire, which he finds in Homer's relation to language, is—according to Pope—the chief character animating every work that can rightly be said to be art. Follow the fire and you follow the work of art. One could elaborate on this by linking this claim with the role of fire in Hölderlin's presentation of Empedocles in his *Death of Empedocles*. Furthermore, it is precisely this fire that is the special province of the artwork that actively resists any effort to grasp and manage it in a language that is itself devoid of such fire. The language of the idea, the language of philosophizing, cannot convey or tame this fire of the poetic work.

Approaching Twombly's paintings, one quickly recognizes that here we find a sort of photographic negative of both the claim and the approach to the assessment of the relation of words and images that we find in Plato. In other words, setting out from a commitment to the disclosive reach of images, Twombly moves to convert even words into the image, all to the end of drawing forward the limits proper to both words and images. In what follows, I want to speak about how I believe this ten-part painting accomplishes this and presents us with the experience of a limit without transgressing it. But I must say at the outset that when I come to speak of Twombly's paintings, I keep hearing da Vinci's caution to those who would speak of painting at all: "Avoid words, unless speaking with the blind."

The installation of this ten-part painting is important to its structure: one sees first a canvas entitled *The Shield of Achilles* in a small entrance room, then one enters a large, brightly lit room with the nine remaining canvases. The canvases have no frames, are quite large, have no signatures, and none of them offers any identifiable representational image. The images seem to float on each canvas without any context. Red is the dominant color of the first canvases, but this red eventually darkens to almost a black, which in turn quickly fades into a foggy, airy grey, and then that seems to change into a gentle blue, which is the color of the water in the "Grotta Azura" on Capri, not far from Twombly's home in Italy. The images that constitute *Fifty Days at Ilium* initially present one with what seems to be a jumble, an almost violent set of quite active, even chaotic, lines, and shapes. The canvases almost seem unfinished so that one seems to be witness to the very process by which these images have come to be. It is often almost as if one is watching the *emergence* of the image here. One might even say that these works present one with something of the process of their own genesis. They feel free, self-rewriting, often searching, elliptical yet intimate, and seemingly unable to conclude. They also frequently remind me of works of graffiti. But unlike the urban graffiti one sees today, which typically stands as the deliberate self-assertion of the artist, these canvases present us with something different, a more ghostly sort of graffiti. If what we see here is like graffiti, then they might best be described as the graffiti of loss or the graffiti of the specter. They are fragmentary, muted, with lines fading into one another and overwritten. Twombly's work often has the character of a palimpsest, the document in which a later text effaces the earlier. Here the words seem to emerge in a ghostly space, forming only in order to dissolve. These almost ephemeral works are also clearly very much about the ruin and decay of the images that constitute them. The images, which are lovingly devoted to nuance despite their large scale, are simply impossible to reproduce, and since reproduction in the present era produces reputation, this has put Twombly's work at a disadvantage. This sense of nuance and of the fading of the image here might best be understood in light of the legend of the origin of drawing which tells us that drawing belongs to memory. The legend is as follows: "facing a separation from her lover of some time, a young Corinthian woman noticed on a wall the shadow of this young man sketched by the light of a lamp. Love inspired in her the idea of keeping for herself this cherished image by tracing over the shadow a line that followed and precisely marked its outline."[14] Memory is the ruin of experience and these images might, in the largest compass of their concerns, need to be seen as a sort of memory-work.[15]

So it is in this series of ten large paintings that Twombly tries to reply to a world as large as Homer's *Iliad*. But the *Iliad* too is the fragment of a larger story; it tells of only about fifty days in the final year of a ten-year war. Ending with a funeral, the *Iliad* nonetheless does not tell the full and final story of the war. It does tell the story of how people die and how these deaths affect the living. At the center of the world of the *Iliad* then we find death. There is hardly a passage without at least one death described, and every death seems to merit its own, singular description. Each of Twombly's paintings needs to be seen as a response to this overwhelming sense of death saturating the *Iliad*. Let me cite just two passages that give some idea of how these deaths are described by Homer. "The veteran Pelagon, one of his closest aides, pushed the shaft of ashwood out through his wound—his spirit left him—a mist poured down his eyes . . . but he caught his breath again. A gust of the North Wind blowing round him carried back the life breath he had gasped away in pain."[16] Another death is depicted as follows: "As a garden poppy, burst into red bloom, bends, drooping its head to one side, weighed down by its full seeds and a sudden spring shower, so Gorgythion's head fell limp over one shoulder, weighed down by his helmet."[17] Each death is singular. Each death marks the end of a life story, a history, and a future. In the end, the *Iliad* is a work in which "The shore is heaped with death and tumult rends the sky."[18] The *Iliad* ends with a funeral which, of course, is a ceremony of transition, of translation from the world of the living to the realm of the dead. Significantly, in Greek, one dies by "darkening," one moves from the region of light to darkness.[19]

When one enters the installation of Twombly's painting, the first canvas of the painting one sees is set apart in a small antechamber; it is entitled *Shield of Achilles*. Its placement is initially quite puzzling if one expects a linear recapitulation of Homer's story since in the *Iliad* the story of Achilles' shield is only told in the eighteenth book, three-quarters of the way through the story of the battles. At that point in the story, Achilles, the real strength and inspirational figure of the Greek army, has elected to remove himself from the battle because he has been offended by the Greek king, Agamemnon.

The battle begins to turn against the Greeks and though he will not accede to the pleas of the other leaders to join the fighting, Achilles does agree to send his most intimate friend, Patroclus, into the battle and agrees to let Patroclus wear Achilles' own armor in the hope of inspiring the Greeks and inducing fear in the Trojans since Patroclus will appear to be Achilles. Homer's description of Patroclus's body being enlarged by a God to fit the armor reads almost like magical realism: Patroclus's body, no match for Achilles' physique, grows to fit the armor as if it was summoned to become greater by the very challenge to fill Achilles' place. Patroclus, of course, is killed by Hector, who takes Achilles' armor as a trophy. Grief now drives Achilles to overcome the rage he feels at Agamemnon and he agrees to enter the battle in order to kill Hector. This rage, fueled by grief that is Achilles' reaction to Patroclus's death, is what Homer speaks of in the *Iliad*'s first words: "Achilles' Wrath, to *Greece* the direful spring of woes unnumber'd, heav'nly Goddess, sing!"[20] It is also the topic of the third canvas in Twombly's painting that presents us with an almost phallic image (the likeness of this phallus to a weapon is evident in several of the canvases) of swirling red, orange, and black—an image that will carry through and repeat itself in several canvases—and that contains the single word "vengeance." Achilles knows from a prophecy that shortly after killing Hector he too will die; nonetheless, his grief, now wedded to his rage, drives him forward to battle. Lacking armor, Achilles' mother, the goddess, Thetis, pleads with Hephaestus, the lame *god of fire*, to fashion a shield for her son. Of course, Twombly's citation of Pope's comment about the kinship of the poetic work with fire needs to be recalled at this point: the act of creation passes through this transmuting fire.

The story of Achilles' grief and of this shield that is to protect him occupies the entire eighteenth book of the *Iliad*, and in many ways it forms one of the great transitional moments in the story. It is a tale that always seems to be concerned with fires: fires blaze out of Achilles' head fueled by grief and rage, and fires fashion the shield that itself repeats images of fire. The shield is designed not only to protect life, it also depicts life on its surface. The shield, in the end, tells the entire story of the whole universe in the images it bears. Its surface is articulated with loving detail by Homer: there are several concentric circles and twelve distinct compartments, each of which has its own world within it. On the shield we find earth and sky, the sea, the sun, and the constellations. We find two noble cities where we see weddings, feasts, and wars, choirs and marketplaces. We encounter human and nonhuman life. Above all, the shield illustrates life in abundance. Nothing less than the entire universe is pictured within its compass: according to Pope, we find "all the occupations, all the ambitions, and all the diversions of humankind."[21] All the loves and hatreds, past and future of human life are depicted. Pope describes the images on the shield as a painting that could be done only by a god. It is, says Pope, the poetic description of the "complete *idea of painting*, and a sketch for what one might call a *universal picture*"[22] (896). It is described as an image, but a living image. It is the image of life seen through the eyes of a god. It is the image become the mirror of life itself. The 1743 edition of the Pope translation of the *Iliad* includes an image of this shield, of this image, an engraving by Jack Liu that is strikingly different in its relation to representation—it strives for some sort of fidelity and accuracy—from the wild swirls with which Twombly presents it. Twombly is intent upon showing how the images on the shield are alive and so in motion.

For my purposes, what is most important about any painterly "representation" of this shield is that it is, strictly speaking, *impossible as a painting.* Television and film—moving images—do raise the stakes of this point, but only by shifting the question to the character of a *series* of images. But introducing the image into the series does not overcome the fact that here we still have to do with the nature of the image. In his *Laocoön*, Lessing spoke of this impossibility, this limit, for the image with respect to this idea of a painting that did not represent life, but was life itself when he wrote: "Obviously, not everything Homer says can be combined into a single picture; the accusation and denial, the presentation of witnesses and the shouts of the divided crowd, the attempts of the heralds to still the tumult, and the decision of the judges are events which follow one another and cannot exist side by side at the same time."[23] Against this limit of the image, Lessing speaks of the different reach of words in this particular situation: "And what are these advantages [of words]? The liberty to extend his description over that which preceded and that which followed the single moment represented in the work of art; and the power of showing not only what the artist shows, but also that which the artist must leave to the imagination."[24] If language is limited by its linearity, the time it takes to unfold its promises, then we equally need to say that painting is limited by its relation to simultaneity. Likewise, while the word is limited by its abstract character, its relation to the invisible universal—which, as Hegel says, has "the divine nature of directly reversing the meaning of what is said, of making it into something else"[25]—it is also, by virtue of this very same characteristic, liberated to speak of what cannot be seen. The image, on the other hand, limited by only ever being able to present what enters the realm of the visible, is by the same token, freed to repeat the visible on its own terms as visible. Twombly's painting strains its own images, letting them fade to the limits of the visible, to the ghostly image, and out of these faded, blank spaces we find words arising as a different kind of image. Here the word serves as an icon highlighting the visibility of the word as it speaks.

In Twombly's series, this painting of a universal painting, a painting done by a god in order to lovingly protect Achilles, greets you before you enter the room with the remaining nine paintings, and its shape and sense of movement carry through each of the subsequent paintings, metamorphosing throughout the series, becoming vengeance, images of battles, fire, even the spirits of dead heroes, finally fading into the ghostly rosetta-like shapes representing the three great heroes of the *Iliad*. Eventually, this shape, first found on this painting of *The Shield of Achilles*, mutates into the hovering image crossed by the words (in blue) "shades of eternal night"—words that refer to death. It is as if the story of the Trojan War was spun out of the images found on Achilles' shield. The image of the idea of painting that is the shield works in several of the parts of this series of paintings so that one must say that it stands as perhaps the central image of the ten canvases. Indeed, the position of the image of the shield in the installation of these canvases is itself testimony to this central role of the idea of the shield: moving the topic of the eighteenth book of the *Iliad* to the first position is but one of the ways of emphasizing that this image of the shield, this "universal painting," will frame the story of the *Iliad* as Twombly retells it. This means that he tells this story not by beginning with the vengeance of Achilles, but by referring to the role of the image itself in the very way the story is told here. The images on Twombly's canvases are very much "about" the role of images in the telling of the story. The image of the shield of Achilles, first in the place of the telling, reminds us of the "self-consciousness" of the images here. But it is also necessary that we see that this image of the shield is augmented in its centrality by another image that appears in one of the large battle scenes. Here at the center of the canvas, tucked away near the bottom, we find the image of an artist's pallet with the words "Artist as" [then there remain scribbles but the writing becomes undecipherable]. The artist belongs to the scene of the battle. The artist's tool, the pallet of paint, is at the margin of the battle scene. It is the presence of the artist that transfigures the carnage of the battle into a work of memory and it is the artist who translated the violence flooding the early images in a poetic work. The artist translates the event into a work of memory and thus into another order.

As one walks into the room, one is placed between images composed almost solely of the proper names of the heroes of the two warring cities and of those gods who have aligned themselves with each side. The gods, who are deathless and always of the same nature, are typically on the upper half of the canvas; the heroes, all of whom will die, are below. As one moves through the room, following the order of the canvases, one notices that the colors are strikingly different: the Achaeans, a culture characterized by its aggressions, are coupled with an angry blood red (the paint is thick here), while the Ilians, a more cerebral culture who will lose the war and whose story of migration will eventually be told by Virgil, are presented with a faded grey and a thin blue that seems to be illuminated by a light from elsewhere. The center canvas, which is the largest canvas of the ten, has three rosetta shapes across its middle, each with a name written just above it. To one's right, Achilles' anger is felt in the violent red shape; the center figure, which is a watery-blue grey, is identified with Patroclus; and finally the third, emptied quatrofoil refers to Hector. Here in the midpoint of this series of ten canvases, there is an echo of the final lines of the *Iliad*: "A solemn, silent, melancholy train: Assembled there, from pious toil they rest, And sadly shar'd the last sepulchral feast, Such honours *Ilion* to her Hero paid, And peaceful slept the mighty *Hector's* shade."[26] Essentially we have here proper names—like the Vietnam War Memorial or the AIDS quilt with their litany of the names of the dead, the pure idiom of the irreplaceable— and as one stands between these memorials one faces the largest of the ten canvases with the seemingly floating symbols of the three figures whose battles form the axis of the story of the *Iliad*. Of course, we would not have any reason to say this were it not for the names attached to these images. Here, the written words, though themselves images emerging out of the iconographic potential of all language, open the surface of the canvas beyond its own pure abstraction. The images beg for words. The words help constitute the image by themselves returning to their own basis as written image.

Each of the individual canvases presents its own specific and internal riddle along with the riddle of the unity of these ten canvases. For instance, there is the strange circumstance of Cassandra's name, which is the largest name, or word, on any of the canvases. What is so strange about that is that she is only mentioned once in the *Iliad*[27] (in connection with a promise that can never be kept). There is also the eerie image and ethereal image of what looks a bit like a cloud and of words that pass into watery blue and that refer in Homer to death and silence that are beyond the reach of grief or any human reach: "Shades of eternal night."[28] Finally, among the images that present puzzles, there remains the one that is in a wildly vivid red—a red that seems to be red as such—made of what looks like blood, sun, fire, and passion, and that refers directly to Homer's own language. Perhaps the most visually and aesthetically striking of the canvases in this series, this image of a fire that consumes is, according to its own legend drawn from Pope's commentary, the very image of the heart of the work of art. "Like a fire that consumes all before it" the work of art transfigures and memorializes these events.

One final point should be noted about the operation of these images. Words form a substantial part of the images on these canvases. Subtracting the words from these canvases would leave them bereft of the bulk of what images there are. But the words do not only function as language; they also, perhaps most of all, work as images of a different sort. Oddly, against expectation, the words here do not become calligraphic—*calligraphy* is the writing of beauty and these words are not calligraphic in that sense since it would be a stretch to suggest that they possess the hallmarks of "beauty." *Zoographīke*, the Greek word for painting, refers to the "writing of life," and in a sense these words want to be something like that, but perhaps the best word we might use to describe the presence of these words here is to say that they are iconographic presences. It is precisely in this iconographic element that we find a communication between word and image, a communication in which each seems to be present as exceeding the other and itself. This passage of word and image into one another—a passage that, at the outset of Western philosophy, Plato took to pose a threat to thinking—is what Twombly finds at the heart of the story that Homer (who, of course, we need always remember was blind and perhaps illiterate)[29] tells. In Twombly's work, word and image seem to meet and somehow communicate at their respective limits. Nothing is illustrated or represented of Homer's text, but much is imparted—above all, much is said about the work-character of both the poetic and the painterly work.

Of course one must also say that Twombly's images try to evoke the relentless series of gruesome killings related in the *Iliad*. The work of death is very much an issue of these canvases. The opening line of the poem—"Achilles' Wrath, to Greece the direful spring of woes unnumber'd, heavenly Goddess sing!"—imagined in the third painting, is traced as it metamorphoses, fading ultimately to the pure white of death. These images, especially in the way proper names punctuate them, also stand as a reminder of the lives and the values of civilized life that war erases. But, at the same time, these images work to give place to the role of the poetic work itself in the telling of this story of death. In this sense, this ten-part painting is a highly reflective work of art.

As one leaves the room of nine canvases, one sees again the wild image of the shield of Achilles and is reminded that these two poles of the human condition—war and peace—and the aspects of human nature corresponding to each—the destructive and the creative—which are at work throughout Homer, are put before us in abstract form on the images on the shield that the god has made for Achilles. From Homer, we hear that there are two cities on the shield, one at peace and one at war. In one city a marriage is being celebrated; the other is besieged by a hostile army and fighting to survive. There are scenes of violence and images of war; there are visions of people working in fields, at play, eating, and dancing. War clearly has a place in the story told on the shield, but it is not the only story told on it. War, which animates and moves the story of the *Iliad*, does not even occupy the largest part of the shield. Rather, most of its surface is covered by scenes of peaceful life. Dance, which is mentioned in detail, seems to play as large a role on the shield as does war. It seems that in dance we find an image of ordered and coordinated, yet free relations between peoples who celebrate their being together. All around the outermost rim of the shield is the stream of the great ocean river that marks the frontier of the known and the barrier separating the living and the dead. The rim of the shield presents that barrier beyond which neither words nor images can reach. Much, very much more "happens" on this impossible shield. All of life, and death too, happens. The painted image of the shield that opens Twombly's series of paintings only serves to prod the memory of one who has already heard or read this story from Homer. But the painted image—which is both the first and final image one sees in this series of canvases—calls vivid attention to what otherwise might be understood simply as a quite magical shield to be used in a war by a great warrior. Twombly helps us grasp more clearly what this shield might really mean. Embedded in the story of the end of the Trojan War we find the story of an image that, as if it were the painting of a god, could tell the story of life itself.

It is, I believe, Twombly's merit to have reminded us that in this great poem, where writing and paintings are each mentioned only once and casually at that, words and images are very much at the heart of what it is that we are given to think in the experience it opens us. We are reminded as well that words—above all, written words—and images alike are the element within which memory pays tribute to the alterity of absence, to what cannot be said and cannot be understood. The quiet, yet crucial, story of memory that might be overwhelmed in Homer's story of brutality and heroism, life and death, courage and terror, is rescued in these images. Something of how images and words do indeed *work* in the poetic work is highlighted in this painting that becomes in this way not simply a commentary on Homer's story, but equally a commentary on itself and the very nature of storytelling at all.

I opened this chapter by speaking of a certain fidelity that holds both words and images to themselves and the imperatives that guide and govern each. My suggestion was that the allegiance of philosophizing to a specific conception of the potential of the word—the conceptualizing potential—and the consequent hostility to the image that emerges out of this commitment to the logic of the concept has been called into question by many philosophers today. Since Nietzsche, we have seen both a scrutinizing of the reach of the concept and a new openness to the power of the image. But it remains a project that is housed completely in the word, no matter how expansively understood. The word retains its Midas-like capacity to convert all that belongs to it into its own peculiar form of abstraction. But what one sees in Twombly's work is the performance of a sort of *infidelity*—from both the side of the word and of the image—in which words and images cross over into one another's own natures. This treason of the word and of the image, this crossing over and translation of natures, is a great impertinence, a lapse in logic. From one point of view, it is impossible. It is no accident that death, another form of crossing and impossibility, is the central theme of these canvases. But it is what we see. In having us see this, Twombly goes a long way toward reframing the assumption of the essential difference between words and images that animates Plato's influential treatment of each in which their essential difference is highlighted. In Twombly's work words and images almost take on each other's nature.

By way of conclusion, let me simply say this. It would, I believe, be a mistake—somehow inappropriate—to try to adjudicate what the two parts of this chapter try to say, as if the contest between words and images could ever be fully settled, as if the debate that Plato set in motion could easily be resolved. But I do believe that one conclusion can be drawn that it would be good for philosophers to bear in mind: namely, that the privilege granted language—more precisely, conceptual language—in philosophical discourse, a privilege that has gone beyond mere privilege and taken on the character of a peculiar hegemony, might need to be placed in question. If nothing else might emerge from these remarks, especially those concerned with the image, it is that the being of the word is wider than the way the word gets enacted in the language of philosophizing. If we bear this in mind, if we take this to heart, then I believe it should encourage us to cast the net of our reflections wider, and in wider forms, than we customarily do today.

CHAPTER TWELVE

LANGUAGE IN THE AGE OF MODERN TECHNICITY: SPEAKING OF FREEDOM AND COMMUNITY ONCE AGAIN

> Of the ideas that were to fashion the twentieth century in ways for the most part pernicious, one that stands out above the others, so far-reaching and indeed immense were its consequences, is the idea of the *good* community ... the evidence before us should at least prompt us to inquire: might there not be something pernicious in the very idea of community, at least when it manifests itself, as has frequently been the case, in a world where technology has extended its grip over the whole planet? This is the crux of the matter: are community and technology somehow incompatible?
>
> —Roberto Calasso, *Literature and the Gods*

In the end, everything for Heidegger comes to be a matter of language. To think, as he understands it, is to engage language in an original manner. It is to listen to how words speak. But during the period that this saturation of thinking by language becomes visible and an ineluctable priority for Heidegger, that is, during the 1930s, he also becomes keenly aware that history belongs to thinking in an equal measure. Taking this force of history seriously is one of the ways in which philosophy learns to address its own times. For us, says Heidegger, this means acknowledging that we find ourselves under the injunction to confront the question of modern technicity. When the effort to think the nature of language is posed in conjunction with this question of modern technicity, the question of language wins its specificity. So, according to Heidegger, the question for us is: how is language deformed and abused in an epoch formed by the logic of modern technicity? We are put before the question of whether or not language can be brought to its most original roots in the present age. These are some of the questions driving Heidegger in his *Beiträge zur Philosophie*. In what follows, my intention is to read that work with an eye to unpacking how it is that these two themes of modern technicity and language intersect. In particular, I am interested in how this intersection shapes what can be said and thought about community and freedom in our times. Let me begin by confessing some prejudices I have about this text in the hope that such an acknowledgment might make the argument I want to make clearer.

First, I believe that *Beiträge zur Philosophie* is a *profoundly intimate work*. One might even say that at times it is so deeply engaged in a process of self-interrogation that it occasionally goes so far as to be self-indulgent. It is unlike most of Heidegger's work in that it was not a text developed in lecture course or for public presentation. Rather, it is best approached by recognizing that in it we find Heidegger wrestling with Heidegger. It is the effort of a great and creative mind struggling to find some clear direction after having suffered a period of great turbulence and confusion. I am referring, of course, to what Heidegger called "the greatest blunder of my life"—his brief and disastrous foray into political life during the Nazi era. In short, I believe that among the central concerns of *Beiträge* is Heidegger's own need to come to terms with the relation of his thought to political life and historical realities. That he might do this elliptically and obliquely, that it might be woefully insufficient, does not diminish the fact that it is Heidegger's way of confronting his own political engagement and even the historical situation in which he wrote.

Second, despite the hermetic quality of this text (something comparable to a 500-page poem by Paul Celan), it needs to be read as fundamentally driven by an effort to diagnose and critique the realities of the time of its composition. This work is a sustained effort to confront historical realities of the present age. But such a claim only makes sense if we recognize that Heidegger sees these realities through a powerfully synthetic, often poetic, sensibility. This lens though which Heidegger views the present age is, if nothing else, a provocation. Let me give an example of just how startling it can be. I am told that when Hitler and Stalin signed the nonaggression pact, Heidegger reacted to the news of this event by saying, "Now the spirits of Dostoevsky and Goethe are united."[1] But one also sees this in the infamous Rectoral Address and in "Tatsache und Gedanken" the appendix to the Rectoral Address composed twelve years later when Heidegger seems to offer a rejoinder to Hitler's use of the word "Kampf" by counterposing it with Heraclitus's notion of *polemos* (a word that Heidegger translates in those texts as "Kampf" as opposed to "Streit," which is his more preferred translation in other texts). In short, I believe that despite its quirks, we would do well to read *Beiträge* as an extended effort to confront historical realties and the contemporary shape of Western culture. But the shift in the perspective from which Heidegger wants to undertake this confrontation is so radical, so basic, that Heidegger finds it necessary to redefine even the vocabulary of the real.

Third, the farthest reaching self-appointed task of *Beiträge* is the effort to grope toward a different form of thinking and speaking about the realities of time. This work *presents itself as a revolutionary work, above all in the matter of language.* But it is important to understand the nature of this revolution. It does not lay out any program, any normative claims for a future. There is no utopian dream woven into this text that would stoke the fires of a positive revolutionary dream. Rather, the revolution here is small and discreet, delicately aimed, and our expectations should not ask something else of it.

This revolution proposed by *Beiträge* is so basic to what must be understood to read this text that some few more preliminary words about its character are necessary. Let me clarify what I mean by this discreet sense of the revolutionary by telling two brief stories. The first is one that Ernst Bloch repeats from a story that Walter Benjamin told him: "The Hassidim tell a story about the world to come that says everything will be just as it is here. Just as our room is now, so it will be in the world to come; where our baby sleeps now, there too it will sleep in the other world. And the clothes we wear in this world those too we will wear there. Everything will be as it is now, just a little bit different." This tiny displacement is what is difficult to explain. It is, of course, not a reference to real circumstances as if this cup needed to be displaced a centimeter, but to the sense of things. What is really displaced in this revolution is us. There are several passages in which Heidegger makes a gesture toward precisely this point. So, for instance, one might refer to the following examples from *Beiträge*: "In philosophical knowing a transformation (a metamorphosis) of the human being who understands takes place from the outset"[2] (14/10); or, "a complete transformation of man into Dasein is required" (475/334); or, "the most stubborn obstacle to originary thinking is found in the unexpressed self-conception which the human being of today has" (61/42). In short, to read *Beiträge* as Heidegger would have us read it is to let oneself be changed. It is a book that wants to say to the reader what Rilke says when he writes that "Du musst dein Leben ändern."[3]

One more story might help clarify the character of the revolution proposed by *Beiträge* by illustrating both how minimal, yet basic, this shift is. On November 4, 1905, Hugo von Hofmannsthal made the following entry in his diary: "A man asked a child, 'Can you touch a star?' And the child answered 'Yes,' and bent down and touched the earth." Nothing is different, everything is new. The revolutionary element in Heidegger's thought is like that: what is effected here is a minimal; nonetheless, there is an elemental shift in relations, perspective, and self-understanding.

My fourth prejudice about this book and how we should read it is that we need to recognize that Heidegger's chief dialogue partners in this venture are critical for understanding what is said, even if these figures are not always so evidently and explicitly present. Hölderlin, Nietzsche, and Jünger have a powerful, even if unacknowledged presence in *Beiträge*. Hölderlin stands out here since he seems to be the object of an almost unqualified admiration. As just one among many examples of how this can be seen, one might point to the passage in which Heidegger asks "to what extent does the poet Hölderlin, who has already gone ahead of us, *now* become our necessity in his singular poetizing and work?" (353/247). One sees this admiration as well in Heidegger's remark that "the historical destination of philosophy culminates in the recognition of the necessity of making Hölderlin's word be heard" (422/297). Hölderlin, who is said to be ahead of our times, will set Heidegger's tongue free, or at least that is the relation to Hölderlin that Heidegger would like to claim for his own. But Nietzsche and Jünger play decisive roles as well, even if not such unambiguously positive roles. Heidegger will draw on Nietzsche for his analysis of metaphysics, Christianity, values, and nihilism. Jünger will be the missing link in Heidegger's analysis of modern forms of technology. In the end, understanding what is going on in *Beiträge* will require seeing how it represents an engagement with these three figures, each of whom is enlisted to the ends of this revolutionary project.

But one other form of literature needs to be understood as haunting this text, even though its name appears only twice in the text proper. I am referring to Greek tragedy, which frames so much of Heidegger's thinking in *Beiträge*. This claim is not easy to justify and document simply with citations from the text such as one could easily do in the case of many of Heidegger's other works of this period (one thinks of course mainly of *Introduction to Metaphysics*, or the lecture courses on Hölderlin).[4] But I believe that the case for the importance of Greek tragedy for *Beiträge* is still quite compelling. The reason for this is simple: tragedy that marks what Hegel referred to as ethical substance as divided within itself, as necessarily conflicted, and the operations of this conflict are the same—in most every regard, certainly every significant regard—as what Heidegger calls here "*das in sich kehrige Ereignis*" (185/130). When Heidegger writes that "the projecting that experiences does not happen in the direction of the representation of a general essence (*genos*), but rather in the originary-historical entry into the site for the moment of Da-sein. To what extent does this happen in Greek tragedy?" (375/261), he is posing one of the most far-reaching questions of this book. He is also suggesting that there is, perhaps, in Western culture a precedent for what his revolution would open up for reflection. In the end, *the lesson of the history of beings, the law of finitude, is the lesson of tragedy in its Greek form.* Above all, it is the lesson of our historical present.

Such are the prejudices, or at least presuppositions, that animate and guide the reading of this text that I want to pursue.

I have suggested that, despite Heidegger's claims to the contrary, *Beiträge zur Philosophie* possesses a deeply political character. Heidegger's lifelong allergy to the word and thought of politics is well known and it is found in this text when he says, for instance, that "all 'political' evaluations . . . must be overcome so that the moments of 'the creators' might find their 'time' " (422/ 297). Consequently, the claim that I want to make—namely, that we must read this work as in some matter deeply committed to the task of formulating a possible politics—is in need of a strong defense. But, even before framing the question regarding political life that I want to put to this work, I need to acknowledge in advance that there are complications that make such a question exceedingly difficult to formulate. There are two reasons for this that need to be made clear: the first concerns Heidegger's own political activities, the second concerns the character of the claims made in *Beiträge zur Philosophie*.

Heidegger's own political engagement and the historical moment of the composition of *Beiträge* render the question of political life here difficult. But *it is no accident* that this work is composed at the inaugural moment of the closure of the political. Likewise, it might well be the case that Heidegger's own political blunder was no accident, no simple human failing. *But*, I would not argue on that account that his one political moment was anything less than a self-misunderstanding on Heidegger's part. In saying this, I am making a distinction between Heidegger's philosophical work and his own efforts to enlist that work to real political ends. It is admittedly a delicate and difficult distinction to make.[5] I do not intend to take up the question of Heidegger's effort to insert himself into the political realities of his time. There is no question of the great stupidity and blindness of that effort. Rather, I want to concede that this insertion of his own language into another language renders the theme of political life significantly more complicated for one who would try to follow through on the promises such language contained for something genuinely new and *fundamentally remote from all that Heidegger once endorsed*. I also want to suggest that we might finally come to better understand how to process this important episode once we work through the political concerns Heidegger formulates in *Beiträge*.

But the second, and perhaps most significant reason, for the difficulty of posing a question regarding political and ethical life here is that something genuinely new is attempted in this work. Let me simply list some of the ways *Beiträge* sets itself apart from what typically passes as a discourse on the character of community, justice, and freedom. First, here we find a critique of present cultural forms that does not legitimate itself with reference to any normative basis. This is the project of critical theory *avant la lettre*. Heidegger rigorously avoids any speculative theory that might set itself up normatively. Instead, he insists on the provisional and transitional nature of what he says, reminding the reader repeatedly that the contribution of *Beiträge* can be only provisional. What we find formulated here is a powerful, relentless, and radical critique of present cultural forms, yet the "grounds" for this critique are never made apparent. Indeed, they could not ever be made apparent. As one reads Beiträge, one question presses forward with increasing urgency: what is it that *enables* the critique that so powerfully animates this text? The second way in which Beiträge sets itself apart from a traditional political philosophy is that in it we find a conception of political and ethical life that is neither based on a notion of human subjectivity, nor governed by the will to realize an idea. Since Plato formulated the relation of knowledge and the political, it has been assumed that knowledge binds us in a community whose character is determined by the idea of community that is opened up by this knowledge. However, Heidegger is no longer guided by this assumption; no knowledge will open the space of political life. Likewise, everything that is said here is said with the dual assumption that we start out from the closure of the metaphysics of subjectivity and that the idea is no longer the paradigm for thinking. This first point means that the starting point for the discourse on community is no longer able to be the subject that could be said to be endowed with rights or encumbered by responsibilities. In other words, the assumptions of the Enlightenment no longer hold good. The second point means that the hegemony of the philosophic over the political has lost its legitimacy. This means that as one reads Beiträge one needs to ask who "we" are (¶ 19). One needs to ask always about "the people."[6] And one needs to ask about what seems to be the "impotence" of thinking (¶ 18) in the face of power.

Another reason that it is so difficult to pose questions regarding political life to Beiträge is that it proposes a conception of political life that is genuinely, rigorously, beyond good and evil. Perhaps nothing is so difficult to accept, and yet nothing as important to understand than this. There is no effort to posit yet another set of values and to establish thereby a calculus of good and evil, right and wrong. This is the greatest challenge of Beiträge with respect to the themes I want to address since it is quite evident that we do not seem to know how to ask about political and ethical life without setting up and positing values. But it is precisely this thetic act, this positing, that Heidegger calls into question and it is the very notion of "values" that he suggests prop up and secure metaphysics. Consequently, something other than a legislative act will define how it is that our being-in-common, our shared life in time, forms itself into something like a political community. As we read Beiträge, we need to ask what is required for us to carry on the questions of community, justice, and freedom without inserting these notions into the realm of values where they are captured by notions of good and evil. Instead of good and evil as the defining categories for thinking through our communal being, what we find in Beiträge are a politics of the self-differentiating event. No longer do we find a will to realize an essence, an idea. We find rather a sense of the political that is thought from out of the history of being. In the end, it is a politics that does not emerge out of a calculus of good and evil, but from an affirmation of the incalculable essence of freedom.

This then is the argument that I want to make in what follows: that *Beiträge* is an extended meditation on the enigma of freedom and that it is an effort to think the relation of this enigma of freedom to the aporia of history as it appears in the present historical juncture. In making this argument, I am taking seriously Heidegger's own claim that "the question concerning the essence of freedom is the basic question of philosophy in which even the question concerning being is rooted" (GA, 31, 300). Here we find a politics of freedom, but this is not the freedom of the subject, not the freedom of a legislative agent such as Kant describes, which is being presented. Rather, what emerges here is a sense of freedom akin to what one finds in Spinoza and Schelling; in other words, it is a sense of freedom that is to be thought in proximity to notions of affirmation and love. Understood in this way, freedom is not a property of a subject, but the ecstasis that is so elemental that it even defines and precedes what we call the "self."

Before moving forward to a further elaboration of the question that I want to put to *Beiträge*, one more presupposition guiding my reading of this text needs to be noted. This one is not only about Heidegger, but more is a more general assumption that I want to make, namely, how it is that we might best use and understand the words "political" and "politics."

By "politics," I want to refer to the play of forces and interests and powers engaged in a conflict over the representation and governance of social existence. By "the political" I want to refer to the operations of words and the form of compulsion proper to words, namely, persuasion, not to violence and force. Following Arendt, I take violence to be an indicator of the absence of the space of the political: to close the space of the political is to enter the space in which power invariably takes recourse to violence. So I take the realm of the political as the space opened up by language and deeds. Its opening, as Arendt suggests, is like a second birth for us that redefines the naked fact of our physical appearance on the earth. The political realm is, again as Arendt reminds us, the realm of freedom: it is by virtue of being free that we enter the political realm, and it is by virtue of being free that the political realm is defined and preserved. Finally, by "the political" I am referring to the space of our plurality, the character of our being-in-common. Clearly, I am drawing on Arendt's work to formulate these conceptions of politics and the political.[7] I believe that her articulation of these notions is fully commensurate with what Heidegger could and would say were he pressed into speaking of these matters. One might see evidence of why this is the case in light of a remark such as the one Heidegger makes in a lecture course on Hölderlin in which he says that "Sophocles is the true thinker of the *polis* in ancient Greece,"[8] and when, in "Origin of the Art Work," he names political founding as among the historical forms of truth. So, in what follows, I want to suggest that in *Beiträge* Heidegger devotes a great deal of his energies to thinking the space of the political—*ta politika*—and that we can even find some indications regarding the politics proper to this space—that is, a way of thinking politics that preserves rather than closes the space of the political. Not by accident does Heidegger carry out this project at the very same moment that politics brutally shuts down the space of the political, and violence, rather than political life, defines the realm of appearance.

Let me now finally pose the question I want to address in this text and outline a strategy for answering it with reference to the resources provided here. The question is simple: what still speaks in terms like community and just in the present age? One might put this question somewhat differently and ask: how are we to understand our being-in-common, the incommensurability of sharing life in time, in an age that is no longer able to understand itself in terms of the will to realize an idea—or ideal—of the common? Put in yet one more form, the question to be asked is: what is to be said of the possibility of saying "we" in the age of the closure of human self-understanding in terms of subjectivity and representation? What, in other words, does the age impose on us in our efforts to preserve the space of our being-in-common, the space of the political, as the realm in which freedom appears? These are the questions to which I believe *Beiträge* contributes something important—especially insofar as it so clearly poses these questions as being asked at the historical moment in which we find the extreme expropriation of the common and the dissolution of politics into the sociotechnical administration of mass society.

To answer these questions in the context of this text, I believe it helps to recognize that there are two distinct "moments" to Heidegger's answers: one might be characterized as "negative" since it is critique and destructive in intention, the other might be called "positive" since it is suggestive in tone. Of course, neither of these moments should be called negative or positive in a traditional sense. There is no negative critique waged from a positive normative ground, and it is important that Heidegger's effort to escape such a traditional framework at least be acknowledged. Nonetheless, there are clearly two aspects of this text, and one is designed to remove elements of Western culture; the other is an effort to open new avenues of cultural life.

What I have called the negative or destructive moment is perhaps the most prominent and extensive element of *Beiträge*. This moment encompasses Heidegger's critique of Western culture and finds its condensation, its most compact formulation, in his analysis of what he calls *Machenschaft*, a word in which we find an analysis of the metaphysical features of Western culture drawn together. Here, as in other texts, Heidegger struggles to engage and critique the West from within itself, but not to do this *as* himself a Western thinker. (As an aside, let me say that the emphasis on "Western" culture is all-important; this is especially true in the case of *Beiträge* which I take to be one of Heidegger's most non-Western works, one that opens up a political sensibility, and a sense of our relation to the earth, that is closer to Lao-Tzu than Plato.) The "positive" moment in Heidegger's effort to open up a new understanding of the possibilities of life at the present historical juncture does not present any "doctrine." There is nothing normative here: no vision of the good life is presented and defended. One does, however, find the effort to engage a form of thinking that he calls "inceptual" and it is in this notion that something—which for the lack of a better word I call positive—appears that holds a promise for a different future. It is, as the word indicates, a thinking that *founds* (and of course, what is founding is always, equally, *disruptive*), and it is a thinking that *loves to begin*. When I take up the notion of "inceptual" thinking, this thinking that sets itself apart, or against, the forms of thinking proper to *Machenschaft*, I will do so by turning to the role of the work of art in its development.

Three themes that emerge in Heidegger's critical analysis of the workings of *Machenschaft* will form the center of my remarks about it: first, the role and significance of the concept of *race*; second, the relation to *nature* as that which appears unbidden by us; and third, the character of *power* proper to the age of *Machenschaft*. But there is one other theme that plays a prominent role in this negative moment that must be addressed first. I am referring to Heidegger's concern with language and above all with his sense that "all elemental words have been used up and the genuine relation to the word has been destroyed" (3/3). The question of language in the present age, the possibilities of speaking and so thinking in the age of *Machenschaft,* almost preempts any other possible question. The reason is simple and clear: if the words we speak are themselves shaped by the logic and imperatives of *Machenschaft*, then even the best effort to overcome such forces will remain, in some essential sense, captive to them. The critique of the culture of *Machenschaft* must begin as an effort to open and refresh the possibilities of language itself. It must begin as an ever to recover language from its abuse, an effort to uncover a genuine relation to the word.

There are two ways in which the question of language gets worked out in *Beiträge*: operatively and thematically. One cannot read *Beiträge* without having the sense that the gates of language are about to slam shut and that all expectations about what it means to read or write a philosophic text are dashed. But what we need to recognize is that Heidegger's struggle with language here is undertaken precisely because he contends that language already has been closed down. To follow the operations of language in this text is to learn to listen to "how" words work as well as to "what" they say. In light of this, one would do well to approach this text with the same sort of interpretive strategies one places on oneself when reading a poem: its *movement*, which is frequently borne by rhetoric rather than conceptual argument, is very much a part of what one needs to follow. This text is a performance and, in the end, is only able to be understood as, and in, a repetition of that performance. The entire text of *Beiträge* is sandwiched between remarks on language: it opens with a reference to the exhaustion and abuse of language in the present age—"all the elemental words have been abused and our genuine relation to them destroyed" (3/3)—and it closes with an allusion to the measure setting possibility of *silence*— "language is grounded in silence. Silence is the most hidden holder of measure.... And so language is measure setting in the most intimate and farthest sense" (510/359). In the end, the movement of *Beiträge*, at least the movement that it would claim for itself, is the path by which language is returned to its essential nature. To get on that path, it is important to see how it is that language was abused in the first place. How, in other words, were even the "essential" words "destroyed"? What is language such that it lets itself be abused? How is this "abuse" detected? How does one find one's way back to the word?

The answer to these questions is, in one sense, quite simple: metaphysics is the name of the force behind the abuse and destruction of language. More precisely, it is the capacity of metaphysics, as a way of thinking and speaking, to cover over and ossify the original event of the truth (or one might better say "truing") of being. The language of metaphysics, a language that submits itself in advance to the logic and presumptions of the idea, freezes and immobilizes the very event—what Heidegger calls *das Ereignis*— that Heidegger argues is most in need of being thought in its vitality. Consequently, the recuperation of the elemental power of words, the project that Heidegger sets for himself in *Beiträge*, needs to be seen as the liberation of the essential relation of language and time (and, of course, that also means setting free the essential relation of language and death, language and mourning, themes that Hölderlin above all advanced).

I will return to the topic of language at the end of this chapter. At this point, I only want to make two further observations regarding language before beginning with the other themes to be addressed. First, I want to suggest that Heidegger is acutely aware that, in our words, we are capable of communicating not just something (such as hunger, thirst, fear), but something of *ourselves*, something of our relation to being as such. He is also aware that the language in which we have come to do this—in the West at least—the language of the idea and the language of the subject distort what it would show. This point is crucial and far-reaching: the vocabulary and even the grammar in which thinking lives are a drag on that which thinking would address. That is why Heidegger's own language seems so forced at times; he is simply trying to push language to open the possibilities of what can be thought. Second, Heidegger argues that though Western philosophy has failed in this project of letting language speak out our relation to being as such, since it prefers certainty to the abyssal truth of time, there remain nonetheless openings in the history of philosophy in which possibilities of such a relation can be detected and these openings merit our attention. In *Beiträge*, and during the years of its composition, Hölderlin's work is repeatedly designated as something of a model for just how it is that language can be brought to say faithfully the event that is most in need of being thought. In the end, it will be necessary for me to follow through on these promises that Heidegger finds in Hölderlin and to say something about what can be learned from him about our relation to time, earth, art, and peoples.

But before that can be done and we can be in a position to appreciate Hölderlin's real achievement in this regard, we need to confront more precisely the forms of thinking that present themselves as obstacles to grasping such an achievement. This means above all seeing more clearly the pervasive force and logic of *Machenschaft* in the present historical juncture since it presents itself as the all-embracing empire from which thinking cannot escape.

The notion of *Machenschaft* needs to be seen as central for any reading of *Beiträge*. But first let me remind you of the questions that will guide even these remarks on *Machenschaft*: what, if anything, still possesses the power to join us in community in the present age? What, if anything, is it that can relate us, and separate us, in a manner that preserves our original freedom? These questions ask what is required if the space of our appearance in common is to be the site for the freedom proper to finite beings who share a life in time to emerge. With that concern in mind, let me turn to the notion of *Machenschaft*.

The analysis and clear critique of the operations of *Machenschaft* as a cultural form and style of thinking constitute a key moment in the development of the space of the political in *Beiträge*. "*Machenschaft*" is the name for the organizing logic and the ruling values of the present shape of the space of the political. If my contention that Heidegger wants us to think the space of the political as the space of freedom is accepted, then it should also be said that *Machenschaft* is the name by which Heidegger thinks the logic by which freedom is repressed in the present historical juncture. To show how *Machenschaft* is to be thought I want to say something about its general character and then to look at three specific forms in which it can be seen to work: the concept of race, the image of nature, and the workings of power.

The notion of *Machenschaft* is not arrived at ex nihilo and so one enters it best by tracing some of the paths in the text that lead to its introduction. Three topics help Heidegger introduce and open up this notion: the analysis of the experience of making, the analysis of the Greek concept of *techne* as an interpretation of this experience prior to the conception of human being as subjectivity, and the analysis of modern technicity as the interpretation of the experience of making in the epoch instituted by the image of human being as a cogito that is thetic in its own nature. Finally, in order to get at this notion, in order to see more clearly what is at stake in it, we need to appreciate the character of its kinship with Western metaphysics and with modernity (these are distinct historical notions too often conflated). The project of overcoming metaphysics requires, as one of its essential dimensions, the critique of these forms of *Machenschaft*. Together these topics paint a portrait of *Machenschaft* as the name for the logic and cultural form that is generated by human beings who still understand themselves as rational animals and who are en route to a self-conception that takes the human as "a technicizied animal" (98/68). In other words, human beings who still do not understand themselves as Da-sein give themselves *Machenschaft* as a rule.

One might best begin to address these issues by noting that before he characterizes the present age as the time of *Machenschaft*, Heidegger designates our ages as a time of *transition* and of *distress*. In a letter to Elisabeth Blochmann from this period, Heidegger writes that this age is to be thought according to that which the Greeks designated as *acme*, as possessing the cutting sharpness of a knife, as the *extremity of time itself*, and that it is only as an extremity of time that the condition of *Machenschaft* can take hold.[9] It is worth noting just how frequently Heidegger uses the word "*äusserste*" when speaking of *Machenschaft*. It is one indication of the fact that Heidegger is telling a story about the *unity* of Western metaphysics and that this story is being told from the point of its eventual *crisis*—that is, from the point at which the very telling of the story indicates that the story itself is becoming different. But we can only inaugurate an understanding of this condition insofar as we grasp the historical moment of its dominance; that is, only insofar as we recognize the transitional character of the present age and insofar as we suffer the distress of such an age.

Heidegger repeatedly insists that "this distress must still be experienced" (25–26/19); in other words, that we find ourselves in the time of "the most extreme distress: the distress of the lack of distress" (107/75), and this means that this is the time in which "the danger grows to the extreme since uprooting is everywhere and—what is even more fateful—because this uprooting already conceals itself, the beginning of the lack of history is already here" (100/69). So it must be said that the distress in which we first detect the domination of *Machenschaft* is a quite peculiar form of distress. Normally distress is signaled by a discomfort, an uneasiness, and this means that it calls attention to itself. One might think of shoes that do not fit and so constantly call attention to themselves. But Heidegger claims that this distress is the distress of an anaestheticization, of a numbing. More precisely, it is the distress that comes from the *loss of history*, the distress of stasis, the distress of the distortion of the event of being. *Machenschaft* is a possible form *only* in the time of such a distortion. It is possible only in the time of an "abandonment of being." This is what Heidegger means when he says "what is this abandonment of being? It arises out of the '*Unwesen des Seyns*' [what is precisely not ownmost to being], out of *Machenschaft*" (107/75). This introduction of the notion of *Machenschaft* couples it with the possibility of what Heidegger refers to as the "*Unwesen des Seyns*," the possibility that being can, in some fashion, disown or displace itself. Asking precisely how this displacement is possible will of course provide an important clue to understanding just what might be meant by being at all.

Later, Heidegger will enlist a similarly strange formulation when speaking of the significance of *Machenschaft*: "Everything now is encased in the security of a path which is planned and exact and steerable, and which masters everything. *Machenschaft* takes '*das Unseiende*' [that which is not a being] into itself protectively by drawing it into the illusion of being; in this way, the ineluctable and enforced desolation of human being is compensated for by 'lived experience' " (406/286). In short, the reign of *Machenschaft* is to be understood as the reign of an illusion, a sort of unreality, that finds a compensation in what Heidegger calls the search for adventures ("lived experiences"). Life is emptied of history, emptied of being, and in its place we fabricate substitutes. Culture gets replaced by Disney World. The simulacrum of history takes the place of history. An illusion reigns and in the place of life we find a *virtual reality*. Indeed, to understand *Machenschaft* we might do well to think of it as the opening through which the very notion of virtual reality has entered contemporary thought.

But more than the possible destination of *Machenschaft*, its *roots* need to be brought to light. Heidegger does this in an extended manner in paragraph 61 of *Beiträge*, and so a closer look at this section might help clarify my point. There, after cautioning against hearing the word "*Machenschaft*" as possessing an evaluative tone, or as connoting something that we "do," Heidegger says that "the name should refer straight away to making (*poiesis, techne*), which of course we know as a human comportment. However, this comportment itself is only possible on the basis of an interpretation of beings in which the '*Machbarkeit*' of beings is brought to the fore, so much so that beingness is defined precisely in the notions of constancy and presence" (126/88).

Before continuing with this passage, before really trying to interpret it, let me simply make the following remark; namely, that this experience of making—of bringing into being, of summoning appearance—is among the most elemental, the most original, experiences for us. And through this power of origination, through an interpretation of how it "works," how it belongs in the world and how we belong to it, we come to understand both our world and ourselves. Furthermore, a circle works here, since through this understanding of the world and ourselves we come to make both the world and ourselves. Our interpretation of the experience of making—a distinctively human experience rooted in the possibility of freedom—confirms itself by concretizing itself, by objectifying itself, in the way we build in nature and the way we recognize ourselves. Here one might well make a reference to Kant's third critique (especially paragraph 43) where he argues that the difference between our relation to making and that of animals is that we create out of, and on behalf of, our freedom. *Art is the greatest document of freedom; it is the homage of freedom to nature that we cannot domesticate.*

Heidegger is deeply committed to thinking through this experience of making and to tracing the trajectory whereby the Western understanding of this experience eventually reaches its summit, its extreme possibility, in that form of making that understands itself as *Machenschaft*. Before returning to the question of how this experience and its determination in the present historical juncture in the Western world is treated in *Beiträge*, let me remind you of the prominence that Heidegger gives this question through his career but above all during the period between 1933 and 1939, that is, from the time of the Rectoral Address (1933), which is the first serious engagement of this question as a question of *techne*, through the "Ursprung des Kunstwerkes" (1935) and *Einführung in die Metaphysik* (1935), up to "Von Wesen und der *physis* bei Aristotles" (1939).[10] In short, this question of the what it means that we "make" something is a bit of a preoccupation during the excessively charged years of the 1930s. After the war, this concern will be picked up again in somewhat modified form in the notion of the "*Gestell*" and its relation to the "*Geviert*" in "Die Frage nach der Technik" (1953), "Bauen, Wohnen, Denken," and the series of lectures entitled "Einblick in das was ist" (1952–1954). I make the references only to situate the passages from *Beiträge* in a larger context and to remind you of the centrality of this question of how we are to understand the experience of making in Heidegger's work. I would also contend that these analyses of making, above all of its interpretation as *techne* in the Greek world, inevitably contribute directly to Heidegger's effort to "deconstruct" Western culture from within itself. In the experience of making that belongs to the possibility of art, Heidegger finds a site of resistance to the very idea of the West, to its animating center: making defines Western "culture," but it does so in terms of some other set of possibilities than those that emerge in the poetic possibilities of making out of freedom.

But let me return to paragraph 61 of *Beiträge* and ask further about the *roots* of *Machenschaft*: "That *something makes itself from itself*, and thus is ready for a corresponding process of making, defines the interpretation of *physis* which gets formulates in the horizon which is open by [the interpretation of the experience of making as] *techne*. What matters now, what is legitimized in this interpretation, is the emphasis upon what can be made and upon what makes itself (cf. the relation of *idea* and *techne*)—in a word: *Machenschaft*" (126/88). Here it might be helpful to recall Aristotle's *Physics* B, I, which perfectly exemplifies the interpretive move to which Heidegger refers here. Aristotle opens by contending that "all things" are by virtue of either *physis* or *techne*. He announces that his intention is to try to understand this enigma of *physis*, of appearances that come into being without out bidding, without our doing. But he also announces that *techne*, the other reason appearances come into being, is more readily intelligible for us because it is an event, a process in which we participate. Consequently, Aristotle analyzes the operations of *physis* by thinking through work of the craftsperson and finds four elements that collaborate in the coming into being of things through our capacity to make things. He then takes these four "causes" as also operating in the realm of appearance proper to *physis*. *Techne* is used as an interpretive model for understanding *physis*. From here it is easy to see how the ontology of nature eventually comes to be an invitation to the onto-technological conception of nature. This technologization of the natural world is, according to Heidegger, the real trademark of modernity.[11]

It should be easy to see now that when Heidegger says that "*Machenschaft* [is] the domination of making and of what is made" (131/92), he is referring to the manner in which the interpretation of our productive nature, this experience of making, as *techne*, as a form of knowledge that we have *at our disposal and which we presume is transparent to us*, comes to govern, to dominate, our understanding of all appearance—even what we do not make, that is, even *physis*—as well as our understanding of ourselves. This possibility of knowledge comes to define the possibility of all being. Heidegger emphasizes the overwhelming predominance of this understanding in the Western world, noting even that "*Machenschaft* contains the *Christian-biblical* interpretation of beings as *en creatum*—regardless of whether this is taken in a religious or secular way" (132/97). But, against this metaphysical and theological conception of making, understood as *techne*, and of the relation of such making to nature, Heidegger wants to argue two points. First, that making is far more enigmatic than we have understood hitherto, and that this becomes most clearly visible to us when we reflect the character of making proper to the *work of art*. Second, he wants to suggest that there is a distinction, a difference, to which we must become sensitive—namely, the difference between *physis* and *techne*—if we are to set free what has been concealed in the present historical juncture. This is why Heidegger says that "*physis is not techne*, indeed, *physis* first makes *techne* experienceable and visible . . . *physis* is not *techne*, i.e. something which belongs to *techne*, the anticipatory knowing which looks to the *eidos* and *re*-presentation. . . . In order for Plato to be able to interpret the beingness of beings as *idea*, not only is the experience of the *on* as *physis* necessary, but also the unfolding of the question along the axis opened by *techne* [through which *physis* is interpreted]" (190–191/133–134).

Once we have come to terms with the *roots* of *Machenschaft*, once we see how it arises out of an interpretation of an experience of making and of the relation of this experience to nature, we do not have to reach far to understand the general remark Heidegger makes about *Machenschaft* when he says: "What does *Machenschaft* mean? That which is set free into its own chains. Which chains? The schema of thoroughly calculable explainability through which everything draws closer to everything else and becomes thoroughly alien to itself, indeed becomes completely other than what is simply alien. The relation of unrelationality" (132/92). In the empire of *Machenschaft*, everything is displaced insofar as the realm of appearances is colonized by the logic of *calculability*. Calculation becomes the standard for the determination of appearance; that is perhaps most clearly expressed in Descartes' fifth and sixth *Meditations*. This is a point Heidegger emphasizes later when he says that we find here "the most extreme intensification of the power of *calculability*. What is at work here is the most indifferent and blind denial of *the incalculable*"(446/314). Here the incalculable refers to *physis*, to appearance that does not submit itself to the laws of our making and the calculus proper to it. To put the same point in the lexicon of Heidegger's text: here the incalculable is being, understood as that which is abandoned in the age governed by the operation of *Machenschaft*.

But this insistence that the determination of being, the horizon of appearance, is calculability is not the most defining feature of Heidegger's understanding of *Machenschaft*. For its most defining characteristic to become clear, one more historical development in the interpretation of the experience of making needs to be noted. Then the extreme nature of *Machenschaft* in the present historical juncture will be evident—and it is this extreme form of *Machenschaft* that first exposes it in its true nature. For this to happen, what still needs to be seen is how the self-understanding of human being forms itself in the notion of *subjectivity*, and how it is that this formation is itself a deformation of an more original freedom. What is interesting here is that Heidegger offers an answer to the question: why did Western metaphysics take as the key notion for the self-understanding of human being the idea that our basic nature is comprehended in the idea of the subject? Heidegger's remarkable reply to this question is that the notion of subjectivity, the view that our deepest nature is found in our being a subject, is itself not founded on any original experience, but is rather the result of, the perfection of, the interpretation of the experience of making that is begun in the ancient world where this experience is thought in terms of *techne*. In short, the very idea of the subject emerges out of a specific interpretation of a more original experience—namely, the experience of making. It is no accident that the full expression of the notion of subjectivity as the notion of the *cogito* happens at the moment when the interpretation of nature as a machine, as the ultimate product of a willful making founded on the calculability of beings, receives its clearest expression. Modernity is the perfection of the view that the realm of appearance is coextensive with the horizon of what is rendered possible by making, whether that making be by a god or human making, and as such modernity requires a notion of a subject as the thetic agent, the willing being, driving the process of making and thus completing it. Modernity thus understands all appearance as produced. A being, more precisely a thetic being, now governs the horizon of possible appearance. Thinking now becomes the re-production, or the re-presentation, of the fabricated world that itself now abides by the law of calculability.

With the satisfaction of the need for theticism to complete the interpretation of the realm of appearance according to the logic of *Machenschaft*, the essential nature of *Machenschaft* is at last able to be understood as rooted in *power*. Here we are in a position to see how the horizon of appearances—which when experienced as the realm of *physis* is experienced as the site of freedom—is colonized and deformed by being defined as the region of beings that are able to be calculated and are governed by the operations of power.

This notion that the essential nature, the real destiny and perfection of *Machenschaft*, is found in power is not developed in *Beiträge*. There the notion of *Machenschaft* is unfolded in terms of connection with "Erlebnis" (cf. especially paragraph 68). In other words, this notion is developed in light of the effort of human being, which understands itself as a subject, to satisfy its desires and in terms of notions of "calculability," "speed," and "size," which are the imperatives governing the empire of beings disclosed under the signature of *Machenschaft*. But in *Besinnung* (1938–1939) and *Die Geschichte des Seyns* (1938–1940), this kinship of *Machenschaft* and *Macht* is one of the central themes, and in these works the role of power in understanding *Machenschaft* is far more elaborately developed than in *Beiträge*. One of the arguments that I would like to make regarding how we must read *Beiträge* is that it cannot stand alone but needs to be read as one part of a trio of texts defined also by *Besinnung* and *Die Geschichte des Seyns*.

It is no accident that the truth of *Machenschaft* becomes clearer to Heidegger during these years in which the struggle for power dominates the space of every appearance and in which the space of political life that is carried on in speech had been closed. Naked violence now occupied that space. Power and violence wed at this historical moment, and Heidegger understands this wedding as the end point, the destiny, of an interpretation formulated at the moment of the incipience of Western culture. That is why he regards the outbreak of the war and the annihilation camps as needing to be understood as events in the history of being. He does not judge these forms of power and violence from the perspective of a humanism that finds them evil. Rather he sees them as epiphenomenal events that expose the destiny of Western metaphysics. There is a critique of the present historical formation of culture, but, as I suggested already, this critique is not governed by any normative ideal, any privileged conception of political or ethical truth. It is, and wants to remain, thoroughly beyond the orbit defined by good and evil. It finds its "roots" in a conception of the truth of being, of an original experience of appearance that was hinted at in the Greek sense of *physis*. But at the same time it is this original experience that has been covered over and obliterated in the present age: this is what Heidegger means when he says that "anxiety in the face of beyng has never been so great as today" (139/97). The place of this original experience has been usurped by something else and power is one of the forms in which this appears. This is what it means to say that Heidegger analyzes the appearance of violence in the present age as the closure of a realm of appearance and not as the violation of an ethical or political norm. It is not on this account less in need of critique; however, the grounds of its critique need to be seen as ontologically, not ethically, "founded."

In the *Geschichte des Seyns* Heidegger suggests that "the essencing of power [*die Wesung der Macht*] is the most extreme form of metaphysics" (69). He also suggests that "power 'needs' power" (75); in other words, that power thrives when it is confronted by power and that "brutality" (76) and "annihilation" (77) are self-affirming goals. Heidegger refers to the peculiar nature of power that unfolds as the truth of *Machenschaft* by saying that "in power, spirit unfolds itself in the most extreme and unconditional manner, and it comes to the point of unrestricted '*Unwesen*'" (78). Power is the culmination, the consummation of the illusion which holds operations, the procedures of *Machenschaft*, in place.

Since my primary concern in this chapter is to work through *Beiträge*, I will not press any further these somewhat later remarks on power. But before leaving these themes and texts I do want to at least refer to the little text *Koinon: Aus der Geschichte des Seyns* (1939–1940), in which Heidegger brings this analysis of power to bear on the world events of the time and says that "the disappearance of the difference between war and peace is testimony to the pressure that power exerts as the definitive standard in the play of world events" (182). This is also the text in which he writes that "the closer power comes to its proper essence—i.e., the more self-empowering power is—the louder and more pregnant is the concern for 'peace and order'" (184). Power empowers itself in the logic of *Machenschaft*. The analysis of power and its contemporary forms needs closer attention than I will give it here. One sees, for instance, how the philosophical grounds for Heidegger's resistance to communism once led him into the delusion that National Socialism offered an alternative, a rupture in the dominance of power rather than its highest expression. Heidegger's analysis of power shows how "*Einförmigkeit*" belongs to the basic character of power and how it is that Heidegger finds this concept of uniformity and power to be most expressed as the "essence of communism" (191). But rather than pursue these themes, let me take up two specific points in which this essence of *Machenschaft* consolidates and concretizes itself, thereby giving shape and distorting our self-understanding and our understanding of the world. I am referring to how race enters into self-understanding and how the notion of an image of *nature* comes to shape our understanding of the world. Both notions are developed in *Besinnung* and *Geschichte des Seyns*, but both, unlike the notion of power that eventually emerges as the essence of *Machenschaft*, are also developed in the *Beiträge* where they are shown to be decisive consequences of the contemporary articulation of *Machenschaft*. In *Beiträge*, it is clear that the overcoming of *Machenschaft*—the overcoming of this extreme form of the abandonment of being—entails an overcoming of both the notion of race and of the contemporary image of nature.

In *Geschichte des Seyns*, Heidegger suggests that "the metaphysical basis of racial thinking is not found in biology, but the metaphysically conceived thought of the subjectivity of all being of beings" (71). In other words, the same web of metaphysics serves as the historical ground for racial thinking as for the interpretation of being as something produced and representable. The argument is clear: the same forces that generate a world that is understood according to the imperatives of *Machenschaft* generate the need for the concept of race to complete our self-understanding. Here the idea that we are subjects—more precisely, rational animals possessing a body and a soul—joins the logic of power, and together they shape our self-understanding in a manner that is destined to serve the ends of the self-assertion of what is dominant with regard to the formations of power.

Perhaps the most important, or at least the most illuminating, passage on the notion of race and its significance as illuminating the deepest forces shaping, and as repressing, the historical present is found in the *Beiträge* (499/347). It is contained in the context of a section dealing with the relation of human being and history, a section that begins with a remark that "up to now human being was never yet historical. On the other hand, man has 'had' and 'has' a history" (492/346). Of course by history Heidegger does not mean "events" or "occurrences" that determine the course of time; rather, history refers to the freedom proper to the realm of appearances. History is how being "happens." From this point of view, *physis* is more "historical" that what is reported in the newspapers. That, in part at least, is what Heidegger means when he says that "only in the essence of beyng itself—and that means at the same time in its relation to the human being who is equal to that relation—can history be grounded" (492/347).

It is in the context of this homage to history that Heidegger speaks once again of race: "It is no accident that 'modernity' brings historicality [which refers to the notion of history understood as occurrences of time] to its genuine place of dominance. This dominance already extends itself so far today . . . that, through the conception of history [*Geschichte*] which is determined by historicality [*Historie*], history is pushed to the point where history is lost. . . . *Blood and race become the bearers of history*. Prehistory [*praehistorie*] gives history [*historie*] the character of validity it possesses today" (493/347). In other words, the notion of race (and of "blood"—we find the vocabulary of National Socialism set to work at this point)[12] becomes the final, the extreme form in which the subject that has severed its roots in *physis,* in the history of being, comes to understand itself. To understand ourselves first off in terms of any conception of race is to confirm the progressive extinction of history, of our free relation to the horizon of appearance understood as *physis*. This self-understanding signals the abandonment of being in the present age. Furthermore, it is not difficult to see how it is that in the era of *Machenschaft*, the age in which production defines the horizon of appearance, the notion of race will be brought together with the notion of production into the very idea of breeding and eventually *eugenics*.[13] This self-understanding belongs to the domain of the human conceived as a rational animal, as a subject. But the domain of being, the horizon of *physis*, cannot be opened from the vantage point of subjectivity. So long as we think out of such a self-understanding, what needs to be thought in the present age will be foreclosed to us. That is what he means when he says that "inceptual thinking finds its most stubborn obstacle in the unexpressed self-conception of human being of today" (61/42). For that domain to be opened, what is needed is the transformation of human being into Da-sein.

But the self-understanding of human being that eventually thinks itself in terms of race is not the only manner in which history (or the historicity of being) is shut out in the age defined by *Machenschaft*. The other signal, or symptom, of this extinction of history is found in the interpretation of *nature* that dominates today. Once again, what needs to be seen is just how the present conception of appearances as what we summon or produce blocks a more original sense of appearance understood as what come to us unbidden. This blockage of the original form of appearance represents an extinction of the original history proper to being. What is difficult to grasp, but fundamental, is that the recovery of the original experience of history, that is, the recovery of *Ereignis*, does not entail a retreat from "nature," such as might be expected in a conception of nature as other than history, "rather, nature is transformed in an original manner"—it becomes *physis*, the region of birth and death, of coming into light and passing away, i.e., it becomes the site of the truth of being" (32/23). But Heidegger is acutely aware that such sense of nature is lost today and so he asks: "What happens to nature in technicity when it is segregated out of beings [in, for instance, nature preserves and natural resources]? The growing . . . destruction of 'nature.' What was it once? The site of the moment of the arrival and the residence of the gods who, when this site was still *physis*, rested in the essencing of being itself. Since this time [of *physis*] nature rapidly became a *being . . .* and after this diminution was reduced still further by the compulsions of calculating *Machenschaft*" (277/195). He concludes this passage by asking "why does the earth remain silent in this destruction? . . . Must nature be surrendered and handed over to *Machenschaft*?" (277–278/195).

In these notions of race and nature—presented as the summits of a thinking guided by the logic of Machenschaft—the "critical," the "negative" moment of Heidegger's critique of the space of appearance, the realm of the political, reaches its highest point. Of course, much more needs to be said about this, but at this point I want to end the presentation of this negative moment and turn now to what I have referred to as the "positive" moment in Beiträge. Obviously, in light of what I have said thus far, that moment will entail the recovery of history, the recovery of physis. It will require that we think differently about ourselves and it will entail a transformation in the language in which we pay tribute to the space of possible appearance.

> Saving means: Not only to evade danger but to set free into what is essential. This infinite intention is the finitude of human being. Out of it humankind is able to get over the spirit of rage. For a long while, I have meditated on this because moral behavior alone does not suffice.
>
> —Martin Heidegger to Hannah Arendt in a letter sent after the war

At the outset, I raised the question of what, if anything, Heidegger's Beiträge might contribute to our understanding of the space of political life, the space of our shared life in history. Further, I asked whether such terms as justice and community might still be brought to have weight in the present age when we find closure of human self-understanding in terms of subjectivity. Finally, I suggested that if we are to appreciate what Heidegger does contribute to these concerns, then we will need to begin by recognizing that political life can no longer be conceived as the will to realize an idea; in other words, we can no longer legitimately appeal to the project that would "produce" a community out of some preconceived concept of what it should be. Rather, we must begin with the realization that the starting point for political reflection must be in the experience of *freedom*, which will need to be acknowledged as the incalculable character of the real site of political life.

In the second part of this chapter, I tried to outline the basic features of the contemporary logic of the distortion of the space of appearance—that is, I analyzed some of the elements of the unfreedom propping up the present forms for Western culture. This was undertaken with the assumption that the obstacles to the experience of freedom that are found in the present age must first be exposed and so destroyed if there is to be any chance of opening the space for a new form of reflection on political life.

To conclude, my task is to say something about the different, the other, sense of how it is that the space of political life might be brought closer in accord with its own deepest nature: as being the site of both history and freedom. To this end, I want to pose the following questions. First, how does Heidegger suggest that we think the space of appearance in a manner that escapes the repressive features of the way appearance is thought and experienced in the age of *Machenschaft*? Answering this question will require both some remarks about Heidegger's understanding of the relation of the work of art to its origin and about the transformation of the human subject into Da-sein. Second, what might be said about the character of our being in common as it is thought from out of the space of appearance once it is understood from out of this "inceptual" thought? In other words, what might be said of the nature of community in light of what we learn about the space of community from Heidegger? Answering this question will require some comments on Heidegger's discussion of "the people" in *Beiträge*. Third, how does a new experience of language belong to this transformation, this other beginning? Let me conclude the introduction of these final questions by saying simply that the space of appearance, which has been closed down by the administration of life in mass society and by the workings of what Heidegger calls *Machenschaft*, has lost its power to gather people together— to relate them and to separate them. This is the difficulty of political life in the present age: not the number of people, but the closure of the space of appearance that enables our being as being in common. Politics needs to be the effort to recover this space and preserve its possibility. The argument with which I want to conclude this chapter is that Heidegger does indeed make an original contribution to the possibility of such a progressive politics tailored for the present age.

It seems clear that a different future will need to open up a sense of the space of appearance as being larger than what we can define and control. This is simply to say that what Heidegger calls the "essencing of being" cannot be found in the orbit of appearances opened up according to the logic of *Machenschaft*. Heidegger repeatedly suggests that under the rule of *Machenschaft* we experience "the metaphysical diminishing of the 'world' which in turn produces a hollowing-out of human being" (495/348). That is another way of saying that in the age of the abandonment of being, the age of the withdrawal of the divine, the withering of the event of being, the space of appearance shuts down by being reduced to that which can be conceived and calculated by a subject. In light of the analysis of the roots of *Machenschaft* as having emerged out of the metaphysical interpretation of the experience of making as an activity governed by a thetic subject, by the *will*, and as realization of an idea, it should be clear that the effort to overcome the determination of the realm of appearance by *Machenschaft* will entail a new understanding of the experience of making. Here Heidegger's reflections on the political and the productive dimension of the work of art are key.

There are at least three ways in which the analysis of the work of art serves Heidegger's effort to open up "inceptual" thinking: first, as providing another model for how we can understand the experience of making; second, as providing a way in which what we do not summon into being and cannot will is revealed to us in its nature as opening up the realm of *physis*, of earth; third, as tragic in its nature, the work of art stands as a memento of the deep, irreconcilable conflict proper to the space of all appearance ["*das in sich kerhige Ereignis*" (185/130)]. While a full discussion of the role of the work of art in the opening up of the space of the political is needed for a more elaborated presentation of Heidegger's contributions to political thought, in what follows I do not intend to do more than give some brief indications of how these features of what is given to be thought in the work of art bear upon the questions I want to put to the *Beiträge*.[14]

Near the end of *Beiträge*, Heidegger writes that "the question about origin of the work of art [which refers us to the experience of making, of *poeisis*] does not aim at a timelessly valid determination of the essence of the art work, which could simultaneously serve as guiding thread for a historically retrospective explanation of the history of art, this question stands in an intimate connection with the task of overcoming aesthetics and that also means with overcoming a specific conception of beings as objectively representable" (503/354). Since 1934, in other words, since the first draft of "The Origin of the Work of Art," Heidegger had been interested in attempting a more original understanding of the claim Hölderlin makes that we "dwell on the earth poetically," that our destiny and our relation to the earth are inseparable from our productive activity. But whereas the dominant conception of this productive activity in the present age is that it is to be thought as *praxis*, that is as a manifestation of a will that produces a concrete effect, Heidegger wants to argue that the essential character of our productive activity is different. More precisely, he suggests that it is closer to what the Greeks designated as *poiesis*, but that we can still see and understand something of this in the present age if we think about the "origin" of the work of art so long as we do this without the assumptions guiding aesthetics. In "The Origin of the Work of Art," Heidegger reminds us that the original Greek sense of *poiesis* did not understand it as "a voluntary process, but in its being a mode of truth, i.e., as an un-veiling, as *aletheia*." It is precisely because of this essential proximity of *poiesis* to truth that Aristotle, who repeatedly theorizes the distinction between *poeisis* and *praxis* as falling within the horizon of human "doing," tended to assign a higher position to *poeisis* than to *praxis*.[15] According to Aristotle, the roots of *praxis* lay in the condition of human being as an *animal*, as a living being, since these roots are constituted by the principle of motion (of the will, understood as the basic unit of desire) that characterizes life. *Poeisis*, on the other hand, constructs the space of appearance in which the human being is able to act. In the Western cultural tradition this distinction between *poeisis* and *praxis* has been progressively obscured: the "doings" of human beings are determined as the production of objects by a will. The central experience of *poeisis*—that is, the truth of coming-into-being—is replaced by another experience, one centered not on this passage from nonbeing into being, but on the being that is the *result* of such a passage. The shift is from the notion that production is a matter of opening a world to the notion that it is the production of objects. The essence of production, conceived in the Greek way (and the way that Heidegger wants to renew), is to bring something into presence (this is why Aristotle says "*esti de techne pasa peri genesin*": "every art is concerned with giving birth"—and why Plato, in the *Symposium*, could link poeitic creation and erotic procreation). Conceived in a Greek sense, production (as both *poeisis* and *techne*) and *praxis* are not the same. Heidegger's concern is to recover this more original sense of production, of making, and to suggest that this might serve as a better "model" for thinking the space of appearance (cf. Aristotle *Physics* B, ii).

In short, the turn to the work of art is a return to its "origins," its sources and conditions, it is *not* a turn to art objects. It is a return to the understanding that artworks are distinguished by virtue of the way they remain close to the event of coming into being from nonbeing. In this sense, art lets *physis* shine in the work. *Art is a making that dwells near this origin of appearing and that is why art always—no matter how old—always has the feel of the new*: it lives at the sources, the origins, of all appearing. This, of course, sets Heidegger's understanding of art in contrast to a view of art that takes it as needing to seek only to emulate the new by being "shocking." Likewise, this means that we need to understand *beauty* as proximity to this event of appearing, not as a matter of any special arrangement of the object, or any "aesthetic" effect. Here one might do well to turn to Kant's *Critique of Judgement*, which goes far toward helping us develop the general insight about the significance of the work of art for ethico-politico reflections.[16]

More could be said about the role of the work of art in opening the space of appearance. To do that, it would be especially important to speak of the struggle of earth and world, and also of what happens to art in the age of technicity. It would be important to understand the turn to abstraction that is the form of art proper to our age. But for now let this suffice so that I might move to one other theme that is crucial in how Heidegger thinks this opening; namely, the transformation of the idea of the subject into Da-sein and from out of this understanding of Da-sein the move to a new understanding of who "we" are. It is from out of this transformation that he wants to develop a nonmetaphysical conception of "the people."

Overcoming a self-understanding of our being as rooted in some form of subjectivity is a complicated matter. It involves, for instance, a reconsideration of how we understand ourselves as bodily beings: "That human being 'consists' of body-soul-spirit does not say much. For the question about the *being* of this unitary thing is avoided when we speak in this way" (50/35). This is a central point that Heidegger will emphasize when he later writes that "from out of the event in which this historical belongingness grounds itself, the foundation arises for why 'life' and body, procreation and sex, lineage, said in basic words: the earth, belong to history and in their own way take history into themselves again, and in all of this only serve the struggle of earth and world. . . . *For because their essence is intimate with the struggle, it is near to the event*" (399/279). Heidegger follows this with the remark that "world and earth in their *struggle* lift life, love and death to their highest moment" (399/280). Later he suggests that Da-sein "should come to be in the innermost order out of which this struggling first takes place" (400/281). In other words, the process whereby the overcoming of our self-understanding in terms of the framework of subjectivity takes place is a process involving a struggle. It is not a simple or an easy matter.

We begin then with this: that Da-sein is the site of a struggle. Furthermore, Heidegger describes the law of this struggle as that of world and earth. It is thus the same struggle opened up by the work of art. But he also describes this as the struggle of love and death, and in saying this adds something new to what needs to be thought. But what is most important to know is that speaking of this struggle that defines Da-sein is another way of naming the *finitude* of Da-sein. In trying to understand this finitude in *Beiträge*, as in *Being and Time*, Heidegger finds it necessary to give *death* a peculiar privilege. We see this in the following remarks, which are only two of the many possible illustrations of this point: "To grasp being-toward-death as the determination of Da-sein and only thus" (284/200), and "death as the highest and most *extreme* testimony of being" (284/200). To understand such initially obscure remarks we might turn to another passage, one that is among the most enigmatic in the text, but does in the end serve as a key to what needs to be said at this juncture. It is found in a section of the text to which Heidegger refers us after he says that "the proper 'being' of human being is thus grounded in a belongingness to the truth of being as such, and this in turn because the essence of being as such . . . contains in itself the call to human being as the call to history" (51/36). After making this remark, Heidegger refers us to section 197 of *Beiträge* that concludes with the passage that is central to what needs to be acknowledged: "Selfhood is the trembling which begins in and is sustained by the fissuring of the countervalency of the struggle" (321).

What this amounts to is the reminder of what was established in *Being and Time*: that the being of Da-sein is *ecstatic*, that is, it is not defined by an "I," a subjectivity or by any form of identity. Rather, in order to grasp the character proper to our own being as Da-sein, we must start from the experience of having always already exceeded what we might eventually construct into a self. Da-sein is this being through which the event of appearance can happen. It is the site of the openness, the clearing, that is the opening of the history of being. This is entirely different from what emerges from an understanding of the 'self' as a subject, as a 'glassy essence' that represents or reproduces a world of things according to ideas. "The projection here that experiences does not occur in the direction of representing a general essence (*genos*), but rather in the original-historical entry in the site of the moment of Da-sein. To what extent does this occur in Greek tragedy?" (374/261). This "self-understanding" is also completely different from a self-understanding that refers us to our capacity for transcendence: "Even when 'transcendence' is conceived differently that it has been hitherto ... even then this determination all too easily displaces the essence of Da-sein" (322/226). That is also why Heidegger says that "the who-question as the enactment of self-reflection has nothing in common with a curious ego-addicted lostness in the grasping after 'one's own' experiences [*Erlebnisse*] (51/36). Rather, "whenever Da-sein is to be grasped, *death* must be defined as the *extreme* possibility of the there [*Da*]" (324/228). The point is this: death, properly understood, irremediably exceeds the resources of a metaphysics of the subject; the subject, which says *ego, cogito sum*, cannot say *ego sum . . . mortuus* even though death is precisely what is most proper to this being and is what is most inalienably its own. This is because the "I" in truth is something other than a subject. Hegel already reminds us that the individual can be the origin and certainly of nothing but its own death. But Heidegger would argue that Hegel still conceived this death as the death of a subject rather than the testimony, the truth, of being itself.

Heidegger suggests that this point has yet to be grasped: "Given that we have barely grasped 'death' in its extremity, how are we ever going to measure up to the rare clue of the last God?" (405/285). But it is clear that this transformation of our self-understanding into Da-sein does begin with, and require, grasping just how it is that death is the highest testimony of being. It is also clear—even if we have "barely" begun to do this—that "*it is only from out of Da-sein that the essence of a people is to be grasped.*" (319/224). It is Da-sein that opens up and opens onto that which constitutes a community.

In light of the relation between Da-sein and death, saying this means that community needs to be thought in relation to death as that which is impossible to inscribe within a metaphysics of subjectivity. Understood in this way, we can say that *community needs to be understood as the presentation to its members of its mortal truth*. This amounts to saying that there is no community of immortal beings, something that Homer's description of the gods makes quite clear. Rather, community is a presentation of the finitude and of the excess that determine finite being. Thus we can say that the death of others—and the way in which such death reveals the character of community to the living—has a privileged role in the exposure of a community to itself. Community is not the space of egos, of subjects that think themselves according to the model of a deathless being; it is rather the space of others. Community is not the fusion of subjects into a higher order, a "we," since that is a coercive gesture no matter how enlightened. Community is rather founded on the knowledge that the other is never able to be grasped or known, never able to be represented or reproduced because in death the other remains forever impossibly out of my grasp. The other remains an unassumeable otherness, a freedom that cannot be legislated. Clearly, no doctrine of community emerges from a thought such as this. What does emerge is a powerful sense of the need for the affirmation of the riddle of others. The solidarity that forges community is rooted in an acknowledgment of the most solitary and impossible truth of Da-sein—namely, that our own ungraspable mortality and the strangeness must be able to find a place if community is still able to possess the power to gather people in their truth.

There are some powerful precedents to be found in the history of philosophy for addressing this thematic of the kinship of death and community. One finds it in Plato's *Republic*, a dialogue that opens and closes with references to death and in between struggles to formulate a sense of the possibility of community. One sees it in Hegel's discussion of *Sittlichkeit* wherever that notion appears. One finds it above all in Sophocles, especially in *Antigone*, which perhaps more than any other work enacts this question of the limits of the possibility of the *polis* as an impossible question wrapped around the riddle of death. That is why Heidegger calls Sophocles "the true thinker of the *polis* in the ancient world;"[17] in Sophocles we see with great clarity that in antiquity the role of tragedy was to remind citizens of the limits of the claims of the *polis* and of the individual. In the tragedy, *community is revealed as that which exposes, rather than sublates, the finitude of its members*. But what does all this really amount to? What must "we" confront, what must "we" think, if we are indeed able to say "we" in the present age and not experience this as a coercive gesture?

In the end, I believe that this means that community will need to begin by recognizing its own limits as a realizable possibility. As such, it will need to understand itself as the preservation of the space of the appearance of differences. To put this point in the language of *Beiträge*, we might say that community will be the realm in which history can happen. It will be the realm in which we find ourselves as belonging to a space of appearance that can, perhaps, be described as something like what is said in the Greek word "*physis*." This means that it will become the realm of birth and death, the region in which we find what we cannot produce, but what we can only celebrate and affirm. It will need to be the realm in which the new can still happen. This means as well that community will need to come to be understood as defined by that which is greater than what we either define, control, or produce; in the end, it will need to be grasped as the site of our dwelling poetically on the earth. The self-formation of peoples will need to be understood as always unfinished, as what Kant called an "infinite task." It will also need to recognize that the capacity of a people to think their own limits and respect the impossibility of community has very much to do with its capacity to open up the world in the work of art. This is not to say that a healthy community needs to produce its own cultural objects, but it does mean that such a community must preserve the space within which its own stories can be told. This capacity requires a boundless generosity to open a space for appearance beyond what we it can control. This, in part, is what Heidegger means when he says that "what compels, what binds, is only the incalculable and unmakeable of the event, the truth of being" (416/292).

One more point, perhaps the most difficult and significant point of all, remains to be mentioned at the end of these remarks. The question of the language proper to the formation of community must be recognized as at the heart of the puzzled posed by the task of forging community. Here I will conclude by simply noting, quite briefly, what it is that Heidegger was able to find in the language of Hölderlin. It is, as Heidegger frequently reminds us, the language of *mourning*, the language of the loving response to the death of the other. But it is also *by the same token* the language of love, the language of connection proper to finite beings. It is, in other words, a language that somehow resists the subsumptive logic of the concept and reminds us that because we are beings who know themselves in the certainty of their death, and because we are beings who can mourn, we are *for that very reason* beings who can love and who are thus able to form impossible communities.

APPENDIX: "MONOLOGUE" BY NOVALIS

There is really something quite mad about speaking and writing: the proper conversation is a mere play of words. One can only be amazed at the ridiculous mistake that people make when they believe that they are speaking about things. Nobody knows the greatest hallmark of language: that it is concerned only with itself. That is why it is such a wonderful and prolific secret: that when one simply speaks for the sake of speaking, one expresses the most splendid and original truths. But if one wishes to speak of something particular, the capriciousness of language lets one say the most ridiculous and perverted things. It is from out of this that a hatred of language grows in some serious people. They notice its playfulness, but they do not notice that contemptible chatter is the infinitely serious side of language. If one could only make people understand that what applies to mathematical formulas applies to language—they constitute a world for themselves—they only play with themselves, express nothing other than their own wonderful nature, and precisely for that reason they are so expressive—and that it is precisely for this reason that the strange play of relationships of things mirrors itself in them. Only through their freedom are they members of nature, and only in their free motion does the spirit of the world express itself and make them the delicate measure and pattern of things. The same is true of language: one who has a fine feeling for its application, its tempo, its musical spirit, one who has perceived the delicate operations of its innermost nature and follows them through the movements of her tongue or her hand, such a person will be a prophet. Conversely, one who knows this, but does not have enough of an ear or sense to write truths such as these, will be mocked by language itself and by derided by me, as Cassandra was by the Trojans. If I believe I have shown in the clearest manner the essence and office of poetry, I nonetheless know that no one will be able to understand me, and I will have said something completely foolish precisely because I wanted to say it at all, and so no poetry comes into being. But what if I had to speak? And what if this impulse to speak were the hallmark of the inspiration of language, of the effectiveness of language in me? and what if my will only wanted what I had to do? could this not then, in the end, be poetry without my knowledge or my conviction, and so make a secret of language understandable? And would I then be a writer who was called, for a writer is only someone who is possessed by language?

NOTES

CHAPTER ONE

1. Immanuel Kant, *Werke* (Berlin: Walter de Gruyter, 1968), Bd. V, pp. 188–189. Henceforth cited as AK followed by the page number of the Akademie edition of Kant. Cf. also AK, 218 and AK, 205: "da doch Schönheit ohne Beziehung auf das Gefühl des Subjects für sich nichts ist," and "Man sieht leicht, daß es auf das, was ich aus dieser Vorstellung in mir selbst mache, nicht auf das, worin ich von der Existenz des Gegenstandes abhänge, ankomme, um Zu sagen, er sei schön." An important consequence of this is that the aesthetic is not bound to the real, but belongs equally—if not in fact to a greater degree—to the imaginary.

2. The phrase is one that Foucault endorses as the postmodern counter to the fundamental claim of modernity. Cf. Michel Foucault, "La pensée du dehors," in *Critique* no. 229, 1966, p. 122.

3. Immanuel Kant, *Reflexionen*, 1820a.

4. Hans-Georg Gadamer, *Wahrheit und Methode* (Tübingen: J. C. B. Mohr, 1975), p. 54. Henceforth cited as WM followed by the page number.

5. Friedrich Nietzsche, *Geburt der Tragödie* (Berlin: de Gruyter, 1988) Bd. I, p. 26. Henceforth cited as GT followed by the page number.

6. The word is typically "belebt" or "Belebung," cf. AK, 219.

7. Gadamer suggests that this shift happens in the era of humanism. Cf. *Gesammelte Werke* (Tübinigen: J. C. B. Mohr Verlag, 1993), Bd. 8, p. 384. Henceforth the *Gesammelte Werke* will be cited as GW followed by the page number; if a volume other than volume 8 is being cited, the volume number will be noted. For an interesting discussion of the absence of natural beauty from the agenda of aesthetic theory, see Theodore Adorno, *Gesammelte Schriften*, Bd 7 (Frankfurt: Suhrkamp, 1972), pp. 97–129.

8. G. W. F. Hegel, *Vorlesung über die Aesthetik* (Frankfurt: Suhrkamp, 1970), Bd. I, p. 25.

9. Cf. my "Economies of Production" in *Crises of Continental Philosophy*, ed. Dallery and Scott (Albany: State University of New York Press, 1991). It is worth noting how much the question of technology, governed by the rule of production according to concepts, belongs to the questions of both art and beauty; both Heidegger, esp. in "Die Frage nach der Technik," and Benjamin, esp. in "Kunst im Zeitalter seiner Technologischen reproducierbarkeit," develop this point.

10. It should be said that some of the most interesting turns in the *Kritik der Urteilskraft* are motivated by Kant's attempt to due justice to this appearance of the non-artefactual. In his *Physics*, Aristotle makes a decisive turn when he faces this very difficulty, but chooses to use the model of the production of the artefact, the *prohairesis*

of the craftsperson, as an interpretative model for understanding the *aitia* of nature. Kant even refuses to speak of natural "products," preferring instead to speak of natural "educts." Cf. AK 371 and 423–424. In the effort to preserve the integrity of nature as not of our own making, Kant comes to resemble Spinoza.

Here it should also be noted that in *Truth and Method* Gadamer criticizes Kant for drawing this conclusion: "Natürlich beruht auch die Bedeutsamkeit der Kunst darauf, daß sie uns anspricht, daß sie dem Menschen ihn selbst in seiner moralisch bestimmten Existenz vorstellt. Aber die Kunstprodukte sind nur um uns so anzusprechen—Naturobjekte dagegen sind nicht, um uns so anzusprechen. Gerade darin liegt das bedeutsame Interesse des Naturschönen, daß es uns dennoch unsere moralische Bestimmung bewußt zu machen vermag. Kunst kann uns dieses Sichfinden des Menschen in absichloser Wirklichkeit nicht vermitteln. Daß der Mensch sich in der Kunst selbst begegnet, ist ihm nicht die Bestätigung von einem andern seiner selbst her.

Das ist an sich richtig. So eindrucksvoll die Geschlossenheit dieses Kantischen Gedankenganges aber ist—er stellt das Phänomen der Kunst nicht unter den ihm angemessenen Maßstab. Man kann die Gegenrechnung aufmachen. Der Vorzug des Naturschönen ist nur die Kehrseite des Naturschönen an bestimmter Ausdruckskraft" (WM, 48).

11. Here is it would be interesting to draw upon Heidegger's early developed of the notion of "formale Anzeige" as a means of addressing the limits of conceptuality.

12. Cf. Hegel, op. cit., pp. 492–520, esp. p. 505, where he says that "Das vollkommene Element worin die Innerlichkeit ebenso äußerlich als die Äusserlichkeit innerlich ist, ist wieder die Sprache" (G. W. F. Hegel, *Phänomenologie des Geistes* [Hamburg: Meiner Verlag, 1952], paragraph number 505; henceforth cited as *PG* followed by the paragraph number) and "so vereinigen sich die besondern schönen Volksgeister in Ein Pantheon, dessen Element und Behausung die Sprache ist" (*PG*, 506).

13. Ibid., p. 564. These words are very different in sensibility than the first words that serve as the epigram of *Truth and Method* where Gadamer cites Rilke saying, "Solang du Selbstgeworfnes fängst, ist alles / Geschicklichkeit und läßlicher Gewinn—/ erst wenn du plötzlich Fänger wirst des Balles, / den eine ewige Mitspielerin / dir zuwarf, deiner Mitte, in genau / gekonntem Schwung, in einem jener Bögen / aus Gottes großem Brückenbau; / erst dann ist Fangen-können ein Vermögen,—/ nicht deines, einer Welt."

14. It is especially important for the question of technology. Once again, Benjamin, who found everything to be allegory, infinitely proliferating, infinitely reproducible, is important here. See also Tzvetan Todorov, *Theories of the Symbol*, trans. Catherine Porter (Ithaca: Cornell University Press, 1982), pp. 189–192.

15. Goethe, *Jubiläumsausgabe*, Bd. 35, pp. 325–326.

16. This is the point at which the erotics of the symbol might be discussed. Cf. A. Carson, *Eros: The Bittersweet* (Princeton: Princeton University Press, 1986), pp. 70–76.

17. Cf. *Anthropologie*, in *Werke*, Bd. VII, paragraph 38.

18. Cf. esp. Sermon 52, "Beati pauperes spiritu," *Meister Eckhart Predigten* (Frankfurt: Deutscher Klassiker Verlag, 1993), pp. 551–563.

19. Though some forms of neo-Platonism and especially Plotinus are quite interesting in this regard. See, for instance, U. Eco, *Art and Beauty in the Middle Ages* (New Haven: Yale Press, 1986), pp. 56–64.

20. He also says the same of maggots (AK, 296) and bird song (AK, 243; 302).

21. Saying this, I am of course doing an injustice to Kant's own claims about what he is arguing since he says quite clearly that "Der Gesmack macht gleichsam den Übergang vom Erkenntnis zum Sinnenriez zum habituellen moralischen Intersse ohne einen zu gewaltsamen Sprung möglich" (AK, 345). But here I agree with Gadamer's suggestion that in the third critique Kant has a tendency to domesticate, to tame, the full radical force of what he is exposing. Heidegger makes a similar claim about Kant in the first critique in his *Kant und das Problem der Metaphysik*.

22. See "Das Ende aller Dinge," in Werke, Bd. VIII, AK, 327–328: "Allein da die Idee eines Endes aller Dinge ihren Ursprung nicht von dem Vernünfteln über den physischen, sondern über den moralischen Lauf der Dinge ... veranlaßt wird."

23. Here it would be interesting to discuss Nicholas of Cusa's notion of a coincidence of opposites.

24. It would be worthwhile to turn here to Nietzsche's remarks about lyric poetry, especially Archilochus, and the identity of lyric poetry with music that leads Nietzsche to say that "the 'I' of the lyric poet resonates out of the abysses of being; his 'subjectivity' in the modern sense of the word is a fiction" (GT, 44).

25. "Reply to Jacques Derrida" in *Dialogue and Deconstruction*, ed. Michelfelder and Palmer (Albany: State University of New York Press, 1989), p. 57.

CHAPTER TWO

1. Heidegger, GA, Bd. 53, pp. 106–107.
2. Gadamer, *Gesammelte Werke*, V, p. 187.
3. Hans-Georg Gadamer, GW, V, p. 193.
4. Jürgen Habermas, *Das Erbe Hegels* (Frankfurt: Suhrkamp, 1979), p. 13.
5. Hannah Arendt, *The Human Condition* (Chicago: University of Chicago Press, 1959), p. 183.
6. Michel Foucault, *The Thought from the Outside*, trans. Brian Masuumi (Cambridge: MIT Press, 1987), p. 13.
7. Ibid., p. 25.
8. Martin Heidegger, *Unterwegs zur Sprache* (Pfullingen: Neske Verlag, 1959), p. 33.
9. Gadamer, WM, 478.
10. E. Canetti, *Der Beruf des Dichters* (München: Hanser Verlag, 1976), p. 5.
11. See Václev Havel, *Living in Truth*, ed. Jam Vladislav (London, Faber and Faber, 1986).
12. Plato, *Republic*, 607a. On this, see my *On Germans and Other Greeks*.
13. Gadamer, GW, V, p. 205.
14. Martin Heidegger, *Was Heisst Denken?* (Tübingen: Niemeyer Verlag, 1954), p. 20. On Heidegger's account of the importance of he relation between writing and speech in the effective history of Greek thought, see *Einführung in die Metaphysik* (Tübingen: Niemeyer Verlag, 1966), p. 49.
15. Aristotle, *Poetics*, trans. Ross, 1451b.
16. Martin Heidegger, GA, Bd. 39, p. 20.
17. G.W. F. Hegel, *Grundlienen der Philosophie des Rechts* (Frankfurt: Surhkamp, 1970), p. 28.
18. Friedrich Nietzsche, *Will to Power*, #822.

19. Friedrich Hölderlin, *Sämtliche Werke*, Bd. II (München: Hanser Verlag, 1992, p. 370.
20. Heidegger, *Unterwegs zur Sprache*, p. 215.
21. That is also the question that runs through the most Platonic of Heidegger's own texts—namely, the *Rektoratsrede* in which the question of the relation of the university to the scientization of knowledge is introduced with a quotation from Aeschylus: "techne d'anagches asthenestera machro." See *Die Selbstbehauptung der Deutschen Universität* (Frankfurt: Klostermann, 1983), p. 11. See my *On Germans and Other Greeks*, chapter 6.
22. Theodor Adorno, *Aesthetische Theorie* (Frankfurt: Suhrkamp, 1970), p. 81.
23. Ibid., p. 17.
24. Heidegger, GA, Bd. 39, p. 87.
25. Hans-Georg Gadamer, *Lob der Theorie* (Frankfurt: Suhrkamp, 1983), p. 45.
26. Gadamer, GW, V, p. 202.

CHAPTER THREE

1. "Kultur und das Wort," in Hans-Georg Gadamer, *Lob der Theorie* (Frankfurt: Suhrkamp Verlag, 1983), p. 23; henceforth abbreviated as *L*. Other references appear in the body of the text abbreviated as follows: *TI* = "Text und Interpretation," in *Gesammelte Werke*, Bd. 2 (Tübingen: J. C. B. Mohr, 1986); *HW* = *Heideggers Wege* (Tübingen: J. C. B. Mohr, 1983).
2. Paul Celan, *Gesammelte Werke* (Frankfurt: Suhrkamp, 1986), Bd. III, p. 197.
3. Hegel, *Phaenomenologie des Geistes*, paragraph 669.
4. See G. W. F. Hegel, *Enzyklopädie der Philosophischen Wissenschaften* (Hamburg: Meiner Verlag, 1969), paragraph 15. For a fuller discussion of the different images of the circle in Hegel and Gadamer, see my "Circles—Hermeneutic and Otherwise," in *Writing the Future*, ed. D. Wood (London: Routledge & Kegan Paul, 1989).
5. Martin Heidegger, *Hölderlins Hymne "Der Ister"* (Frankfurt: Klostermann Verlag, 1984), p. 76. Henceforth abbreviated as *HH*.
6. Jacques Derrida, *De l'esprit* (Paris: Galilée, 1987), p. 17.
7. Walter Benjamin, *Gesammelte Schriften*, Bd IV, 1 (Frankfurt: Suhrkamp, 1980), p. 12.
8. Friedrich Hölderlin, *Sämtliche Werke*, Bd. V (Stuttgart: Kohlhammer, 1982), p. 266.
9. Friedrich Hölderlin, "Bemerkungen zu Oedipus," in *Sämtliche Werke*, Bd. V, ed. Beissner (Stuttgart: Kohlhammer, 1982), p. 196.
10. Benjamin, op. cit., p. 18.
11. Among the several such comments Heidegger made on this move from Greek to Latin, see *Der Satz vom Grund* (Pfullingen: Neske Verlag, 1957), p. 164, and *Einführung in die Metaphysik* (Tübingen: Niemeyer, 1966), pp. 10–11.
12. Martin Heidegger, *Was Heisst Denken?* (Tübingen: Niemeyer Verlag, 1971), p. 51.
13. Elias Canetti, *The Tongue Set Free*, trans. J. Neugroschel (New York: Continuum, 1979), p. 1.

14. Friedrich Hölderlin, "Das Höchste" quoted in HH, 62.
15. G. W. F. Hegel, *Philosophie der Geschichte* (Frankfurt: Suhrkamp Verlag, 1970), p. 14.

CHAPTER FOUR

1. This is said pointedly by Anne Michaels in *Fugitive Pieces* (New York: Knopf, 1996), p. 21: "Athos didn't want me to forget. He made me review my Hebrew alphabet. He said the same thing everyday: 'It is your future you are remembering.'"
2. In saying this, I am taking issue with Aristotle's claim that "the difference between poetry and history is that the former relates things that have happened, the latter things that may happen. For this reason poetry is more philosophical and more serious than history" (*Poetics*, 51b6ff). I would suggest instead that poetry and history are similar occupations, and, as the practice of poetry in Greece demonstrated, very much in the service of one another—both are, at bottom, fundamentally concerned with the moral enigma of finite life. On the notion that the full meaning of time is only to be understood morally, see Kant's "Das Ende aller Dinge" in *Werke*, Bd. VII (Berlin: de Gruyter, 1968), pp. 327–339.
3. G. W. F. Hegel, *Vorlesung über die Philosophie der Geschichte* (Frankfurt: Suhrkamp Verlag, 1978), p. 38.
4. Ibid., p. 73.
5. Hans-Georg Gadamer, *Wahrheit und Methode* (Tübingen: Siebeck, 1990), p. 305ff.
6. Sophocles, "Oedipus at Colonus," in *The Three Theban Plays*, trans. Robert Fagles (New York: Penguin Books, 1984), lines 608–610.
7. On the specifics of the muses, see the entry in *Der Kleine Pauly: Lexikon der Antike*, ed. K. Ziegler and W. Sontheimer (München: DTV, 1979). Of note is the legend that has Hyacinth, who comes into being and rules only for a single season, as the child of the muse of history. See also the discussion of the various muses and their relation to "sung speech" in Marcel Detienne, *The Master of Truth in Archaic Greece*, trans. J. Lloyd (Cambridge: Zone Books, 1996), pp. 40–52.
8. Nicole Loraux, *The Invention of Athens: The Funeral Oration in the Classical City*, trans. A. Sheridan (Cambridge: Harvard University Press, 1986), p. 3.
9. On the differences between the representation of the invisible in literature and in art, as well as the problem of the representation of identities among the dead (who have no body), see Emily Vermeule, *Aspects of Death in Early Greek Art and Poetry* (Berkeley: University of California Press, 1979), esp. pp. 1–41.
10. Of course the literature of such journeys is quite large in antiquity and after, and ranges from what one finds in Dante's *Divine Comedy* to Valery's *Eupalinos*.
11. This same ambiguity frequently represented on the grave stele where one might find images of the living and the dead shaking hands and thus indicating a sort of unity or connection between them, while one equally finds images of the living and the dead simply not able to even see one another. On this see *The Greek Miracle: Classical Sculpture from the Dawn of Democracy*, ed. Diana Buiton-Oliver (Washington: National Gallery of Art, 1993), esp. images number 32 and 34.
12. On the figure of Tireseus, see my "What we didn't see," in *The Silverman Lectures* (Pittsburgh: Dusquense University Press, 1995), pp. 39–53, or modified in

The Presocratics after Heidegger, ed. David Jacobs (Albany: State University of New York Press, 1999). The image of blindness is so central to the Greek poetic imagination and its conception of the relation of the poetic to the just that it was necessary for the Greeks to think of their preeminent poet, Homer, as blind. We do not even know if there was an individual poet named Homer, but we do know that all the images of Homer, whose name *Homeros* is also the nickname for those who were blind and hostage to that blindness, represent him as blind.

13. Homer, *The Odyssey*, trans. R. Fagles (New York: Viking, 1996), line 235.

14. Ibid., line 237.

15. Hölderlin, op. cit., 268.

16. Among the most powerful expressions of this is the remark made by Achilles in Hades that "I would rather by on the soil, a serf to another, to a man without lot whose means of life are not great, than rule over all the dead who have perished" (lines 489–491). It is a remark for which Plato condemns Homer in *Republic*, Book III.

17. Vermeule, op. cit., 29. It is worth noting that while the living do not seem to exert any pressures on the dead or their world, the dead are a central preoccupation for the living. The dispute that drives *Antigone* turns on this question of the relation of the living and the dead.

18. G. W. F. Hegel, op. cit., p. 35.

19. Ibid., p. 38.

20. Ibid., p. 103.

21. See the chapter "Observing Reason" and the nature of the organic bodies in the *Phaenomenologie des Geistes*, Hegel, op. cit., pp. 183–254.

22. G. W. F. Hegel, *Phaenomenologie des Geistes* (Hamburg: Meiner Verlag, 1952), p. 29.

23. Ibid., 148.

24. See my *The Ubiquity of the Finite* (Cambridge: MIT Press, 1988), pp. 85–89, for a fuller treatment of the question of death for Hegel.

25. See my "Why I am so happy" in *Research in Phenomenology*, Vol. XXIV, 1994, 3–14.

26. Hegel, op. cit., p. 12.

27. Ibid., p. 98.

28. Ibid., p. 74.

29. Here Gadamer, who otherwise owes much to Hegel, might stand apart. His unwillingness to highlight the notion of the "end" of metaphysics or the idea of "post"-modernity, an unwillingness to grant any sort of privilege to the present age that would set it apart, means that his is able to read history much more as a matter of episodes that move without any necessary destination. No "crisis" of history defines the present age and thereby the history that might be said to produce such a crisis.

30. Hegel, op. cit., 15.

31. One sees this, for instance, working in section 74 of *Being and Time* where the notion of "generation" needs to be understood as marking the site of a conflict in history.

32. This issue forms the central concern of Lacoue-Labarthe's *La fiction du politique* (Paris: Christian Bourgois Editieur, 1987). Reiner Schürmann made this point in several of his works as well. On this, see my "Changing the Subject: Heidegger 'the' National and Epochal" in *Graduate Faculty Philosophy Journal*, Vol. 14, No. 2–Vol. 15, No. 1, 1991, 441–464.

33. "Für Kreon oder für Antigone: Der slowenishce PEN tagt," *Frankfurter Allgemeine Zeitung*, 28 Mai 1996, Nr. 122, p. 35. Or "Ancient Passions that Illuminate Today's Tragedies," *New York Times*, November 29. 1998.

34. On this, see my "Can Law Survive?" in *The University of Toledo Law Review*, Vol. 2, Nr. 1, Fall 1994, pp. 147–158.

35. See my "Lyrical and Ethical Subjects: The Ordeal of the Foreign and the Enigma of One's Own" in *Philosophy Today*, Vol. 40:1, Spring 1996, 188–196.

36. Celan is the one very notable exception to this. See his Bremen Lecture in Paul Celan, *Gesammelte Werke*, Bd. III (Frankfurt: Suhrkamp Verlag, 1983). On the relation of history and the poem, see "Catastrophe," P. Lacoue-Labarthe and "The Realities at Stake in the Poem," C. Fynsk in *Word Traces* (Baltimore: John Hopkins University Press, 1994).

37. Hölderlin, op. cit., Bd. II 374.

38. Ibid., Bd. I, 621.

39. Walter Benjamin, "Über den Begriff der Geschichte," in *Gesammelte Schriften*, Bd. I, 2 (Frankfurt: Suhrkamp, 1980), pp. 697–698.

40. Ibid., p. 697.

41. Martin Heidegger, *Die Selbstbehauptung der deutschen Universität* (Frankfurt: Klostermann, 1983), p. 19. The line in Greek is *"ta megala panta episthale"* at *Republic*, 497d,9.

42. Benjamin, op. cit., p. 698

CHAPTER FIVE

1. Martin Heidegger, *Der Satz vom Grund* (Pfullingen: Neske Verlag, 1978), pp. 146–147, henceforth abbreviated as SG. Other works by Heidegger cited in the body of this text are abbreviated as follows: US = *Unterwegs zur Sprache* (Pfullingen: Neske, 1975): H = *Holzwege* (Klostermann: Frankfurt, 1972). Works by Nietzsche cited in the body of the text are abbreviated as follows: GD = "Götzen-Dämmerung" in *Werke* III, ed. Karl Sclechta (Frankfurt: Ullstein Verlag, 1976); Z = "Also Sprach Zarathustra" in *Werke* II; GT = "Geburt der Tragödie" in *Werke* I: FW = "Die Fröhliche Wissenschaft" in *Werke* II; SM = "Sprache und Music" in *Nietzsche Werke: Fragmente aus 1869–1871* Bd. II; W = "Words and Music" a translation of "Sprache und Musik," in *The Complete Works of Friedrich Nietzsche*, ed. O. Levy, trans. M. Mügge, Vol II (New York: Macmillan, 1924), pp. 29–47. The English translation contains five pages not found in the *Werke* edition.

2. G. W. F. Hegel, *Phänomenologie des Geistes* (Hamburg: Meiner, 1952), p. 163.

3. Michel Foucault, *The Thought from the Outside*, trans. B. Massumi (Cambridge: MIT Press, 1987), p. 13.

4. Ibid., p. 25.

5. Hans-Georg Gadamer, *Wahrheit und Methode* (Tübingen: J. C. B. Mohr, 1965), p. 450.

6. Besides a few passing references to Beethoven's late quartets and a special remark dedicated to Mozart (that makes no reference to any musical work in particular) on the two hundredth anniversary of his birth (SG, 117–118), one finds, so far as I know, only a very short letter in which Heidegger refers to Stravinsky's "Symphonie of Psalms" and "Persephone" (D, 113).

7. G. Steiner, *Real Presences: Is there anything 'in' what we say?* (London: Faber and Faber, 1989), p. 19.

8. Philippe Lacoue-Labarthe, "The Echo of the Subject," trans. B. Harlow, in *Typography*, ed. C. Fynsk (Cambridge: Harvard University Press, 1989), p. 145. On the relation of sight and speculation in the formation of the metaphysical tradition, see Hans-Georg Gadamer, *Wahrheit und Methode* (Tübingen: J. C. B. Mohr, 1975), pp. 432–449. For a clear statement of the Greek privileging of sight, see Aristotle, *De sensu*, 473a3, and *Metaphysics*, 980b23–25; on music, see *Politics*, 1339a14ff.

9. G. Bruns, *Heidegger's Estrangements* (New Haven: Yale University Press, 1989), p. xv.

10. This is the case in two very different, yet equally influential, recent readings of Nietzsche: M. Blanchot's "L'expérience-limite" in *L'entretien infini* (Paris: Gallimard, 1969), and A. Nehamas's *Nietzsche: Life as Literature* (Princeton: Princeton University Press, 1987). There are, of course, exceptions. Besides the Lacoue-Labarthe piece already cited, see, for instance, M.A. Gillespie, "Nietzsche's Musical Politics" in *Nietzsche's New Seas*, ed. Gillespie and Strong (Chicago: University of Chicago Press, 1988), pp. 117–149.

11. On the figure of "woman" in Nietzsche's work, see David Krell, *Postponements* (Indianapolis: Indiana University Press, 1986), and Drucilla Cornell, "Disastrologies" in *Praxis International*, 9:1/2 April & July 1989, pp. 183–191. On the relation of women and music, see Eva Rieger, "Dolce semplice"? in *Feminist Aesthetics*, ed. G. Ecker (Boston: Beacon Press, 1985), pp. 135–149.

12. See also the same remark in the letter to Köselitz dated March 21, 1888.

13. Friedrich Hölderlin, "Brot und Wein" in *Sämtliche Werke*, Bd. 6, ed. D. E. Satler (Darmstadt: Luchterhand, 1979), p. 102.

14. E. Bloch, *Prinzip Hoffnung*, III (Frankfurt: Suhrkamp, 1973), p. 1243.

15. Nietzsche, *Die fröhliche Wissenschaft*, p. 13.

16. Nietzsche, *Die Wille zur Macht*, #822.

17. See "Über den Fetischcharakter in der Musik und die Regression des Hörens" in *Dissonanzen: Musik in der verwalteten Welt* (Göttingen: Vandenhoeck & Ruprecht, 1972), pp. 9–45. Also interesting in this context is Adorno's "Musik, Sprache und ihr Verhältnis im gegenwärtigen Komponieren" in *Schriften* Bd. 16 (Frankfurt, Suhrkamp Verlag, 1978), pp. 649–664.

18. Jacques Attali, *Noise: The Political Economy of Music*, trans. Brian Massumi (Minneapolis: University of Minnesota Press, 1985), p. 51.

19. See esp. *Republic*, 398ff. Full discussion of the political place of music for Plato would need to address the relation that he, like Nietzsche, claims that music bears to both mourning and woman.

20. See, for instance, his *Politics*, 1340a 18–19.

21. Adorno, "Fetischcharakter," p. 31.

22. Edison patented his phonograph in December 1877, the year after Nietzsche published his *Richard Wagner in Bayreuth*.

23. W. Benjamin, "Das Kunstwerk im Zeitalter seiner technischen Reproduzierbarkeit," *Gesammelte Schriften*, I, 2 (Frankfurt: Suhrkamp, 1974), p. 474.

24. Ibid., p. 477.

25. Bloch, *Prinzip*, p. 1246.

26. See Igor Stravinsky's criticisms of "mechanically reproduced music" in his *Poetics of Music*, trans. A. Knodel and I. Dahl (Cambridge: Harvard University Press, 1942), esp. pp. 134–135.

27. See Theodor Reik, *The Haunting Melody* (New York: Farrar, Straus, 1953), p. 250.

28. Martin Heidegger, *Nietzsche*, Bd. I (Pfullingen: Neske Verlag, 1961), p. 119. The passage, full of echoes and puns, resists translation, but means "we live insofar as we [are a] body."

29. Attali, op. cit., p. 143.

30. Lacoue-Labarthe, "Echo," p. 193.

31. For a more extended treatment of these issues in Heidegger, see my "Changing the Subject: Heidegger, 'the' Epochal, and National" in *Graduate Faculty Journal of the New School*, "History and Catastrophe" in *Heidegger: Toward the Turn*, ed. J. Risser (Albany: State University of New York Press), and "Ruins and Roses: Hegel and Heidegger on Sacrifice, Memory and Mourning" in *Endings*, ed. R. Comay and J. McCumber (Evanston: Northwestern University Press).

32. Friedrich Hölderlin, *Sämtliche Werke*, ed. F. Beissner (Stuttgart: Kohlhammer, 1943), Bd. IV, p. 282.

33. See *US*, p. 65ff.

34. Martin Heidegger, *Was heisst Denken?*, p. 20

CHAPTER SIX

1. Cf. Kant, *Grundlegung*, AK, 408. It is this paradox of exemplarity that leads Kant to the final description of human moral being as simultaneously exposing each individual as sovereign and subject, and to the peculiar concept of autonomy that is proper to such individuals.

2. Hegel, *Phaenomenologie des Geistes*, paragraph 110.

3. Ibid., paragraph 807.

4. Cf. Kant, *Kritik der Urteilskraft*, AK, 219.

5. Though, as Gadamer rightly notes, this does not mean that aesthetic experience is to be understood in an abstract opposition with conceptual knowing. Cf. his *Gesammelte Werke*, Bd. 8, 192.

6. Ibid., pp. 122–130.

7. Cf. Kant, *Anthropologie*, paragraph 38.

8. But the case is quite clear: the beauty of nature is superior to the beauty of works of art. Cf. for instance Kant, *Kritik der Urteilskraft*, AK, 299–300. It is worth noting that this exclusion of the question of nature seems to begin already in Hegel for whom the beauty of nature is manifestly inferior to that found in artwork. Adorno is right when he says that, since Hegel, natural beauty has been illegitimately dropped from the agenda of aesthetics since Kant; cf. his *Aesthetische Theorie*, chapter 5, where he makes some gestures toward remedying this problem. Here Gadamer's otherwise remarkably sensitive reading of Kant, especially in *Truth and Method*, must be included in this problem.

9. Curiously, Kant himself does not do this. In fact, the example he gives of a symbol—the peppermill and the despot—really qualifies more as allegory than as symbol. The truly symbolic is much more akin to what Aristotle means by metaphor in the *Poetics*. On this, see my "Stereoscopic Thinking and the Law of Resemblances," in *American Continental Philosophy* (Bloomington: Indiana University Press, 2000). See also, J.-F. Courtine, *Extase de la Raison* (Paris: Galilée, 1990), pp. 45–68.

10. The question of freedom appears only briefly in *Truth and Method* and then chiefly in the context of the theme of universal history, not as a problem of moral life.

11. See the epigram to this chapter.

12. On this, see especially Gadamer's treatment of the "logic of question and answer" in *Truth and Method*, pp. 375–386.

13. See the epigram to this chapter.

14. This is the point at which the need for free speech is to be thought.

15. Schelling, *Philosophische Untersuchungen über das Wesen der menschlichen Freiheit*, p. 351.

CHAPTER SEVEN

1. Paul Celan, "Sprachgitter," in *Paul Celan: Gesammelte Werke*, Bd. I (Frankfurt: Suhrkamp Verlag, 1986), p. 167. All further citations from Celan's work have been taken from the three volumes of that edition. In subsequent citations, the bibliographical data will be given following the citation with (first) the Roman numeral referring to the volume number and the (second) Arabic number referring to the page number in that volume. The translations here are my own; however, I have consulted translations by Michael Hamburger [*Poems of Paul Celan* (New York: Persea Books, 1988)], Katherine Washburn and Margret Guillemin [*Paul Celan: Last Poems* (San Francisco, North Point Press, 1986)], and Rosmarie Waldrop [*Paul Celan: Collected Prose* (Manchester, Carcanet Press,1986)].

2. Maurice Blanchot, *The Writing of Disaster*, trans. A. Smock (Lincoln: University of Nebraska Press, 1986), p. 57.

3. See, for instance, M. Heidegger, *Unterwegs zur Sprache* (Pfullingen: Neske Verlag, 1975), pp. 52–76. Henceforth this text will be cited as *US* followed by the page number.

4. George Steiner spoke eloquently of the problem facing those writing in German after the Holocaust when he writes:

> Let us keep one fact clearly in mind: the German language was not innocent of the horrors of Naziism. It is not merely that a Hitler, a Goebbels, and a Himmler happened to speak German. Naziism found in the language precisely what it needed to give voice to its savagery. . . . A language in which one can write a "Horst Wessel Lied" is ready to give hell a native tongue. How should the word "spritzen" recover a sane meaning after having signified to millions the "spurting" of Jewish blood from knife points?). . . . That is what happened under the Reich: not silence or evasion, but an immense outpouring of precise, serviceable words . . . words were committed to saying things that no human mouth should ever have said and no paper made by man should ever have been inscribed with. . . . Languages have great reserves of life. . . . But there comes a breaking point [*Language and Silence* (New York, Atheneum, 1967), pp. 121–124].

5. Bitter almond is the smell associated with gold cyanide. See, for instance, the associations of "bitter almond" with death, the association for Celan as well, in Gabriel Garcia-Marquez's *Love in the Time of Cholera*.

6. Georges Bataille, *Visions of Excess*, trans. A. Stoekl (Minneapolis: University of Minnesota Press, 1985), p. 13.

7. Peter Szondi, "Lecture de Strette: Essai sur la poésie de Paul Celan," in *Critique*, Vol. 27, No. 288, 1971, p. 388.

8. This is the point at which one might begin to discuss Celan's language in terms of the sublime. See, for instance, Kant's *Kritik der Urteilskraft* AK, 271 where Kant remarks that the sublime "only reveals itself aesthetically through sacrifice." For an interesting discussion of thinking as sacrifice, a discussion that lead to remarks on language in the poem, see Heidegger's "Nachwort zu: 'Was ist Metaphysik?' " in *Wegmarken* (Klostermann: Frankfurt, 1978), pp. 307–309.

9. Here one finds a special resonance with the first words of Canetti's autobiography, *The Tongue Set Free*, trans. J. Neugroschel (New York: Seabury, 1979), p. 3.

10. Adorno defines the living relevance of philosophy with much the same sensibility when he begins *Negative Dialektik* (Frankfurt: Suhrkamp, 1977), p. 15, with the remark that "philosophy, which once seemed to be overcome, remains alive because the moment of its realization was passed by." Likewise, in the epilogue of "Origin of the Ar Work," Heidegger defines the situation of art in terms of its own destination in what Hegel defined as its death.

11. One regard in which the body extends itself in a manner that is to be thought through the relation of language and the body is suggested by Osip Mandelstam who writes that "the *Inferno* and especially the *Purgatorio* glorify the human gait, the measure and rhythm of walking, the foot and its shape. The step, linked to breathing and saturated with thought: this Dante understands as the beginning of prosody." Quoted in Bruce Chatwin, *Songlines* (New York: Viking, 1987), p. 230. For a fascinating set of reflections on the relation of language and land, one should consult *Songlines* and its discussion of the meaning of Aboriginal "songlines." See also *US*, 235 where Heidegger speaks of "step," "call," and "breath" in the poem, ultimately leading him to say that "step [. . .] and call and breath hover around the rule of the word."

12. See Katharine Washburn's introduction to her translation of *Paul Celan: Last Poems* where she cites Celan's inscription (presented to Michael Hamburger) saying that he was "ganz und gar nicht hermetish" (p. vi).

13. See, for instance, Hans-Georg Gadamer, "Celans Schlussgedicht," in *Argumentum e Silentio*, ed. A. D. Colin (Berlin: Walter de Gruyter, 1987), p. 60. For a detailed reading of Celan's "Atemkristall," see Gadamer's *Wer bin Ich und wer bist Du?* (Frankfurt: Suhrkamp, 1976). There are many remarks in that reading that would be worth careful attention; in particular, see the comments on "readiness for death" in the poem (17) and those on the "wound" and "pain" of reading (78).

14. Compare, for instance, Heraclitus, Fr. 51: "how a thing agrees at variance with itself; it is an attunement turning back on itself."

15. Such stretching of language beyond itself is equally the effort of the translator. One should not neglect Celan's work as a translator, but regard it as a practice belonging to his poetic practice. For a discussion of the intersection of poetry and translation, see my "Hermeneutics and the Poetic Motion" in *Translation Perspectives*, Vol. V, 1990, pp. 5–18.

16. G. W. F. Hegel, *Philosophie der Geschichte* (Frankfurt: Suhrkamp, 1970), p. 12.

17. Here one would do well to compare Freud's comment that all works of art bear a "date-stamp" as the enduring trace of memory in all poetic practice and as raising the question of the repetition at work in all art. See S. Freud, *Collected Papers*, Vol. 4 (New York: Basic Books, 1977), p. 177.

18. J. Derrida, *Schibboleth: pour Paul Celan* (Paris: Galilée, 1986), p. 87.

19. See, for instance, G. Vattimo, "The Shattering of the Poetic Word," in *The End of Modernity* (Cambridge: Polity Press, 1988), pp. 65–78.

20. W. Benjamin, "Über den Begriff der Geschichte," in *Gesammelte Schriften* Bd. I.2 (Frankfurt: Suhrkamp, 1980), p. 701. See also my "Heidegger and the Greeks / History and Catastrophe," in *Heidegger Toward the Turn: Essays on Texts of the 1930's*, ed. J. Risser (Albany: State University of New York Press).

21. Cited in O. Pöggler, *Spur des Worts* (Freiburg: Alber Verlag, 1986), p. 250. For discussions about the two meetings between Heidegger and Celan, see pp. 259–271. See also G. Baumann, *Erinnerung an Paul Celan* (Frankfurt: Suhrkamp, 1986), p. 65–70.

22. I suspect that Celan would have understood the deeply perplexing comment made on the eve of the war by a now forgotten poet: "it is all over now, if I were really a poet I could have prevented the war." Quoted in E. Canetti, *Der Beruf des Dichters* (München: Hanser Verlag, 1976), p. 5.

23. A. D. Colin, "Celan's Poetics of Destruction," in Colin, op. cit., p. 167.

24. Jünger's essay is, of course, "Über die Linie," in *Sämtliche Werke* Bd. 7, Essays I (Stuttgart: Klett-Cotta, 1980), pp. 239–280. Heidegger's text was retitled and published as "Zur Seinsfrage," in *Wegmarken* (Frankfurt: Klostermann, 1978), pp. 379–419. Also relevant is Jünger's "Über den Schmerz," in *Sämtliche Werke* Bd. 7, Essays I, pp. 145–191.

25. Martin Heidegger, *Beiträge zur Philosophie (Vom Ereignis)* (Frankfurt: Klostermann, 1989), p. 510. Of course, the full sense of silence in Celan is related to many other specific concerns not present in Heidegger. See, for instance, S. Wolosky, "Mystical Language and Mystical Silence in Paul Celan's 'Dein Hinübersein'," in Colin, op. cit.

26. Theodore Adorno, *Aesthetic Theory*, trans. C. Lenhart (London: Routledge & Kegan Paul, 1984), p. 444.

27. This relation of voice and body is also felt as the curious alienation from one's own voice when one is speaking a "foreign" language. Nowhere else is the alien element of another language felt as palpably as in the voice of the speaker.

28. This is the point from which one can understand the full significance of Heidegger's remark that "anxiety robs us of words" [*Wegmarken* (Frankfurt: Klostermann, 1972), p. 111.]

29. Elaine Scarry, *The Body in Pain* (New York: Oxford University Press, 1985), p. 33. One of the many interesting aspects of the reflections on the relation of language and pain in this book is the one that leads Scarry to describe a torturer as "a colossal voice" and the victim of torture as "a colossal body." Those remarks lead to further insight about the relation of voice and power.

30. The discussion of "blue" in Heidegger's text on Trakl ("Die Sprache im Gedicht") needs to be called into question. Here it would be helpful to refer to Gottfried Benn's remarks on "blue" in "Probleme der Lyrik," in *Gottfried Benn: Gesammelte Werke* I (Stuttgart: Klett-Cotta, 1977), p. 504 and p. 512. One of the curious features of both Heidegger's and Benn's very curious remarks on "blue" is that at some point both give lists of colors and then proceed to attach "meanings" to those colors, both include blue on that list, and both omit only blue from the subsequent list of determinate meanings (see *US*, 74–75; Benn, 504). I am indebted to Werner Hammacker for the reference to Benn.

31. One sees the extent to which this effort goes in Heidegger's remark that "only a being that speaks, i.e. thinks, can have a hand" [*Was Heisst Denken?* (Tübingen: Niemeyer Verlag, 1971), p. 51.].
32. The phrase is Yeats in "The Mother of God," in *The Collected Poems of W. B. Yeats* (New York: Macmillan, 1979), p. 244.
33. Kant, *Kritik der Urteilskraft*, AK, 277.
34. M. Heidegger, *Hölderlins Hymnen: 'Germanien' und 'Der Rhein'* (Frankfurt: Klostermann, 1980), p. 87.
35. Derrida, op. cit., p. 83.
36. Paul Valéry, *Cahiers* (Paris: Pleiade, 1973), Vol. I, p. 1126. Quoted in Jean Starobinski, "Monsieur Teste Confronting Pain," in *Fragments for a History of the Human Body*, Part II, ed. M. Feher (Cambridge: MIT Press, 1989), p. 371.
37. Freidrich Hölderlin, "Im Walde," in *Hymns and Fragments by Friedrich Hölderlin*, trans. R. Sieburth (Princeton: Princeton University Press, 1984), p. 226.

CHAPTER EIGHT

1. Ludwig Wittgenstein, "Lecture on Ethics," *Philosophical Review*, 74 (1965): 11.
2. Hans-Georg Gadamer, *Gesammelte Werke*, Bd. 8, p. 258.
3. Martin Heidegger, *Gesamtausgabe*, Bd. 54, p. 125.
4. Hans-Georg Gadamer, *Gesammelte Werke*, Bd. 1, p. 423.
5. Plato, *Phaedrus*, 247D.
6. Martin Heidegger, *Unterwegs zur Sprache* (Pfullingen: Neske, 1972), p. 203.
7. Gadamer, GW, Bd. 8, 278.
8. Plato, *Cratylus*, 422e–423.

CHAPTER NINE

1. Hegel, *Phänomenologie des Geistes*, paragraph 8.
2. Adorno, *Negative Dialektik*, p. 15.
3. E. Levinas, *Totalité et Infini*, p. 13.
4. Schelling, *Briefe über Dogmatismus und Kritisimus*, p. 336.
5. Kant, *Reflexionen*, 1820A.
6. Hölderlin, *Der Grund des Empedocles*, IV, 154.
7. Roberto Calasso, *The Marriage of Cadmus and Harmony* (New York: Vintage, 1993), 279–280.
8. Adorno, *Aesthetische Theorie*, p. 97.
9. Salman Rushdie, *The Ground Beneath Her Feet*, pp. 465–466.
10. Hegel, *Aesthetics*, p. 43.

CHAPTER TEN

1. Hans-Georg Gadamer, *Wahrheit und Methode* (Tübingen: J. C. B. Mohr, 1960), p. 450.
2. Plato, "Cratylus," 427D, trans. Jowett, in *Collected Dialogues*, ed. Hamilton and Cairns (Princeton: Princeton University Press, 1961).

3. Hans-Georg Gadamer, *Das Erbe Hegels* (Frankfurt: Suhrkamp Verlag, 1979), pp. 90–91.
4. Ibid., p. 91.
5. Martin Heidegger, *Gesamtausgabe*, Bd. 53, pp. 79ff.
6. Ibid., p. 76.
7. Hans-Georg Gadamer, "Text und Interpretation," in *Gesammelte Werke*, Bd 2, p. 334.
8. "Kultur und das Wort," in *Lob der Theorie* (Frankfurt: Suhrkamp, 1983), p. 23.
9. Martin Heidegger, *Unterwegs zur Sprache* (Pfullingen: Neske Verlag, 1975), p. 37.
10. Hans-Georg Gadamer, "Unterwegs zur Schrift," in *Gesammelte Werke*, Bd. VII (Tubingen: J. C. B. Mohr, 1991), p. 258.
11. Ibid., pp. 261–262.
12. Hans-Georg Gadamer, *Wahrheit und Methode* (Tübingen: J. C. B. Mohr, 1960), p. 156.
13. Hans-Georg Gadamer, "Writing and the Living Voice," in *Applied Hermeneutics*, ed Misgeld and Nicholson (Albany: State University of New York Press, 1992), p. 66.
14. Ibid., p. 65.
15. Hans-Georg Gadamer, "Hermeneutics and Logocentrism," trans. Palmer & Michelfelder, in *Dialogue and Deconstruction* (Albany: State University of New York Press, 1989), p. 124.
16. Walter Benjamin, "Ursprung des deutschen Trauerspiels," in *Gesammelte Schriften*, Bd. I, 1, p. 384.
17. *WM*, p. 391.
18. Ibid., p. 393–394.
19. So far as I have been able to discover, among the 5053 languages that are said to be in existence today, all possess the possibility of being written.
20. See especially *Theatetus*, 203A–204A in which the question of the whole and parts is illustrated by means of a discussion of the relation between letters forming a syllable. There Theatetus points out that consonants are "not articulate sound" and "inexplicable," while vowels are "a sound" but no account can be given of them either (203B). One curious point is how frequently Plato links the discussion of writing with Egpyt. That is the case in the *Phaedrus*, *Timaeus*, and *Philebus*.
21. See, for instance, *Phaedrus* 274D, 276C, *Charmides* 159C, 160A, *Protagoras* 326C, *Laws* VII.809E, *Philebus* 18B, *Theatetus* 203B. Reference to the letters of the alphabet even plays a role in a decisive move in the *Republic* when Socrates suggests that "I think we should employ the method of search that we should use if we, with not very keen vision, were bidden to read small letters from a distance, and then someone had observed that these same letters exist elsewhere larger and on a larger surface" (368D–E). Platonic dialogues also frequently employ an analogy between the general process of education, but especially education with regard to laws, and the specific process of learning to form the letters of an alphabet. (Foucault makes a similar point when discussing the pervasive nature of discipline when he discusses the process whereby handwriting is taught in the schools. See Michel Foucault, *Discipline and Punish*, trans. Sheridan (New York: Random House, 1979), p. 152. The general point is simply to note that Plato is indeed fascinated by the Greek alphabet. It was,

as scholars have noted, a remarkable invention, since "The Greek sign, and this for the first time in the history of writing, stands for an abstraction, the isolated consonant" (K. Robb, "Poetic Sources of the Greek Alphabet," in *Communication Arts in the Ancient World*, ed. Havelock and Hershbell, 1978, p. 31).

A point about the Greek alphabet worth further reflection is just how it became the basis or the Greek way of writing numbers. On this, see also my "On Counting, Music, and the Stars," in *The New Yearbook for Phenomenology and Phenomenological Philosophy*, III, 3, 179–191.

22. G. W. F. Hegel, *Phänomenologie des Geistes* (Hamburg: Meiner Verlag, 1952), paragraphs 315/316.

23. Martin Heidegger, *Was Heisst Denken?* (Tübingen: Niemeyer Verlag, 1971), p. 51.

24. Martin Heidegger, GA, Bd., 54, p. 119.

25. Martin Heidegger, GA, Bd. 54, p. 125.

26. Ibid., p. 125. I should note that the passage that I omitted from the citation refers to the substitution of the typewriter for the pen ("und wenn das Schreiben der Maschine übertragen ist"). Much of Heidegger's concern in his remarks about script is guided by the effort to exhibit the "'metaphysical' essence of technicity" (p. 127) via a discussion of the way in which the typewriter "conceals the essence of writing and script" (p. 126), thereby "accelerating the destruction of words" (p. 129). The question of the technics of writing is not insignificant here. A fuller treatment of that question would need to pay attention to the fact the pen was a radical innovation of Greek writers introduced for use on papyrus. While Egyptians wrote with the stem of a rush cut on a slant to form a brush that painted words, the Greeks devised a pen out of the stiff hollow reed called *kalamos*, which was sharpened to a point that produced a fine line. See E. G.Turner, *Athenian Books in the Fifth and Fourth Centuries B.C.* (London: H. R. Lewis, 1952), p. 11; also A. Carson, *Eros: The Bittersweet* (Princeton: Princeton University Press,1986), pp. 58–60.

27. GA, Bd., 54, p. 124.

28. Op. cit., p. 119.

29. Op. cit., p. 125.

30. As does the way language spoken shapes the face in exercising its muscles.

31. Gadamer, *Wahrheit und Methode*, p. 395.

32. Gadamer, "Unterwegs zur Schrift," p. 261.

33. Ibid., p. 264.

34. Here one might also consider Merleau-Ponty's text "L'oeil et l'esprit," as well as Nietzsche's *Geburt der Tragödie*.

35. Heidegger, GA., Bd. 54, p. 125.

CHAPTER ELEVEN

1. For instance, see *Republic* 420c–421c, 500e–501c, 579b–598c, 603a–603b.

2. Cited in Plutarch, *Moralia* 346–347. On this kinship of painting and poetry, see also Aristotle, *Poetics* 47a, Horace, *Ars Poetica* 361–365, Longinus, *De sublimitate* 17.20, Augustine, *In Ioannis Evangelium* 24.2.

3. On this, see Jacques Taminiaux's *Poetics, Speculation, and Judgment* (Albany: State University of New York Press, 1993), pp. 171–185, and David Michael Levin's *The Philosopher's Gaze* (Berkeley: University of California Press, 1999), Michel

Haar, *L'oeuvre d'art* (Paris: Hatier, 1994), and Véronique Fóti, *Visions Invisibles* (Albany: State University of New York Press, 2003).

4. Martin Heidegger, "Bemerkungen zu Kunst-Plastik-Raum," p. 8.

5. Obviously, the return of art to the service of the divine in the Christian era signals a retreat of art from this set of possibilities. Significantly, Hegel's analysis of art in the *Phenomenology of Spirit* regards art as housed in the framework of religious consciousness. On this, see my "Why is Spirit such a slow learner?" in *Research in Phenomenology*, 2001.

6. But Hegel also argues that this path on which art enters into its proper nature is not completed in the Greek world, but must wait until the period of Romantic art. That is because "the true content of romantic art is absolute inwardness... [and] in this pantheon all the gods are dethroned." See, Hegel, *Aesthetics*, Vol. 1, p. 519.

7. Pliny, *Natural History*, 35.29. Cited in Carson, *Economy of the Unlost*, p. 47.

8. For a more detailed discussion of this set of issues in Aristotle, see my *On Germans and Other Greeks*, chapter 2.

9. On this, see John Sallis, *The Force of Imagination* (Bloomington: Indiana University Press, 2000) and *Shades* (Bloomington: Indiana University Press, 1998).

10. Martin Heidegger, *Nietzsche* (Pfullingen: Neske Verlag, 1962), p. 119.

11. Friedrich Nietzsche, *Geburt der Tragödie*, p. 20. For an excellent discussion of this, see John Sallis, *Crossings* (Chicago: University of Chicago Press, 1991).

12. See *Republic* Book X where he complains that tragedy feeds the soul a diet of "threnody."

13. Curiously, in the text—Book II line 780 of the Greek—Pope will translate this passage differently in order, I believe, to fit the meter of the surrounding lines. And so he will translate in the text as: "Now, like a deluge, covering all ground, the shining armies sweep along the ground; swift as a flood of fire, when storms arise, it floats the wide field, and blazes to the skies."

14. Runciman, *The Origin of Painting* (1771), cited in Derrida, *Memoirs of the Blind* (Chicago: University of Chicago Press, 1993), p. 49.

15. That ruins are the proper metaphor for memory is something that Benjamin knew well and spoke to in his reference to Klee's painting *Angelus Novus* in "The Theses on the Concept of History."

16. Homer, *Iliad*, translation by Fagles, Book V, lines 795–802.

17. Ibid., Book III, lines 349–452.

18. *Iliad*, Pope translation, Book XII, line 562.

19. See Ruth Padel, *In and Out of the Mind* (Princeton, Princeton University Press, 1992), p. 78.

20. *Iliad*, Book I, lines 1–2.

21. Ibid., p. 889 (Pope commentary).

22. Ibid., p. 896.

23. Gotthold Ephraim Lessing, *Laocoön: An Essay on the Limits of Painting and Poetry*, trans. Edward Allen McCormick (Baltimore: Johns Hopkins University Press, 1962), pp. 99–100.

24. Ibid., p. 99.

25. G. W. F. Hegel, *Phänomenologie des Geistes* (Frankfurt: Meiner Verlag, 1952), paragraph 110.

26. *Iliad*, Pope translation, Book 24, lines 1012–1016.

27. Ibid., Book XII, line 424.

28. Ibid., Book XI, line 900.
29. See Bernard Knox's introduction to Robert Fagles's translation of *Iliad*, p. 7ff. Pope held to the view that Homer was indeed a "writer." His preface begins with the words: "Homer is universally allow'd to have had the greatest invention of any writer."

CHAPTER TWELVE

1. I cannot verify this story, but do believe that it is credible both because it comes from a credible source whom I trust, but also because it fits well Heidegger's way of thinking through political events.
2. Martin Heidegger, *Beiträge zur Philosophie: Vom Ereignis* (Frankfurt: Klostermann Verlag, 1989). English translation by Emad and Maly, *Contributions to Philosophy (From Enowning)* (Bloomington: Indiana University Press, 1999). All future references to this work are cited in parentheses by the page number for the German edition followed by the page number for the English translation. Most of the translations here are my own. For some comments on how I believe this text might need to be read, as well as some concerns about the translation, see my "Strategies for a Possible Reading," in *Companion to Heidegger's "Contributions to Philosophy,"* ed. Scott, et al. (Bloomington: Indiana University Press, 2001).
3. R. M. Rilke, "The Archaic Torso of Apollo."
4. On this, see my *On Germans and Other Greeks*, chapter 6.
5. On this, see my "The Baby and the Bathwater: On Heidegger and Politics," in *Heidegger and Practical Philosophy*, ed. Raffoul and Pettigrew (Albany: State University of New York Press, 2002), pp. 159–172.
6. On this, see Robert Bernasconi, "The Double Face of the Political and the Social," in *Research in Phenomenology* 26, 1996, pp. 3–24.
7. Hannah Arendt, *The Human Condition* (Chicago: University of Chicago Press, 1998).
8. Heidegger, GA, Bd. 53, pp. 106–107.
9. See *Martin Heidegger–Elisabeth Blochmann: Briefwechsel 1918–1969*, ed. Joachim Storck (Marbach am Neckar: Deutsche Schillergesellschaft, 1989), pp. 48–49.
10. See my "Economies of Production," in *Crises in Continental Philosophy*, ed. Dallery and Scott (Albany: State University of New York Press, 1990), pp. 145–157.
11. Cf. Hobbes: "nature is the art" or Leibniz, *Monadology* where nature is likened to an "organic machine." Heidegger will find this such a pervasive tendency of modernity that he will even include Kant's third critique as an example of this tendency.
12. Nazi conceptions of race turned more on the idea of "blood" rather than "skin." The complicated notion of race—especially as it develops in Germany at this point—needs further attention. On this, see Bernasconi and Lott, eds., *The Idea of Race* (Indianapolis: Hackett Press, 2000).
13. This is the point at which the "decoding" of the human genome might need to be taken up and thought.
14. See Philippe Lacoue-Labarthe, *La fiction du politique* (Paris: Christian Bourgois, 1987).
15. On this, see Robert Bernasconi, "The Fate of the Distinction between *Praxis* and *Poiesis*," in *Heidegger Studies*, 2 (1987), pp. 111–139.
16. See Hannah Arendt, *Lectures on Kant's Political Philosophy* (Chicago: University of Chicago Press, 1982).
17. Heidegger, GA, Bd. 53, pp. 106–107.

INDEX

Achilles, 26, 154–58, 160, 198
Adorno, Theodor, 22, 29, 36, 54, 68, 69, 75, 98, 99, 118, 120, 128, 141, 151, 193, 196, 200, 203–5
Aeschylus, 196
Aesthetics, 11, 19, 64, 70, 150, 186, 193, 201
Aesthetic experience, 4, 7–9, 11, 13–15, 17, 59
Agamemnon, 155
Aletheia, 24, 185
Allegory, 15, 194
Alphabet, 106, 111, 135, 137, 197, 206
Antigone, 29, 41, 55, 125, 150, 189
Aphrodite, 125
Apollo, 11, 27, 147
Apollinian, 67
Arendt, Hannah, 21, 57, 58, 169, 183, 195, 209
Aristophanes, 15, 51
Aristotle, 17, 25, 26, 27, 55, 69, 80, 106, 108, 110, 120, 145, 146, 148–51, 176, 177, 185, 186, 193, 195, 200, 207, 208
Art, 9–14, 27–29, 35, 37, 55, 63, 67, 69, 94, 120–22, 127, 129, 142–60, 173, 176, 184–87, 193, 201, 203
Atali, Jacques, 68, 72, 200, 201
Audibility, 105, 107–12
Augustine, 109, 207
Auschwitz, 22, 31

Bakhtin, Mikhail, 30, 71
Bataille, Georges, 93, 202
Baudelaire, Charles, 74
Beauty, 7–15, 18, 70, 84, 85, 122, 126, 150, 186, 193, 201
Beethoven, Ludwig van, 63, 70, 199

Benjamin, Walter, 33, 39, 41, 44, 50, 52, 53, 56, 57, 58, 69, 70, 75, 96, 120, 136, 138, 143, 165, 193, 194, 196, 197, 200, 204, 206
Benn, Gottfried, 204
Bernasconi, Robert, 209
Birth, 54, 67, 186
Blanchot, Maurice, 63, 75, 92, 98, 200, 202
Blindness, 51, 67, 113, 167, 198
Bloch, Ernst, 67, 165, 200
Elizabeth Blochman, 131, 174
Blood, 51, 124, 158, 159, 181, 202, 209
Body, 34, 41, 52, 67, 70–75, 92, 94, 100, 101, 110, 125, 137, 186, 203, 204
Böhlendorf, Casimir, 56, 57
Borges, Jorge Luis, 23
Breath, 94, 99, 203
Bruns, G., 200

Caesura, 41, 57
Calasso, Roberto, 54, 128, 163, 205
Canetti, Elias, 22, 42, 195, 196, 203, 204
Carson, Anne, 194, 207, 208
Casandra, 151, 191
Catastrophe, 54, 56, 57, 92, 93, 201
Celan, Paul, 36, 44, 91–99, 101, 102, 164, 196, 199, 202, 203
Community, 1, 19, 21, 27, 29, 30, 35, 59, 68, 69, 72, 150, 151, 163, 164, 167, 168, 170, 188–90
Concept, 4, 8, 10, 11, 13–16, 27, 79, 81–83, 146, 152, 161, 162, 173, 193
Conceptual, 79, 80
Conceptualization, 1, 13

211

Creon, 150
Crisis, 20, 54, 56, 57, 133, 174, 198
Cornell, Drucilla, 200
Courtine, Jean-François, 201
Cratylus, 131
Culture, 20, 26, 43, 95, 170, 176, 179

Da Vinci, 148, 154
Deaf, 106, 109, 111–13
Death, 2, 51, 53, 55, 71, 72, 74, 93, 94, 100, 101, 118, 122, 123, 126, 144, 149, 150, 155, 160, 161, 172, 188, 189, 198, 202
Deleuze, Gilles, 143
Derrida, Jacques, 39, 53, 54, 104, 120, 143, 196, 204, 205
Descartes, 178
Destiny, 53, 54, 56, 57, 66, 185
Detienne, Marcel, 197
Dike, 24, 51, 151
Dionysus, 11, 27, 51, 70, 71, 73, 147
Dissonance, 11, 36, 37, 73–75
Divine, 16, 81, 85, 125, 144, 184
Dostoevsky, 164
Dream, 11, 52, 67

Eco, Umberto, 194
Empedocles, 117, 121–26, 129, 154
Eros, 15, 134
Ethical life, 1, 2, 19, 118, 121, 127, 168
Ethics, 17, 18, 117, 119, 120, 129
Evil, 1, 4, 78, 120, 168, 169, 179
Exemplarity, 14, 15

Finitude, 2, 4, 5, 11, 14–18, 35, 38, 47, 48, 63, 82, 83, 85–89, 100, 125, 126, 131, 133, 166, 183, 188, 189, 197
Forgetting, 49, 50, 96
Foucault, Michel, 22, 63, 143, 193, 195, 199, 206
Fragmentary, 29, 154, 155
Freedom, 1, 2, 13, 18, 48, 50, 77–89, 117–22, 125, 127, 163, 164, 167, 169, 173, 176, 178, 179, 183, 201
Freud, Sigmund, 24, 203
Fynsk, Christopher, 200

Gadamer, Hans-Georg, 4, 9–17, 20–24, 27–31, 33–36, 38, 40, 41, 43, 49, 78, 79, 83, 84, 86–88, 104, 105, 107, 109, 113, 114, 120, 131, 132, 134–36, 138, 139, 143, 193, 194, 195, 196, 197, 198, 199, 200, 201, 202, 205, 206, 207
Garcia-Marquez, Gabriel, 202
Genius, 8, 10, 11, 13, 84
Gestell, 75, 176
Goethe, Wilhelm, 15, 20, 164, 194
Good, 1, 4, 78, 120, 152, 163, 168, 169, 179
Greek, 20, 26, 41, 52, 55, 56, 63, 84, 121, 127, 142, 144, 145, 166, 170, 174, 176, 179, 188, 195, 197, 198

Haar, Michel, 208
Habermas, Jürgen, 195
Hades, 51, 52, 58
Hammacker, Werner, 204
Hand, 41, 107, 110, 114, 137, 139, 153, 205
Harmony, 36, 73, 74, 100, 122
Havel, Václev, 2, 3, 195
Hector, 156, 158, 159
Heidegger, Martin, 4, 9, 10, 12, 19, 20, 22, 25–29, 38, 39, 40–43, 52–58, 61–75, 78, 79, 92, 95, 97, 98–101, 103, 104, 106–9, 113, 114, 119, 120, 131, 132, 134, 137, 139, 145, 148, 150, 163–90, 193, 194, 195, 196, 198, 199, 201, 202, 203, 204, 205, 206, 207, 208, 209
Hegel, G.W.F., 12, 26, 27, 35, 37, 38, 40, 43, 44, 49, 52, 54–56, 62, 63, 80, 81, 96, 108, 118, 119, 129, 137, 138, 144, 148, 157, 166, 189, 193, 194, 196, 197, 198, 199, 201, 203, 205, 207, 208
Heraclitus, 23, 36, 73, 123, 164, 203
Hermeneutic Circle, 38, 196
Hermeneutics, 29, 33, 37, 38, 45, 78, 79, 83, 88, 89, 131–34
Herodotus, 113
Hexis, 28

INDEX   213

History, 1, 19, 26, 35, 37, 43, 44, 47–59, 61, 62, 69, 92, 95, 95, 139, 155, 163, 181–83, 187, 189, 197, 198, 201
Hobbes, Thomas, 209
Hoffmannsthal, Hugo, 165
Hölderlin, Friedrich, 4, 10, 19, 20, 22, 28, 35, 39, 40–42, 44, 52, 56, 57, 64, 66, 73, 93, 102, 147, 150, 153, 166, 169, 172, 173, 185, 189, 196, 107, 108, 199, 200, 201, 205
Holocaust, 101, 202
Holy, 16, 100, 132
Homer, 22, 26, 51, 144, 149, 151–53, 155–57, 159–61, 198, 208
Humanism, 2, 82, 84, 85, 120, 127, 193
Hyperion, 121, 122, 125

Icon, 107, 135–39, 141, 157, 159
Idea, 14, 20, 81, 142, 147, 151, 154, 156, 163, 168, 170, 172, 176, 184
Ideality, 106, 108, 146, 147
Idiom, 81, 82, 95, 133, 150–52
Image, 11, 15, 52, 62, 105, 106, 111, 112, 135, 136, 139, 141–44, 146–48, 151–54, 157–62, 173, 196, 197, 198
Imagination, 14, 26, 118, 157, 198
Ineffable, 1, 16
Inexpresssible, 15, 206
Intimacy, 3, 4, 125
Intuition, 1, 14, 16

Judgment, 1, 4, 7, 11, 85, 86, 150
Jünger, Ernst, 97, 166, 204
Justice, 167, 168

Kant, Immanuel, 4, 5, 7–18, 27, 49, 55, 59, 78–87, 89, 100, 120, 121, 122, 129, 146, 147, 152, 169, 176, 186, 189, 193, 194, 195, 197, 201, 203, 205, 209
Keller, Helen, 42
Klee, Paul, 57, 208
Knox, Bernard, 209
Krell, David, 200
Kushner, Tony, 58

Lacan, Jacques, 65
Lacoue-Labarthe, Phillipe, 54, 65, 66, 198, 200, 201, 209
Lao-Tzu, 171
Law, 18, 36, 55, 79, 80, 82, 83, 87, 152, 166, 206
Legibility, 105, 106
Lessing, Gotthold Ephraim, 157, 208
Levin, David Michael, 207
Levinas, Emmanuel, 43, 92, 205
Limits, 2, 9, 11, 17, 35, 37, 40, 43, 45, 48, 51, 53, 59, 61, 63, 75, 85, 125, 132, 139, 144, 150, 157, 160
Loraux, Nicole, 197
Love, 40, 71, 72, 74, 93, 101, 124, 126, 129, 133, 169, 187
Lyotard, Jean-François, 43
Lyrical subject, 4, 7, 8, 17
Lysias, 138

Machenschaft, 119, 170, 171, 173–84
Mahler, Gustav, 70
Mandelstam, Osip, 203
Marx, Karl, 54, 151
Meister Eckhart, 16
Memory, 30, 43, 44, 49–52, 56, 74, 93, 96, 138, 139, 155, 158, 160, 203
Mendelssohn, 65
Merleau-Ponty, Maurice, 143, 205
Metaphor, 32, 83, 146, 201
Metaphysics, 1, 2, 4, 13, 16, 20, 23, 27, 54, 63, 66, 67, 71, 78, 79, 81, 83, 87–89, 137, 138, 168, 172, 175, 176, 180, 184, 188, 198, 207
Michaels, Anne, 187
Midas, 139, 161
Mimesis, 25, 29, 40, 137, 145, 146, 148
Modernity, 61, 63, 177, 178, 181
Mourning, 29, 42, 56, 72, 93, 101, 150, 151, 172, 190, 198
Mozart, Wolfgang, 199
Music, 11, 24, 27, 35, 61–76, 136, 139, 195, 198

Names, 30, 132, 144, 160
Nature, 11–13, 17, 85–87, 116–29, 171, 173, 176, 177, 182, 183, 193, 194, 201

Nazis, 20, 58, 97, 180, 182, 207, 209
Nehamas, Alexander, 200
Nicholas, of Cusa, 195
Nietzsche, Friedrich, 3, 4, 7, 9, 10, 11, 12, 27, 28, 47, 53–55, 63–76, 97, 120, 127, 147–49, 161, 166, 193, 195, 200, 207, 208
Non-human, 121, 127, 156
Novalis, 191

Odysseus, 51, 151
Oedipus, 118, 125, 126, 149
Okri, Ben, 55
Origin, 93, 119, 186

Padel, Ruth, 208
Pain, 37, 52, 67, 74, 93, 98–101, 204
Painting, 24, 136, 139, 142, 143, 145, 156, 207
Parmenides, 134, 137
Patroclus, 156, 158
Performance, 2–5, 121, 172
Phaedrus, 133, 134
Physis, 176, 177, 181–83, 185, 189
Plato, 20–25, 27, 28, 30, 38, 44, 51, 55, 58, 65, 69, 80, 107, 108, 110, 125, 128, 133, 135, 136, 138, 140, 142, 142, 145, 146, 149–54, 160–62, 168, 171, 177, 186, 189, 198, 205, 206, 207, 208
Play, 10, 145
Pleasure, 7, 31, 122, 145, 150
Plotinus, 194
Plutarch, 207
Poetry, 17, 20–22, 29, 30, 31, 34, 36, 37, 40, 44, 65, 79, 104, 132, 133, 142, 145, 195, 197, 207
Pöggler, Otto, 204
Poiesis, 175, 185, 186
Polis, 25, 27, 29, 30, 44, 68, 69, 151, 170, 189
Political life, 1, 21, 30, 31, 164, 167 168, 183
Political realm, 19–31
Pope, Alexander, 152, 153, 156, 159, 208
Postmodernity, 21, 62, 198
Power, 24, 27, 53, 171, 173, 179–81, 204

Praxis, 23, 29, 185, 186
Production, 10, 12, 13, 16, 28, 119, 142, 185, 193
Proust, Marcel, 52

Race, 171, 173, 181, 183, 209
Reading, 139
Reflection, 4, 28, 115, 128
Reik, Theodor, 201
Relation, 2, 7, 19, 41, 64, 71, 73, 77, 82, 86, 100, 118, 123, 126, 132, 136, 142, 171
Repetition, 28, 36, 63, 68, 73, 75, 95, 152, 203
Representation, 5, 13, 18, 28, 40, 50, 62, 135, 144, 170
Reproducibility, 65, 69, 73, 194
Reproduction, 40, 75, 76
Rieger, Eva, 200
Rilke, Rainer Maria, 91, 117, 194, 209
Risser, James, 204
Robb, K., 207
Rushdie, Salman, 128, 205

Sacrifice, 43, 44, 82, 93, 124, 202
Sallis, John, 208
Scarry, Elaine, 204
Schelling, Friedrich, 1, 8, 9, 27, 55, 56, 77, 78, 87, 88, 120, 121, 134, 147, 169, 202, 205
Schema, 15, 147
Schiller, Friedrich, 14,
Schürmann, Reiner, 198
Script, 105–7, 110, 112, 114, 133–37, 141, 149, 207
Secret, 13–18, 36
Silence, 16, 34, 36, 37, 44, 83, 91–96, 98–101, 103, 106, 109, 110, 113, 114, 125, 133, 172, 202
Simonides, 142
Singularity, 8, 54
Socrates, 23, 66, 133–36, 138–40, 151
Sophocles, 20, 39–41, 55, 64, 148–50, 169, 189,197
Song, 3, 63, 68, 73, 106, 124, 149, 195, 197
Sound, 34, 99, 105, 106, 108, 109, 114, 134–36

Speculation, 16, 65, 167
Spinoza, 120, 169, 194
State, 20, 23, 25, 37
Steiner, George, 200, 202
Story-telling, 24, 54, 158, 161
Stravinsky, Igor, 99, 200
Subject, 1, 7–18, 22, 28, 30, 35, 119, 126, 169, 172, 179, 184, 188, 201
Subjectivity, 4, 7, 21, 63, 168, 170, 174, 178, 181, 188
Sublime, 12, 17, 202
Symbol, 10, 14–17, 84–88, 159, 201
Szondi, Peter, 203

Tacitus, 49
Taminiaux, Jacques, 207
Taste, 7, 8, 10, 11, 15, 17, 18, 150
Techne, 174, 175, 177, 178, 186
Technology, 28, 65, 70, 75, 118, 119, 126, 143, 163, 166, 176, 182, 194
Theuth, 135, 139
Theory, 23, 65, 142–45, 149
Threshold, 2, 126
Time, 19, 37, 50, 56, 58, 62, 67, 73, 74, 96, 97, 113, 123, 134, 139, 148, 172, 173, 175
Tireseus, 51, 151, 197
Todorov, Tzvetan, 194
Tragedy, 41, 54, 55, 67, 68, 117, 118, 121–23, 127, 147, 166, 185, 188, 189
Trakl, Georg, 204
Translation, 4, 33–45. 83, 85, 104, 105, 132, 133, 144, 152, 153, 203
Truth, 4, 12, 15, 25, 27, 48, 67, 120, 141, 155, 172

Twombly, Cy, 144, 152–58, 160, 161

Unbidden, 11, 129
Universality, 8, 17, 29, 33, 72, 80, 81, 83, 99
Unsayable, 1, 24, 29, 93, 113
Untranslatability, 15, 34, 36, 38, 39, 42, 95

Valéry, Paul, 101, 205
Van Gogh, Vincent, 63
Vattimo, G., 204
Vermeule, Emily, 197, 198
Violence, 30, 57
Virgil, 158
Visibility, 149, 157, 169, 170, 179
Voice, 3, 25, 34, 43, 96, 99–101, 109, 110, 112–14, 134, 135, 202, 204

War, 19, 22, 97, 155, 158, 159–61, 204
Wieseltier, Leon, 48
Will, 64, 67, 168, 170, 184, 185
Witness, 102
Wittgenstein, Ludwig, 61, 205
Word, 3, 4, 11, 14, 27, 34, 41, 44, 64, 71, 83, 87–89, 98, 105–15, 124, 132, 134, 137, 140, 141, 144, 146, 148, 157, 161, 171, 172, 203, 207
Writing, 25, 103, 106, 107, 195, 206, 207

Yeats, William Butler, 205

Zarathustra, 66, 71
Zeus, 50

www.ingramcontent.com/pod-product-compliance
Lightning Source LLC
Chambersburg PA
CBHW070337240426
43665CB00045B/2155